ELITES, CRISES, AND THE
ORIGINS OF REGIMES

ELITES, CRISES, AND THE ORIGINS OF REGIMES

edited by
Mattei Dogan
and
John Higley

ROWMAN & LITTLEFIELD PUBLISHERS, INC.
Lanham • Boulder • New York • Oxford

ROWMAN & LITTLEFIELD PUBLISHERS, INC.

Published in the United States of America
by Rowman & Littlefield Publishers, Inc.
4720 Boston Way, Lanham, Maryland 20706

12 Hid's Copse Road
Cumnor Hill, Oxford OX2 9JJ, England

British Library Cataloguing in Publication Information Available
Library of Congress Cataloging-in-Publication Data Available

ISBN 0-8476-9022-9 (cloth : alk. paper)
ISBN 0-8476-9023-7 (pbk. : alk. paper)

Printed in the United States of America

∞ ™ The paper used in this publication meets the mimimum requirements of
American national Standard for Information Sciences—Permanence of Paper
for Printed Library Materials, ANSI Z39.48–1984.

Contents

Acknowledgments

This book grew out of the work of the Research Committee on Political Elites of the International Political Science Association. The committee has in recent years treated a variety of topics that relate to the functioning of elites in modern societies, including studies of charismatic leadership, parliamentary recruitment, cabinet ministers, and higher civil servants. We are grateful to Fundación Encuentro in Madrid and especially to its president, José María Martín Patino, and executive officer, Giovanna Bombardieri, for invaluable support in generating the book. We also thank colleagues, especially Juan Linz, and anonymous reviewers for constructive comments and suggestions during the course of our editorial work. Finally, we thank Tong-yi Huang, at the University of Texas at Austin, who helped us prepare the manuscript for publication.

Mattei Dogan
John Higley

Part I

Theoretical

1

Elites, Crises, and Regimes in Comparative Analysis

Mattei Dogan and John Higley

Most political regimes, whether authoritarian or democratic, are born in abrupt, brutal, and momentous crises. Crises are the birth certificates of regimes: they mark their start; they can be found in the histories of nearly all countries; and they are commemorated by solemn ceremonies, days of remembrance, and many symbols. Crises involve sharp confrontations among political elites, and they often produce changes in elite composition and functioning that are manifested by new or significantly altered regimes. Especially in moments of crisis, political leaders and elites possess significant autonomy and latitude for maneuver. The choices they make at such moments are frequently decisive for the outcomes of crises and for the regimes that follow. Political elites are never wholly independent actors, but neither are they simply the puppets of larger class, economic, ethnic, or religious forces.

Comparativists who study political regimes have customarily given priority to gradual processes of political development, comprising incremental changes and evolutions stretching over generations. This approach reflects the convergence of comparative politics with sociology and social history. Although beneficial in many respects, it has led comparativists to neglect momentous crises and to overemphasize the *longue durée*. The idea that regimes emerge in step with changing economic conditions, mass beliefs, political cultures, and other glacial processes of social maturation ignores the seminal importance of sudden and dramatic crises in the making of regimes and the forging of national political histories.

We believe that it is time to return to the study of how crises affect political elites and regimes. Comparativists must bow before the enor-

mous historical fact that most regimes are born in crises and elite confrontations; they originate in political impasses and elite power
struggles fraught with the potential for great violence. It is necessary
to reestablish this fact and to admit that theories that ignore the pivotal
roles played by crises and elites in the birth of regimes have limited
validity.

A perusal of the circumstances in which most European regimes
were born supports our belief. The British regime's birth occurred in
England's great political crisis of 1688–89, the so-called Glorious Revolution, when Tory and Whig elites rid themselves of the detested James
II and established a parliamentary regime that has lasted to this day.
Today's regime in Sweden stems directly from the crisis of 1808–9, during which time the country, governed by the incompetent Gustav
Adolf IV, was in economic disarray and was threatened by Russian and
French-Danish military invasions; as in England, leaders of opposing
elite camps unseated the monarch and in five weeks negotiated a new
and lasting parliamentary regime. In Amsterdam in the winter of
1813–14, the basic structure of today's Dutch regime was created in a
fusion of elites from previously disparate Dutch provinces amid the
collapse of French military occupation; it was consolidated constitutionally in the subsequent political crisis of 1848. The latter year also
witnessed the brief civil war in which the modern Swiss regime originated. In France, crises in 1789, 1799, 1814, 1830, 1848, 1852, 1871, 1940,
1945, and 1958 spawned the revolutionary, dictatorial, monarchical,
and several republican regimes that have made up the tumultuous
French political record. Paralleling that record, Spain's several authoritarian, monarchical, and republican regimes during the past two centuries were all born in crises, the most recent of which began with
Francisco Franco's death in 1975.

In Germany during the twentieth century, elites were reconfigured
and new regimes were produced in four major crises: those of 1918–19,
1932–33, 1945, and 1989. Austria and Italy experienced two crisis-
generated elite and regime changes during the first half of the century:
in Austria, the downfall of the Austro-Hungarian Empire in 1918 and
the onset of an authoritarian regime under conditions of civil war in
1934; in Italy, the consolidation of the Mussolini fascist regime in a
crisis during 1924–25 and that regime's demise toward the end of
World War II. Portugal's long-lived and authoritarian Estado Novo regime originated in a sharp economic and political crisis in 1926, and
its successor, today's democratic regime, was created in the crisis of
1974–75, when a losing effort to retain African colonies culminated in
coups and power struggles among military and political elites. Similarly, in Greece in July 1974, a crisis that arose from the involvement of

the colonels' regime in a coup against the government of Cyprus and an ensuing Turkish invasion of Cyprus precipitated an elite reconfiguration and the rebirth of a democratic regime in Athens.

The list of crisis-induced elite and regime changes extends far beyond Western and Southern Europe. In Russia, the Soviet regime was, of course, born in the great revolutionary crisis of 1917–18, and it collapsed in the space of a few months during another severe crisis in late 1991. The Soviet regime's weakening during 1988–89 produced political crises throughout East Central Europe from which diverse postcommunist regimes emerged. The regime in Mexico today dates back to a political crisis that started with the assassination of president-elect Alvaro Obregón in July 1928; Japan's democratic regime was born in total military defeat and occupation at the end of 1945; Iran's theocratic regime originated in a crisis during late 1978 and early 1979, when the shah was forced to abdicate and an Islamic republic was proclaimed; in South Africa, a crisis that climaxed between June and September 1992 provided the incentive for elites to create a substantially new and more inclusive democratic regime.

This book explores these and other crises and their effects on elites and regimes. Its premise is that political regimes are deeply imprinted by the genetic crises and elite disruptions in which they are born. By studying crises and the elite changes they involve, much can be learned about the origins and trajectories of political regimes. This is not a simple undertaking, however, because the relation between elites, crises, and regimes is extraordinarily complex and variable. First, some political crises do not lead to significant elite and regime changes. The dramatic *tempête* in France in May 1968 produced widespread panic among elites and the political class, but it was nevertheless contained without important changes among French elites or the regime of the Fifth Republic. To take another example, the armed confrontation between the Russian government's executive and parliamentary branches in Moscow in October 1993 was clearly a crisis, but it produced few changes in elite makeup and regime functioning. Second, some regimes originate in circumstances that fall short of profound crises. A number of the recent transitions from authoritarian to democratic regimes in Latin America (Peru in 1980, Uruguay in 1984, Brazil in 1985, Chile in 1989) involved the negotiated transfer of government power from military to civilian elites in situations that were undoubtedly tense but hardly crises. Third, there can be significant elite changes, accompanied or unaccompanied by crises, without any clear regime change taking place. The gradual, electorally driven circulations of political elites in countries with stable, politically representative regimes illustrate this pattern: witness Britain over the past two centuries and the succession of sixteen political dynasties, from the Adams to the Kennedy families, in the United States (Hess, 1966).

Adding to the complexities, crises take many forms, and their intensities vary. As Alan Knight observes in chapter 2, there is no simple metric by which major crises can be distinguished from minor ones. Crises have a subjective component, so that what we as observers might regard as a major or a minor crisis may well be perceived as the opposite by actors who are embroiled in it; needless to say, it is actors' perceptions that count. To give one example, comparativists observing Chile during 1973 might have had a hard time identifying a climactic crisis, but military and right-wing political leaders in July and August that year felt the political and economic situation to be so dire that seizing power and liquidating Salvador Allende and his government was to them essential. Nor is there any easy way to distinguish between simmering crises and sudden, crippling ones. As Michael Burton and John Higley note in chapter 3, Colombia has long been beset by guerrilla insurgencies, and many outside observers would say that Colombia has been in continual crisis throughout the past half century. But since the late 1950s and down through President Ernesto Samper's recent entanglement with drug cartels, there has been no crisis explosive or powerful enough to reconfigure elites or change the regime; conversely, as Burton and Higley show, the crisis in Colombia that did produce elite and regime change, during 1957–58, had little connection to ongoing guerrilla insurgencies.

To make the puzzle still more complex, crises frequently involve more than elite confrontations. Mass protests, riots, strikes, uprisings, and assorted terrorist actions are often prominent features of crises, helping to shape their severity and paths. Many students of politics hold that mass discontents and pressures greatly limit elite autonomy, and never more so than during crises. Is it, therefore, wrong to focus primarily on what happens to elites in crisis situations? Should one instead concentrate on mass and "structural" forces? This is one of the issues most frequently raised in comparative politics and political sociology. Although we cannot hope to resolve it, exploring the relation between elites, crises, and the origins of regimes yields much evidence about the political intersections of elites and mass publics.

Characteristics of Crises

Because the term "crisis" is so casually and routinely used by politicians, commentators, and scholars to characterize all manner of events and situations, its meaning must be specified. By *crisis* we mean an abrupt and brutal challenge to the survival of a political regime. A crisis most often consists of a short chain of events that destroy or drastically weaken a regime's equilibrium and effectiveness within a period of days or weeks. More rarely, a crisis is a chain of individually small but cumulating events and power confrontations that unfold over several years. In either sense, crises should not be confused with the "historical crises" of center-periphery, church-state, land-industry, and owner-worker cleavages on which scholars associated with the school of political development focused during the 1960s (e.g., Lipset and Rokkan, 1967; Binder, 1971). Although those lasting cleavages generated many specific power struggles, they were not crises as we think of them.

Typically, crises involve a sudden flaring of belligerence by one or more of the elite groups that are jockeying for government power, a rapid escalation in the volume and intensity of political actions, and a clear change in the flow of power exertions among elites, as well as greatly increased elite insecurities. There is always much uncertainty about the outcomes of crises, and this uncertainty is immediately and intensely felt by the supporters and opponents of an existing regime. Unlike palace intrigues aimed at changing the pecking order among individual actors, crises have far-reaching implications. They threaten to involve large segments of elites, and even of society, in violent actions more or less immediately. The Algerian crisis in France in May 1958 was a prototypical case: in a single week of high drama, General Charles de Gaulle reentered French political life and agreed to become premier, and in so doing he staved off impending civil war.

It is necessary to distinguish crises not only from lasting cleavages and the changing power balances they gradually produce, but also from the assorted "affairs" and scandals that are often dubbed "crises" by commentators and journalists. The Dreyfus affair, which dominated French public life between 1894 and 1906, or the Watergate and Iran-Contra scandals, which respectively preoccupied American politics during the early 1970s and mid-1980s, were not crises in our sense. The Dreyfus affair involved a heated moral, intellectual, and ultimately political debate about justice in France. The American scandals centered on breached codes of political behavior and standards of political rectitude among government officials and institutions. But these long-running disputes and revelations did not challenge the survival of the French and American political regimes, nor did they gravely weaken either regime's equilibrium and effectiveness.

Crises are potentially major turning points in politics. They go beyond the pushing and shoving, the tactical maneuvers and surprises, that capture headlines and are the stuff of everyday politics. Thus, a "government crisis" brought about by the loss of a parliamentary majority (as occurred more than fifty times in Italy between 1947 and 1997), by revelations of corrupt or immoral practices among the high and mighty (as happens recurrently in all countries), or even by the sudden demise of a powerful chief executive (such as the murder of Sweden's prime minister Olaf Palme in 1986) are not in themselves crises, though they may sometimes be part of the backdrops to crises.

A Rough Inventory of Crises

Specifying what we mean by political crises is a first step. However, the circumstances in which crises occur and the forms they take are so diverse that it is impossible to group them in a few tidy categories. It is nevertheless useful to assay several main kinds of crises and to explore their somewhat differing effects on elites and regimes. We propose the following rough, admittedly incomplete and overlapping, inventory.

One kind of crisis often occurs when territories achieve national independence. Especially after a violent secession struggle, national independence may involve the ascendancy, *ex abrupto*, of a new political elite. The new elite's functioning, as well as the character and effectiveness of the regime it erects, are usually highly uncertain. There is much initial disorganization; new political institutions are unfamiliar and untested; the new regime's writ is not everywhere obeyed; different groups want to go in different directions or in the same direction at different speeds; there are old rivalries and scores to be settled; economic and other resources are in short supply. In 1948 there were 46 independent national states recognized by the United Nations; today there are more than 190, many of them in old countries that have been resurrected. Not infrequently, their births or rebirths have occurred in crises from which deeply divided political elites and harsh authoritarian rule have stemmed. A good example is the chaotic struggles that attended the Belgian Congo's abrupt independence in June 1960 and their legacy of dictatorial rule by Joseph Mobuto over what came to be known as Zaire.

A second, especially stark kind of crisis arises from defeat in warfare. The responsibility for defeat is almost always sheeted home to the political and military elites who presided over it. Where they are not annihilated, these elites, as well as the regime they operated, are destroyed politically. An ancient example was the overthrow of democracy in Athens following the disastrous defeat of the naval fleet sent to Sicily in 415 B.C. Some twentieth-century examples are the crises arising from military defeats of the German, Austro-Hungarian, Russian, and Ottoman imperial regimes at the end of World War I. Still deeper crises arose from the devastating defeats suffered by the Japanese and German Nazi regimes in World War II. Other instances of political crises stemming from defeats in warfare include France after the Franco-Prussian War in 1870–71, Portugal after failure in its African colonial wars in 1974, Greece indirectly by the Turks in Cyprus that same year, and Argentina in 1983 after losing its war with Britain over the Falkland Islands. In each case, the existing regime either was destroyed or was so gravely weakened by defeat that there followed a period of great political uncertainty while surviving and emerging elites maneuvered for power.

A third kind of crisis, and one that has received much study, is "revolution." The quotation marks are necessary because there is no agreed definition of revolution (for a typology of revolution, see Dobry, 1992). But whatever is precisely meant by the term, most historians and comparativists agree that revolutions have punctuated the modern political record. As the American historian Crane Brinton (1965) shows in his "anatomies" of the English, French, Russian, and (more dubiously, in our view) American revolutions, they constituted political crises of the highest order. Revolutionary crises involve interregnums in which all the expectations of normal political life cease to obtain, there is for the moment no clearly constituted regime, and political power is up for grabs. Recent scholarship on revolutions links them closely to defeats in warfare (the Russian and Chinese communist revolutions) or to fiscally enervating foreign adventures such as those France undertook during the 1780s under Louis XVI (Skocpol, 1979, 1994).

A fourth kind of crisis that might be distinguished involves the withdrawal of foreign support for ruling elites and the regimes they operate. A physical analogue would be the cracks that temperature changes create in the polar icecaps, so that great icebergs drift away and later melt. When foreign support is withdrawn (the "temperature" changes), elites dependent upon that support lose much of their capacity to rule, so that deep "cracks" at the elite and regime level quickly open. This approximates what happened in the countries of East Central Europe once the Soviet Union signaled, during 1988 and early 1989, that it would no longer use force to shore up communist elites and regimes in the region. In less than a year, eight countries recovered their national independence and established new regimes, although most entrenched elites survived by shedding their communist mantles, adopting nationalist idioms, and reveling in testimonies about their country's ancient lineage. However, the withdrawal of foreign support for a regime often occurs in the midst of, and due to, a crisis that already challenges the regime in question. It was in such circumstances that the United States withdrew its support for the Batista regime in Cuba in late 1958, for the shah's regime in Iran during the last weeks of 1978, and for the Marcos regime in the Philippines at the start of 1986. The withdrawal of foreign support can thus be more like the proverbial straw that breaks the camel's back, greatly fueling and perhaps even shaping the outcome of an already existing crisis.

Political "implosions" may constitute a fifth kind of crisis. As happened to the Austro-Hungarian Empire in 1918, a radical decompression or a rapid and grave weakening of state apparatuses (the military, police, the central administration) takes place. Ruling elites suddenly find themselves without support from any quarter, their capacities sclerotic, and their decisions and edicts largely ignored. But violent struggles between ruling and challenging elites, accompanied by mass uprisings or military defeats by hostile foreign powers, are not central aspects of the situation. Implosions, in other words, are not the same as revolutionary crises. Although the societies in which implosions occur suffer great distress, most institutions and elites manage to survive, and there is no chaotic interregnum when power is "in the streets." There is, however, much disarray among political elites; regime leaders are discredited and forced to leave politics; their lieutenants hastily repackage themselves politically or move to elite positions outside politics; hodgepodges of leaders and cliques reconstitute the decompressed state, possibly with new territorial boundaries. Reflecting the trauma of implosion crises and the positional scrambles they entail, political elites become badly fragmented; elite relations and political game rules are in flux, and conflicts proliferate. All of this makes the character and direction of postimplosion regimes uncertain.

Implosion crises result from a concatenation of accumulating economic malfunctions, spreading corruption among elites, and greatly increased difficulties in keeping national states that are culturally and regionally segmented intact. They consequently take the form of a self-dissolution, of self-destruction—a kind of collective political demission or resignation. One example is the decision of the Hungarian Socialist Workers' Party on October 7, 1989, to dissolve itself (1,059 delegates to the party congress voted for dissolution, and only 159 resisted it). Or consider the Czechoslovak communist regime's relinquishing of power in the space of ten days during November 1989. The Soviet regime imploded quite suddenly and unexpectedly during the autumn months of 1991, even though dissipative tendencies had been evident for some time. Under the postcommunist Russian regime that followed, living standards dropped precipitously, with roughly half of all economic activity taking place underground and outside state control or regulation. The Yugoslav regime imploded with nearly equal suddenness during 1990–91. The hecatomb of much of the Italian political elite between 1991 and 1994 in a whirlpool of revelations about corrupt practices is another interesting case, although the regime itself never quite imploded.

Weak political regimes in the countries of sub-Saharan Africa seem particularly vulnerable to small-scale implosion crises. In this region, states are skeletal, in part because they are beset by vertical political cleavages between ethnic groups with regional bases, rather than by horizontal cleavages based on social class. Consequently, instead of revolutions there are successive small implosions followed by the ascendancy of new but short-lived ruling cliques. Whether more sweeping implosions will occur in such multiethnic and territorially fragmented states as Indonesia, or in the somewhat culturally and regionally divided China, is a question of great importance.

Do economic disasters constitute another distinct kind of crisis? Stephen Haggard and Robert Kaufman (1995) think so, and they are certainly not alone in this belief. They argue that a sharp deterioration in a country's aggregate economic performance may challenge its political regime by adversely affecting a wide segment of the population and by forcing ruling elites to adopt dramatically different policies. The new policies alienate the coalition of groups that benefited from the previous, failed policies and supported the elites. If the new policies do not quickly reverse the economic deterioration, and if the ruling elites are unable to fashion a new and powerful coalition to support those policies, the elites may be overthrown and the regime replaced. Like defeats in warfare, economic disasters may thus constitute crises in which elites are reconfigured and regimes are changed. In Germany during the Great Depression, economic collapse and mass unemployment, preceded by a catastrophic monetary inflation during 1923–24, climaxed in the brutal political crisis and elite machinations that unfolded during December 1932 and January 1933, following the Nazi Party's strong performance in 1932 elections. Its outcome was the harsh Nazi dictatorship that followed Hitler's ascendancy as chancellor at the end of January 1933, the Reichstag fire, which he used as a pretext for assuming emergency powers less than four weeks later, and the rigged elections he engineered in early March 1933. Similarly in the Soviet Union, as Jack A. Goldstone discusses in chapter 5, ever more dire economic circumstances during the 1980s lay behind Mikhail Gorbachev's increasingly divisive efforts to reform the Soviet system. The result was a profound political crisis during August and September 1991 in which the Soviet regime was effectively destroyed.

It is clear, however, that not all economic disasters produce elite-

and regime-destroying crises. Anglo-American and Scandinavian elites and democratic regimes survived the Great Depression, Mexican elites and the PRI regime weathered severe economic crises in 1982 and 1994–95 (discussed in chapter 4), and during 1992–93 elites and regimes in Venezuela and Peru were badly shaken but not destroyed by failed coups and constitutional confrontations that were in great measure fueled by steep economic declines. It thus appears that only in some conditions—the central feature of which may be the presence of elites that are already deeply divided and therefore unable to implement effective new policies—do economic disasters constitute highly destructive crises.

Another, more indistinct kind of crisis involves sudden breakdowns of unstable democratic regimes. In Europe twenty-two new democracies emerged overnight from the cataclysm of World War I, and eight older democracies survived the war: those in Belgium, Britain, Denmark, France, Italy, the Netherlands, Norway, and Sweden (Spain and Portugal might be added, though nascent democratic regimes in both countries soon fell in crises during the 1920s). Born in war-induced crises and upheavals, only two of the twenty-two new democratic regimes (Finland and Ireland) were still functioning at the start of World War II in 1939. Among the older democracies, as already noted, Italy succumbed to a fascist regime when a chain of crises involving postwar insurrections and Mussolini's 1922 "march on Rome" climaxed in the crisis triggered by the Fascists' murder of Socialist leader Giacomo Matteotti in June 1924. By 1939, Europe was a cemetery of twenty-one collapsed democracies, each of them destroyed in a crisis during which nondemocratic forces seized power. But admittedly, the crises in which sudden democratic breakdowns occur are highly variable in their forms and intensities, so that it is difficult to speak of a generic "democratic breakdown crisis."

A coup d'etat is often a central feature of such breakdown crises, and coups figure importantly in the other kinds of crises we have surveyed. We are reluctant, however, to view coups as a distinguishing feature of crises. Most coups are limited to skirmishes over the control of a few strategic buildings. They reveal the weakness of states and are manifestations of fights and rivalries among political leaders and cliques. But most coups merely alter political pecking orders in small ways (for example, the numerous and recurring coups by cliques of military officers in many African countries). Only where the state is strong may a coup result in a substantial replacement of elites and a change of regime. Coups led by the two Napoleons in France (1799 and 1852), by Col. Gamal Abdel Nasser in Egypt (1952), and by General Augusto Pinochet in Chile (1973) are good examples. They might constitute another kind of crisis or perhaps help to specify the heterogeneous "breakdown crisis" we have mentioned, but we see no obvious way to separate the relatively few consequential coups from the many inconsequential ones.

It will be apparent that the kinds of crises we have canvassed often overlap and compound each other. To take a particularly elaborate example, defeat in warfare followed by an implosion crisis led to a revolutionary crisis in Russia in 1917. After disastrous military setbacks at German hands and mass troop desertions, strikes and demonstrations broke out in St. Petersburg on March 7, 1917. One week later, Nicholas II abdicated, and a political implosion of the tsarist regime occurred. A month later, the run-up to a revolutionary crisis began with the arrival of Lenin, and that crisis climaxed with the Bolsheviks' seizure of power on November 7, 1917. Similarly in Turkey during 1917, military defeat of the Ottoman regime was followed by the regime's implosion and by the emergence of a charismatic leader, Kamal Ataturk, who then reconstituted the state and initiated a modernizing process (Dogan, 1984). A comparable sequence of military defeat, political implosion, and the emergence of a "providential" leader (Marshall Philippe Petain) unfolded in France in 1940.

We do not mean to suggest that in a given country and time there is but one kind of crisis or that crises always and everywhere consist of a few brief and clear-cut events. Rather, we are focused primarily on crises as important phenomena in the study of elites and the origins of regimes. Our rough inventory helps, we hope, to accomplish this aim. It is relevant to note that only one of the seven kinds of crises we have distinguished—the revolutionary crisis—appears among the four modes of transitions from authoritarian regimes that Terry Lynn Karl and Philippe Schmitter (1991) have outlined. Among their three other transition modes, elite "pacts" specifying a programmed alternation in power may or may not modify the basic character of a regime. Some pacts do indeed have this consequence, but as Burton and Higley argue in chapter 3, many do not. The "imposition" mode Karl and Schmitter discern in the Soviet transition is, we believe, better viewed as a regime implosion. Similarly, whereas Karl and Schmitter treat the Yugoslav regime's disintegration as illustrating a fourth "reform" mode, events since they constructed their typology more clearly indicate an implosion. Finally, a series of cases they evaluate as "difficult to classify" are for us crises that arose from defeats in warfare: Japan and Germany-Austria in 1945, Greece and Portugal in 1974, Argentina in 1983. Other cases unclassified by Karl and Schmitter underwent elite and regime changes during crises that stemmed from the sudden withdrawal of foreign support: Hungary, Poland, Czechoslovakia, Romania, and Bulgaria in 1989. It is necessary, moreover, to consider all kinds of crises and regime changes, not just exits from authoritarian rule. Crisis-generated replacements of authoritarian regimes by other dictatorships and breakdowns of democratic regimes must also be studied.

Crises and Elite Change

"Elite" is a word that is used almost as casually and routinely as "crisis." In some sociological studies, however, "elite" is given a more precise meaning by estimating the size of a social system's top level. One example is tsarist Russia at the end of the eighteenth century, in which the individuals who monopolized ruling functions have been estimated to number nine thousand men (LeDonne, 1993, 288). Obviously, there are difficult questions about the definition and criteria of "eliteness." In 1947, the Hungarian communist government deported some ten thousand "capitalists" from Budapest and other large cities to rural villages. In 1941, Stalin's secret police agents decapitated the Polish army, executing some fifteen thousand officers at Kalinin, the Katyn Forest, and Starobel'sk. Certainly, all of those Hungarian businessmen and Polish officers were not "rulers," though many analysts and observers would see them as part of their country's "elites." The French "political class" has been estimated at three thousand persons in 1990, even though various *Who's Who?* compilations numbered France's "visible elites" at approximately twenty thousand persons (Dogan, 1994).

The size of political elites or of a strictly defined political class depends on a country's size. For countries the size of Germany, it is plausible to think in terms of a few thousand persons who head the major institutions, organizations, and political movements and who are able to take, force, or impede political decisions on a regular basis (Hoffmann-Lange, 1992). For countries the size of the United States, the most plausible number is closer to ten thousand persons (Dye, 1983). Located in an array of hierarchies and sectors, political elites usually display widely varying interests and stances, including antiregime stances in many countries. There are, of course, tens or hundreds of thousands of people in a modern society who resemble elites in levels of education, wealth, and other social characteristics and whose second-echelon positions in powerful institutions, organizations, and movements enable them also to influence political decisions. But the political influence of these persons is usually intermittent, indirect, and limited to specific issues pertaining to the organizations and movements in which they are located. They are better thought of as "shadow elites" or what Gaetano Mosca (1939) calls the "second stratum." By *political elites* we refer only to holders of strategic positions in powerful organizations and movements, including dissident ones, who are able to affect national political outcomes regularly and significantly.

Political elites are the critical actors in crises. Indeed, many crises are initiated by the actions or inactions of leaders and tiny groups at the top of the political pyramid. Political fights among elites occur precisely because it is unclear who will win them, and their outcomes are seen to depend upon the actions that various leaders and elite groups may or may not take. We contend that, especially in crises, the "makers of history" enjoy a latitude of action. We adduce as evidence the innumerable memoirs and testimonies of political leaders recalling the crises they faced, the hopes, doubts, and fears they harbored, and the choices they made on the basis of assumptions they knew were frail. The search by historians for causes, determinisms, and "necessary" outcomes of crises comes later, when the dust has settled. If, by some magic, historians could do their job in advance of crises, then crises would not occur because the potential losers would adopt a different strategy. In working such magic, however, historians would do away with most of political history.

There are few political crises that do not alter the composition and functioning of elites in important ways. Crises and elite change are closely related. Getting a better grip on the genetic importance of crises, therefore, requires comprehending the kinds of elite changes they may induce. This is the province of elite theory, the seminal contributions to which were made by Mosca, Vilfredo Pareto, and, to a lesser extent, Robert Michels early in the twentieth century, even though all three elite theorists too often neglected the role of crises in propelling elite change.

Elite Composition

Crises most often affect the composition of political officeholders (e.g., cabinet ministers, party leaders, and parliamentarians). Changes in the makeup of bureaucratic, economic, and other elites who stand at some distance from the corridors of government power are usually less pronounced, though crises also frequently produce important changes in the composition of military elites. Japan in 1945 is an excellent example, and it is the subject of detailed analysis by Hiromitsu Kataoka in chapter 9. According to the Potsdam Declaration of August 2, 1945, only persons who had not been associated with the defeated Imperial regime could hold high political office in postwar Japan. In an early study, Hans Baerwald (1959) found that some 210,000 Japanese notables who survived the war were purged by the American occupation authorities. Kataoka confirms Baerwald's estimate for notables, though he adds on the basis of more recent research, that altogether some 640,000 persons were purged from Japanese public life during the years after 1945. Four of every five of those purged were military officers; but 16.5 percent were former political leaders and activists. However, the upper reaches of the formidable Japanese government bureaucracy were left virtually intact. Out of a total bureaucratic elite "talent pool" numbering 8,300 officials, fewer than one percent were purged. Likewise, the largest part of the business elite escaped the purge. As General Douglas MacArthur explained, some of the most able business leaders were removed because they were "born and bred as feudalistic overlords who held the lives and destiny of the majority of Japan's people in virtual slavery and geared the country with both the tools and the will to wage aggressive war" (quoted in Baerwald, 1959, 93). Nevertheless, Baerwald found that only 468 of a total of 2,395 private enterprise owners and managers were removed, while Kataoka, in chapter 9, calculates that fewer than one percent of the top business elite were purged. Baerwald concludes that "on the basis of statistical evidence it is fallacious to believe that the purge substantially altered the composition of Japan's leadership in these [bureaucratic and business] fields of endeavor; the purge was, at best, only temporarily and partially effective in changing the economic leadership of Japan" (93).

In Germany, too, most business and bureaucratic elites survived the Nazi takeover in 1933, and they also survived the Nazi regime's total defeat in 1945, as Ursula Hoffmann-Lange recounts in chapter 8. Although its members collaborated actively with Hitler's government, the business elite remained intact, and it largely retained its autonomy during the Third Reich. With only a few exceptions, the business elite was similarly unaffected by the Nazi regime's destruction. As Hoffmann-Lange (chapter 8) and also Herve Joly (1995) show, business leaders moved from the Nazi regime to the Federal Republic regime during and after 1945 without difficulties. Most high-level German bureaucrats also survived the Nazi regime's destruction, even though the occupying authorities gave priority to recruiting and promoting new bureaucrats untainted by Nazi associations. Studying the demise and replacement of the Ottoman and Chinese imperial regimes early in the twentieth century, Fred Riggs (1994) has found an altogether similar continuity of administrative and business elites, despite the Turkish and Chinese regime changes.

Six possible effects of crises on political elite composition can be distinguished:

— Some elite persons and groups remain untouched and retain their positions, with each case being of special interest,
— Some are obliged to accept less powerful and prestigious but still politically influential positions,
— Some are pushed out of politically influential positions and forced to take up more nonpolitical and specialized positions,
— Some are obliged to accept obscure positions (e.g., an ambassadorship in a peripheral country) or other cushioned sinecures,
— Some manage to undergo "ideological conversions" at early points so that they survive politically in the postcrisis regime,
— Some incumbents of elite positions, as well as some positions themselves, are simply eliminated, although the sectoral proportions vary and must be investigated in each case. This is the most significant effect of crises on elite composition, but it is also the most difficult to measure and evaluate.

The extent of such changes in the composition of political elites differs among the several levels of a political hierarchy: at the apex or nucleus of the political system, at immediately adjacent echelons, or at middle ranks. The amount of change also differs between a nation's capital and its regional and local centers. The extent of elite replacement depends, additionally, upon similarities and differences between the old and the new regime: if both are authoritarian or both are democratic—what Juan Linz and Alfred Stepan (1996) call "within-type" regime transitions—the replacement is likely to be less substantial than in "out-of-type" transitions from authoritarian to democratic regimes or vice versa.

Most crises, in any event, engender a change of guard at the elite level, although the new guard does not necessarily appear overnight. New elites often emerge piecemeal, coming from "shadow elites," from prisons, from exile, and from underground organizations. These new elites are seldom able to take charge of a crisis in its early stages. However, by the time a new regime is instituted, there is a significantly altered set of elite groups, at least some of which have had little or no previous experience in top-level power positions.

Elite Relations and Behavior

In order to assess changes in elite functioning that occur as a consequence of crises, we suggest distinguishing between political elites that

are fundamentally disunited and those that are "consensually" or
"ideocratically" united. Disunited elites are marked by pervasive dis-
trust and fear. The groups making them up adhere to differing codes
of political conduct, view politics in winner-take-all terms, dispute the
worth of political institutions, and engage in unrestrained, often violent struggles for government power. Where a political elite is disunited, an irregular seizure of executive offices through a coup or elite-
led uprising is probable during a crisis. Its result is usually an authoritarian regime operated by the group or groups that carry out the power
seizure. Although crises and the elite struggles they involve may sometimes open the way to more democratic regimes, a new democratic
order is likely to be short-lived unless elites have somehow managed
to become more united during the crisis that produces that order.

There are, however, two distinct configurations of united political
elites. In one, all or nearly all groups belong to a dominant party or
movement, and they uniformly profess its ideology, religious belief, or
ethnonationalist creed—an "ideocratic" configuration that is primarily
coerced (Piekalkiewicz and Penn, 1995). Such an "ideocratically
united" political elite usually originates in a revolutionary crisis during
which an extremist group gains the upper hand, destroys most of its
rivals, and dictates that henceforth anyone who possesses or aspires to
power must conform to the extremist group's doctrine and organizational base: examples include the Russian Bolsheviks from 1921, Yugoslavia's League of Communists from 1945, Mao's communists in China
from 1949, Castro's communists in Cuba from 1961, and the Shia fund-
amentalists in Iran from 1980. An ideocratically united political elite
may also be created when a foreign power imposes an extremist group
on a country following conquest in warfare, as occurred in East Central
Europe after World War II and in South Vietnam in 1975. Because of
their exceptional capacity to identify and weed out "troublemakers,"
regimes created by ideocratically united elites tend to be long-lived.

In the other configuration of united elites, groups are affiliated with
competing parties, movements, and beliefs, but they share a consensus
about rules and codes of restrained political competitions. Such "consensually united" political elites have sometimes originated in fundamental compromises and accommodations negotiated by leaders of
warring elite camps. As Burton and Higley discuss in chapter 3, such
sudden and deliberate "elite settlements" appear to occur only during
profound crises that threaten elite bloodletting but at the same time
provide key leaders with strong incentives and sufficient autonomy to
"settle" the most basic disputes between their respective camps. The
much-analyzed Glorious Revolution of 1688–89 in England was the
classic instance of an elite settlement (see chapter 3 and, inter alia,

Mansfield, 1964; Rustow, 1970; Weingast, 1997). Consensually united political elites have also originated through political cooperation in operating "home-rule" governments in colonial territories and through unifying elite struggles for national independence (e.g., American, Australian, Canadian, Indian, and New Zealand elites under and then against British rule; Norwegian elites under and then against Swedish rule during the nineteenth century; Senegalese elites under and then against French rule before and after World War II). Once political elites become consensually united, their competitions for electoral and other support are restrained and conducive to the peaceful, politically binding elections that are the hallmark of stable democracies, or at least of liberal oligarchic regimes like those in the English-speaking and Scandinavian countries before universal male suffrage was introduced.

These distinctions between disunited and two types of united elites are, of course, simplifications. In reality, political elites in all countries compete continually for advantage, and none is ever fully united. Similarly, most political elite groups have nothing to gain in a war of all against all, so probably no political elite is ever completely disunited. Elite professions of ideocratic unanimity always conceal doctrinal disputes and much jockeying for power; a voluntary elite consensus about the rules and proprieties of restrained competitions is always fraying and in need of reinforcement; disunited elite expressions of unbridgeable oppositions are often belied by secret deals. The extent to which political elites are disunited or united thus fluctuates with changing circumstances, and the ambiguities and secretiveness of elite behavior make its assessment difficult. Nevertheless, we believe that shifts from one to another of these basic patterns of elite functioning can be observed in a significant number of countries, and we contend that these shifts usually occur during or immediately following political crises.

Studying the relation between crises and regime changes must therefore involve assessments not only of the changing compositions of political elites but also of changes in their disunited or united functioning. In revolutionary crises, wholesale change in both the composition and functioning of elites is likely. In other kinds of crises, there may be significant change in one but not the other aspect. In crisis-induced settlements, for example, there is usually little change in elite composition but a fundamental change in elite functioning. In most crisis-induced overthrows of authoritarian rulers, conversely, there is usually significant change in elite composition but no basic change in elite functioning; the authoritarian rulers are replaced by a congeries of cliques and factions that continue the disunited pattern that sparked or contributed to the crisis in the first place. In chapter 8, Hoffmann-Lange discusses how the disunited pattern continued in

Germany down to the Nazi regime's onset; in chapter 9, Kataoka traces the same pattern among Japanese elites from the Meiji Restoration of 1868 until the end of World War II.

Crises and Regime Change

A political regime is the basic pattern by which government decision-making power is organized, exercised, and transferred in a society. We may speak, for example, of monarchical or republican, parliamentary or presidential, and authoritarian or totalitarian regimes (Linz, 1975). A regime is not necessarily synonymous with the current wielders of government power—a "Chirac regime" in France or a "Clinton regime" in America at the time of this writing. Chief executives such as Jacques Chirac and Bill Clinton and the governments (or "administrations," in the more accurate American term) they lead come and go according to electoral fortunes, scandals, party splits, and much else; but the basic pattern of organizing, exercising, and transferring government power among its successive holders may nevertheless persist, and in some countries it has done so over long periods. Thus, in Britain there have been many Tory, Whig, Liberal, Labour, and assorted coalition governments since the Glorious Revolution; but government executive power has been continuously organized, exercised, and transferred in accordance with the principles and processes of a sovereign, popularly and periodically elected parliament that were agreed by contending elites in that seminal crisis. Britain has, in effect, had but one slowly evolving political regime during the past three hundred years. In France since 1789, by contrast, the organization, exercise, and transfer of government power has oscillated between five republican, three monarchical, and two "imperial" regimes, plus an authoritarian one (the Vichy regime during World War II), each of which was born in a major crisis.

Comparativists have constructed many typologies of regimes, but we are content to use the most familiar and basic one: traditional (monarchical), authoritarian, totalitarian, and democratic regimes. Each type can be unstable or stable according to the occurrence or nonoccurrence or the perceived likelihood or unlikelihood of irregular seizures of government power through coups and uprisings. The composition and functioning of political elites is, we contend, the most important determinant of the type of regime that exists in a country. There are, of course, other determinants of regimes, but none is as critical as the configuration of elites. Where elite composition changes only gradually and where elite groups are consensually united, stable democratic regimes evolve and persist over long periods (e.g., the Anglo-American and Scandinavian democracies); where elite composition changes even more slowly but where elite groups are ideocratically united, relatively stable totalitarian regimes persist and perhaps evolve toward a post-totalitarian condition (e.g., the Soviet Union from 1922 until 1991, or the Chinese communist regime from 1949 to the present; for a discussion of the posttotalitarian condition, see Linz and Stepan, 1996). On the other hand, where there are sizable changes in elite composition during crises and where elite groups remain disunited, a succession of unstable authoritarian regimes, perhaps interrupted by unstable and short-lived democratic regimes, is the usual pattern (e.g., all Latin American countries during the nineteenth century and most African countries during the past forty years).

Between these stable democratic, stable totalitarian, and unstable authoritarian poles, however, there are several complex patterns and possibilities. At least eleven "itineraries" of regime change that are associated with crises and with the changed elite compositions and patterns of elite functioning that crises produce can be identified (see table 1.1).

These itineraries do not exhaust the modern record of regime changes, and our classification of some of the typical cases can be disputed. Our purpose is to highlight the importance and variability of crisis-induced elite changes in the origins of regimes. The itineraries listed involve different patterns of elite replacement and elite functioning, but several complications need to be mentioned. As regards elite replacement, one complication is hierarchical level: the higher the level, the greater the extent of replacement. In many regime changes, as noted earlier, the entire group of uppermost political rulers is replaced, while the turnover of political elites at middle levels is more limited. A second complication, also commented on earlier, is sector: elite replacement is almost always greater among top-level political leaders than among other powerful elite groups such as high-level bureaucrats, business leaders, or prominent clergy. A third complication is geographic: elite replacement is usually greater in the political capital of a country than in its provincial cities and towns. A fourth complication is simply the size of the political elite: the smaller and more concentrated the top of the political hierarchy, compared with middle and lower levels, the greater the rate of the top elite's replacement. Still another complication is time: if a regime has been long-lived, an entire generation of previous political leaders will have died by the time a regime change occurs, and there will accordingly be that many fewer experienced leaders available for top positions; conversely, if a regime

TABLE 1.1

Itineraries of Regime Change and Associated Patterns of Elite Change

Regime Itinerary	*Elite Composition/ Functioning*	*Typical Cases*
Traditional to stable democratic	From notables to professional politicians, progressively chosen in free elections/Consensual unification of elites	England, 1688–69; Sweden, 1808–9; Netherlands, 1813–14
Traditional to authoritarian	Annihilation of ruling class/New elites are disunited	Turkey, 1922; Egypt, 1952; Ethiopia, 1974
Traditional to totalitarian	Annihilation of ruling class/New, ideocratically united elite takes over	Russia, 1917–22; Yugoslavia, 1945; Iran, 1979–81
Unstable democratic to stable democratic	Hecatomb of a political class/Consensually united elite begins to form	France, 1958–62; Italy, 1992–94
Unstable democratic to authoritarian	Replacement of politicians by military and bureaucratic elites/Elites disunited	Portugal, 1926; Spain, 1936–39; most East European countries, 1919–39
Unstable democratic to totalitarian	Persistence of bureaucratic and business elites/New, ideocratically united political elite represses opposition elites	Italy, 1922–26; Germany, 1933
Authoritarian to new authoritarian	Opposition elites annihilated/Ruling elites remain disunited	Indonesia, 1965
Authoritarian to stable democratic	Authoritarian ruler toppled/Consensual unification of remaining elites	Costa Rica, 1948; Colombia, 1957–58; Venezuela, 1957–58
Authoritarian to totalitarian	Annihilation of ruling elites/New, ideocratically united elite takes over	Most East European countries, 1945–48
Totalitarian to posttotalitarian	Rise of technocratic elites/ Ideocratically united ruling elite begins to fragment	Hungary, 1970s–80s; U.S.S.R., 1970s–90s; China 1990s
Posttotalitarian to stable or unstable democratic	Ruling ideocratically united elite implodes/ Consensual fusion or fragmentation of surviving elites	Hungary, 1989; U.S.S.R.-Russia, 1991

is short-lived, leaders of one or more earlier regimes may reappear rapidly to construct a new regime.

In studying the relation between elite change and regime change, it is also necessary to take into account "conversions" or adaptations by political leaders and elites. Elite replacement may be limited because many persons and groups suddenly convert to a new regime and its principles. A famous example was the chief rabbi of Toledo who became Catholic bishop of that city when Queen Isabel ascended to the Spanish throne in 1474. Such conversions may occur at all levels of a political hierarchy, and through them elites may retain their positions or obtain comparable ones. The existence of political chameleons is well known in French history, and the world has recently witnessed more or less wholesale conversions to liberal democratic principles among the former communist elites of Eastern Europe.

Finally, a change of political elites is possible only if there is an organized opposition and thus a reservoir of counterelites. A new ruling elite cannot be created ex nihilo. When their communist regimes fell between 1989 and 1991, the countries of Eastern Europe were not pluralist societies. Apart from Poland, where the communist regime had always been more authoritarian than totalitarian (Higley and Pakulski, 1995; Linz and Stepan, 1996), there were no free parties, no free trade unions, and no economic forces independent of the state, and in the Orthodox countries of the region there were no relatively independent church hierarchies. Because of the absence of counterelite power bases under communist rule, it is not surprising that large proportions of postcommunist elites have consisted of persons who were prominent in the communist regimes.

Crises, Elites, Regimes: Questions about Causation

We have argued that political crises are pivotal events that frequently produce changes in elites and regimes. The historical and contemporary political record on this point is indisputable. Put in the form of a simple causal model,

$$\text{political crisis} \rightarrow \text{elite change} \rightarrow \text{regime change}$$

As we have seen, however, the relation between crises, elites, and regimes is not so straightforward. When it is "unpacked," as we have begun to do in this chapter and as Alan Knight does in the next chapter, the causal arrows quickly start to point in both directions. Crises effect changes in elites and regimes, to be sure, but elites and regimes often create crises. Many crises involve, but they also derive from, elite confrontations and regime weaknesses. The danger of tautology is evident: elites and regimes change during crises that elites and regimes create.

One way to reduce the circularity is to look for conditions in which the preponderant flow of causation is from crises to elites and regimes and for other conditions in which the preponderant flow is in the reverse direction, from elites and regimes to crises. Crises created mainly by exogenous forces—conquests by foreign powers, fluctuations in world markets that create local economic disasters, as well as calamitous earthquakes, fires, and floods—may independently cause changes in elites and in the regimes elites operate. Similarly, crises that originate in dramatically altered situations of mass populations—the onset of famines, diseases, and population explosions or sudden mass migrations into territories—occur more or less independent of existing elites and regimes, yet they may serve as catalysts of elite and regime change.

We are interested, however, in more overtly political crises: the achievement of national independence, defeat in warfare, a revolutionary outbreak, a mainly endogenous economic disaster, an implosion of elite and regime power bases, a democratic breakdown. As Knight worries in chapter 2, most political crises have important origins in elites and regimes themselves, and their analysis is indeed uncomfortably tautological. At the same time, Knight contends, most political crises have important mass or "structural" causes. To this extent, it is not crises themselves that explain elite and regime change but, rather, the mass and structural conditions that fuel crises in which elite and regime changes then take place. In Knight's view, our claim that political regimes originate in crises and elite confrontations is at best only half the story, and at worst it ignores the most important causes of political change, which are the conditions and forces that shape mass discontents and propel mass actions. Moreover, Knight argues, there are reciprocal relations between elites and mass publics, so that elites compete for the support of mass publics, which the latter are always capable of withdrawing, and there are also reciprocal relations between regimes and mass publics, so that regime strength or weakness shapes the probability and success or failure of antiregime mass mobilizations.

Somewhat contrary to Knight, we regard the idea that mass publics may revolt or otherwise force a regime change without emerging or existing political elites mobilizing and leading them to be as misleading as the notion, before Pasteur discovered microbes, that "agents" of diseases are generated spontaneously. We do not ignore the occurrence of sudden, essentially "eliteless" peasant *jacqueries*, worker riots, or student demonstrations. These take place sporadically in nearly all known societies and historical periods. In a discussion of mass uprisings in Mexico—especially the self-proclaimed "Zapatista" uprising that occurred in the state of Chiapas on January 1, 1994—Knight, in chapter 4, highlights the importance of such events. But more or less spontaneous manifestations of mass discontent (the Kwangju uprising in South Korea in 1980, the Tiananmen Square protests in Beijing during May and June 1989) do not by themselves topple regimes. One reason is that they are almost always too local and short-lived to have such a momentous effect. For masses to bring down regimes, especially modern regimes with all the firepower they deploy, serious organization and the articulation of a clear leadership or elite that can plan and direct a mass assault on the bastions of power is essential.

Our skepticism about the importance and independence of mass publics in producing crises and the elite and regime changes they entail is not widely shared among comparativists. Knight takes direct issue with us in the next chapter, and he argues cogently for the proposition that, especially during crises, mass publics play decisive roles. Is it in times of crisis that elite autonomy wavers and contracts, as he suggests, or is it precisely at moments of traumatic events that the freedom of political leaders and elites to make decisions, wisely or foolishly, is greatest? Burton and Higley argue in chapter 3 that in the kinds of crises that produce elite settlements, elites are very much in control; indeed, settlements are possible only where this is so. Hennie Kotzé's detailed account in chapter 10 of how elites maneuvered and largely controlled the crisis in which South Africa's regime was transformed during the early 1990s supports and further illustrates Burton and Higley's argument. Assessing the Soviet Union's collapse in 1991 as stemming from a true revolutionary crisis, Jack A. Goldstone similarly concludes, in chapter 5, that the crisis unfolded primarily from the top down—from changes in elites—rather than from the bottom up. Indeed, much of the recent writing about the Soviet regime's dramatic implosion highlights the absence of mass actions (e.g., Fish, 1995; Hough, 1997; Kotz, 1997).

The competing views of elite or mass causation fit different historical circumstances. Neither is universally valid, and each can be supported with numerous examples. But precisely because of this, naive theories that pretend to universal validity fail. In March 1917 in St. Petersburg, thousands of civilians and soldiers played the decisive role. But during the forty-eight hours between the assassination of Caesar and the meeting of the Roman Senate, only a handful of individuals played the crucial, and exclusive, role. If forced to choose between the competing views, we believe that the weight of historical evidence is that leaders and elites are the substantially autonomous and thus decisive actors in crisis situations.

The following chapters explore how patterns of crises have affected political elites and regimes in a score of countries. All the authors are less interested in why these crises occurred—questions of complex causation and historical contingency that require full-fledged historical studies—than in their consequences for elites and political regimes. We suggest that three propositions emerge:

—The crises studied greatly challenged existing regimes and the political elites that operated them, so that substantial elite and regime change was unavoidable.

—The character of successor regimes was a product of the choices that leaders and elites made during the crises, and those choices are best understood in terms of the changed composition and functioning of elites.

—The crises were profound enough to ensure that there could be no going back, that is, that the new elite configurations and regimes were likely to persist, absent another deep crisis.

In sum, the crises and elite and regime changes dealt with in this volume were watershed events in the politics of the countries where they occurred. They demand a central place, despite their contingent and impetuous character, in explanations of political change.

References

Baerwald, Hans. H. 1959. *The Purge of Japanese Leaders under the Occupation.* Westport: Greenwood Press.

Binder, Leonard, ed. 1971. *Crises and Sequences in Political Development.* Princeton: Princeton University Press.

Brinton, Crane. 1965. *The Anatomy of Revolution.* Rev. ed. New York: Vintage Books.

Dobry, Michel. 1992. *Sociologie des Crises Politiques.* Paris: Fondation Nationale des Sciences Politiques.

Dogan, Mattei. 1984. "Attaturk et de Gaulle: analogies entre deux personalites charismatiques." In *Attaturk, foundateur de la Turquie moderne,* eds. Ali Kazancigil and Ergun Özbundun. Paris: Masson.

———. 1994. "La Classe Politique Francaise." *Encyclopaedia Universalis.* Paris: Universalia, 115–21.

Dye, Thomas R. 1983. *Who's Running America? The Reagan Years.* Englewood Cliffs N.J.: Prentice-Hall.

Fish, M. Steven. 1995. *Democracy From Scratch: Opposition and Regime in the New Russian Revolution*. Princeton: Princeton University Press.

Haggard, Stephen, and Robert R. Kaufman. 1995. *The Political Economy of Democratic Transitions*. Princeton: Princeton University Press.

Hess, Stephen. 1966. *America's Political Dynasties from Adams to Kennedy*. New York: Doubleday.

Higley, John and Jan Pakulski. 1995. "Elite Transformation in Central and Eastern Europe."*Australian Journal of Political Science* 30 (November): 415–35.

Hoffmann-Lange, Ursula. 1992. *Eliten, Macht und Konflikt in der Bundesrepublik*. Opladen: Leske & Budrich.

Hough, Jerry F. 1997. *Democratization and Revolution in the U.S.S.R., 1985–1991*. Washington D.C.: Brookings Institution Press.

Joly, Herve. 1995. *Patrons d'Allemagne: Sociologie d'une elite industrielle 1933–1989*. Paris: Presses de Sciences Politiques.

Karl, Terry Lynn, and Philippe Schmitter. 1991. "Modes of Transition in Latin America, Southern and Eastern Europe." *International Social Science Journal* 128 (May): 269–84.

Kotz, David, with Fred Weir. 1997. *Revolution From Above: The Demise of the Soviet System*. London: Routledge.

LeDonne, John P. 1993. "The Ruling Class: Tsarist Russia As the Perfect Model." *International Social Science Journal* 136 (May): 285–300.

Linz, Juan J. 1975. "Totalitarian and Authoritarian Regimes." In *Handbook of Political Science: Macropolitical Theory*. ed. Nelson Polsby and Fred Greenstein, 175–412. Reading Mass.: Addison Wesley.

Linz, Juan J., and Alfred Stepan. 1996. *Problems of Democratic Transition and Consolidation*. Baltimore: Johns Hopkins Univ. Press.

Lipset, Seymour Martin, and Stein Rokkan. 1967. "Cleavage Structures, Party Systems, and Voter Alignments: An Introduction." In *Party Systems and Voter Alignments: Cross-National Perspectives*, ed. Seymour Martin Lipset and Stein Rokkan, 1–64. New York, Free Press.

Mansfield, Harvey. 1964. "Party Government and the Settlement of 1688." *American Political Science Review* 68 (June): 933–46.

Mosca, Gaetano. 1939. *The Ruling Class*. Edited and revised by Arthur Livingston, translated by Hannah D. Kahn. New York: McGraw-Hill.

Piekalkiewicz, Jaroslaw, and Alfred Wayne Penn. 1995. *Politics of Ideocracy*. Albany: State University of New York Press.

Riggs, Fred. 1994. "Mandarins, Retainers, Transients and Functionaries." Paper presented at the World Congress of Sociology, Bielefeld, Germany.

Rustow, Dankwart. 1970. "Transitions to Democracy: Toward a Dynamic Model." *Comparative Politics* 2 (April): 337–63.

Skocpol, Theda. 1979. *States and Social Revolutions*. New York: Cambridge University Press.

———. 1994. *Social Revolutions in the Modern World*. New York: Cambridge University Press.

Weingast, Barry. 1997. "The Political Foundations of Democracy and the Rule of Law." *American Political Science Review* 91 (June): 245–63.

2

Historical and Theoretical Considerations

Alan Knight

The extensive literature on democratic transitions and consolidations focuses, obviously, on regime change of a democratic kind. The analysis pursued in this volume covers a much wider universe: crises in general and their relation to regime transformations of whatever kind (authoritarian to democratic, democratic to authoritarian, and other permutations). If the larger universe, by affording a bigger sample, facilitates comparison, it also involves problems. We may agree on a reasonably clear definition of democracy as involving adherence to procedures of free contestation, wide citizen participation, and protected civil liberties, although problems arise in applying it in borderline cases (e.g., Mexico).[1] However, the other concepts we are invited to juggle present greater problems. As regards *elite*, the suggested definition is clear enough, but it can lead to problems in practice. More serious, *crisis* lacks any clear or agreed definition; it does not figure in most book indexes or conceptual guides; it is used in a wide and contrasting variety of ways.[2] Historians have debated at length the "general crisis of the seventeenth century" (e.g., Parker and Smith, 1978); Ernest Carr (1939) wrote of the twenty-year crisis which followed World War I; closer to home, Merilee Grindle (1996) discussed the 1980s and 1990s as an era of crisis for countries in Latin America and Asia.

In the preceding chapter, Mattei Dogan and John Higley favor a tighter, exclusively political, usage. For them, crisis consists of "a short chain of events that destroy or drastically weaken a regime's equilibrium and effectiveness within a period of days or weeks." Occasionally, they add, a crisis may involve several years of "individually small but cumulating events and power confrontations." However, the ensuing typology of crises they present includes both generic phenomena (e.g., national independence movements, revolutions, "implosions") and specific examples (the Chinese Revolution, the Italian and German fascist seizures of power, the "implosion" of the Soviet Union), which would seem to stretch this tight formulation, in some cases to the breaking point. Dogan and Higley do, of course, recognize that it is necessary to distinguish political crises from longer processes of regime change. However, they do not offer a method for so distinguishing, and, in fact, the examples they cite seem to embrace both longer processes and shorter crises (plural), tightly interrelated. For them, the German crisis of 1932–33 began with the 1923–24 inflation (or even, we might add, with the 1918 Versailles settlement). These events, coupled with the 1929 Great Depression, culminated in the machinations that put Hitler in power at the end of January 1933. So, we have a crisis spanning at least four years. If we unpack the other cases—the Italian fascist takeover, the Chinese Revolution—we find similarly extended processes, punctuated by conjunctural crises: in Italy, the March on Rome and the Matteotti crisis; in China, the Long March, the Japanese invasion and final defeat in 1945, the communist victory of 1949. Most social revolutions and—though I am less familiar with the category—most "implosions" would, I suspect, follow such an extended, multi-crisis pattern.

If "elites" and "democracy" are, therefore, relatively clear concepts with which to work, "crisis" remains problematic. Lacking any tight procedural definition, and apparently capable of application to a huge universe of diverse historical phenomena, "crisis" is a standing invitation to ex post facto rationalizations (alias hunches); we see a crisis when and where we want to. The distinctions drawn between real crises and elite games of musical chairs, or between crises and longer processes of regime change, seem somewhat intuitive, a shaky foundation for a rigorous comparative theory.

Finally, I think a further element of confusion, possibly of tautology, creeps in when crisis and elite configuration are spliced together. Given the definition of elites ("holders of strategic positions in powerful organizations and movements, including dissident ones, who are able to affect national political outcomes regularly and significantly"), it follows that a serious political crisis must involve a challenge to "the basic configuration of elites" (if it does not, it fails to constitute a serious political crisis and falls within the musical chairs category); while, conversely, a challenge to the basic elite configuration must involve a serious political crisis (possibly a crisis *manqué*, if the elites remain intact; otherwise, a "successful," i.e., transforming, crisis). Thus, the basic proposition of Dogan and Higley that regimes are "born in abrupt, brutal, and momentous [political] crises,"—that is, that rapid changes in elite configuration involve crises and that "successful" political crises involve rapid changes in elite configuration—would seem to follow from the respective definitions of *elite* and *crisis*.

But their proposition is not therefore trivial, for at least two reasons. First, the definitions themselves embody theoretical assumptions— about elites and regimes—that we might wish to accept, reject, or qualify. Second, an important historical argument is also conveyed— namely, that regimes are usually formed in brief, violent, unstable conjunctures. In place of gradual evolutionism, we have a form of political creationism or, at least, sharply "punctuated equilibrium."

If we are to consider the validity of both of these points—the theoretical and the historical—I think we have to go somewhat beyond the consideration of crisis offered in the Dogan and Higley *mise-en-scéne*. In this chapter, therefore, I briefly address the concepts under discussion. In chapter 4, I apply these concepts to the particular case of Mexico and—briefly and by way of comparison—Latin America more generally. My conceptual discussion concerns, chiefly, "crisis," but it also touches on the related question of elites.

Crisis

First, it is reasonable to talk of serious crises that are not strictly political and are not associated with regime transformation. (The relevance of this point will become apparent; my aim is to expand the universe of "crises" beyond those that are strictly political and perhaps tautologically associated with regime transformation). Economic crises may not involve political consequences tantamount to regime transformation: the Great Depression—or, if you prefer, the specific crisis of the 1929 Wall Street crash—toppled Weimar democracy but left the American and British regimes intact. Demographic crises, triggered by epidemics, can transform society while leaving regimes in place: for example, the Black Death of the fourteenth century, the plague of the 1660s in England, cholera epidemics in the nineteenth century. Serious military crises, including military defeats, do not necessarily lead to political regime-transforming crises: for example, the North's initial defeats in the American Civil War, the Battle of the Marne (1914), Dunkirk (1940), Russian defeats in 1812 and 1941, which were respectively survived by tsarism and Stalinism.

Why are some "crises" (conventionally and reasonably defined) associated with regime transformation and others not? Three approaches

to this question present themselves. First, there must be some attempt
to calibrate the seriousness—the "criticality"—of crisis: of its scale,
depth, and impact. This is not necessarily achieved by a typology of
categories of crisis (independence, revolution, implosion, etc.), useful
though such a typology may be for other purposes. Without such calibration, we may retrospectively discern crisis wherever and whenever
we want. Or we may deny "crisis" to conjunctures that were, in fact,
"critical" but did not produce the expected outcome (i.e., regime transformation). I return to this point later.

   Second, in seeking such a calibration (and I do not mean a strictly
quantitative assessment, which I think would be impossible), we need
to distinguish between subjective and objective dimensions. Did a
given crisis—be it economic, military, demographic, political, or some
combination—have the objective capacity to bring about rapid change,
specifically, regime transformation? This can be formulated in Dogan
and Higley's terms: did the crisis "destroy or drastically weaken a regime's equilibrium and effectiveness?" But also, subjectively, did con-
temporaries see the crisis as genuinely "critical," as pregnant, in
Dogan and Higley's words, with "uncertainty . . . immediately and
intensely felt by the supporters and opponents of an existing regime"?
We could term these, respectively, the "etic" and "emic" assessments
of crisis: the first retrospective, detached, and objective; the second con-
temporaneous, involved, and subjective (Harris, 1979, 32). The latter is
clearly important, since the notion of crisis necessarily embodies a
strong subjective element. Is a crisis that no one perceives as a crisis
really a crisis? Can we, in other words, talk of a crisis *manqué* or—a
historical commonplace—a crisis-in-the-making, one that will "go critical" once subjective perceptions register "crisis"? After all, most full-
blown crises start with certain "objective" events, whose final impact
depends upon the reaction of elites—and mass publics.

   If everyone behaved like former British Labour Party prime minister
Jim Callaghan during Britain's "winter of discontent" in 1978–79, crises would be rather rarer in the world. It will be recalled that Callaghan
returned to Britain from a relaxing summit meeting in the Caribbean
and, fresh off the plane, airily dismissed talk of crisis, despite wholesale public sector strikes and shutdowns. Referring to Callaghan's glib
dismissal, the *Sun's* headline—CRISIS? WHAT CRISIS?—hammered another nail into the Labour Party's coffin and helped ensure the election
of Margaret Thatcher a few months later. If readers and voters had
believed Callaghan, the outcome might have been different. My point
is that sometimes crises, or panics, are highly subjective and bear little
relation to "objective" events. Perceptions of immanent uncertainty
and impending doom (or deliverance) are woven out of events that

are, to the dispassionate eye of the historian, objectively unremarkable (hence, "acritical"). Millenarian movements may be the most obvious examples, and it is topical to recall the foreboding with which our early medieval ancestors greeted the end of the first millennium. But there are plenty of secular examples of the subjective genesis of crisis: the Great Fear during the French Revolution; the contrasting hopes and fears about a division of the plantations that swept the American South at Christmas 1865; even the more extreme forms of paranoia conjured up by American Red Scares in 1919 and the late 1940s. Moods of crisis, therefore, enjoy a considerable autonomy from objective events; and for a crisis to count as a crisis, such a subjective mood must be present. Hence, a rough schema emerges (see table 2.1).

My third consideration involves another distinction, perhaps yet more crucial, between externally and internally generated crisis. The meteor-asteroid that plummeted into the Gulf of Mexico, shrouding the earth in a dark pall and ending the era of the dinosaurs, was clearly the carrier of an exogenous crisis (for the dinosaurs, at least).[3] If, however, humankind terminates its own era in a deathly nuclear winter, we will have only ourselves to blame: the crisis, and ensuing ecotransformation, will be thoroughly endogenous. In historical events, of course, the distinction is harder to make with clarity, but it is one that historians grapple with regularly, if not always successfully. Was the demise of a particular regime endogenously or exogenously caused? Were the doomed elites luckless dinosaurs or culpable humans? The question is obviously important, since in the first case the regime cannot be blamed for its demise, in the second it connived at its own destruction. Or, in social science jargon, in the first case the determining crisis was a thoroughly independent variable, in the second it was dependent upon prior elite failings (*inter alia*). This is clearly important for our consideration of crisis and elite reconfiguration, for it makes us think about whether elites bring crises (and ejections from power) upon themselves or whether they are the hapless victims of *fortuna*.

Although important—and historiographically familiar—such questions are not usually easy to answer; indeed, they have often generated major debates. Revolutions—classic, if extreme, regime transformations—have traditionally been interpreted in terms of endogenous, sociopolitical factors. More recently, however, revisionist scholars, some taking their cue from Theda Skocpol (1979), have stressed exogenous causes: the international arena, great power rivalry, military expenditure and defeat. World War I offers a sterling example. Did the Russian Revolution derive essentially from the war (no war, no revolution, no regime transformation); or was the war, at best, a catalyst or accelerator (bearing in mind the precedent of 1905 and the fact that the Russian

TABLE 2.1
Emic and Etic Dimensions of Political Crises

Emic = subjective	+	*Etic = objective*	→	
No perception of crisis	+	No objective problems	→	Business as usual; elites in charge
(panic assuaged) ←		← (problems resolved)		
Perception of crisis	↔	Critical problems		
(panic → problems) →		→ (problems → panic)		
Panic unassuaged	+	Problems unresolved	→	Full-blown crisis; elite authority and autonomy lost

No crisis

Potential crisis

Actual crisis

war effort was far from being a story of uninterrupted defeat)? Maybe the causal arrow flew the other way: the 1917 revolution, following the "dress-rehearsal" of 1905, signaled the delegitimization of the old regime and, as a result, the collapse of the war effort. Depending on our interpretation, we will place more weight either on exogenous factors (e.g., German military strategy) or on endogenous ones (e.g., the oppression of tsarism). In doing so, we will imply whether the fall of tsarism resulted from bad luck or bad politics.

An important rider to this argument must be noted. The relation between warfare and regime varies greatly over time. Cash is traditionally the sinews of war, hence fiscal resources always count. But success in, for example, medieval warfare did not depend directly on economic mobilization and political capacity. These counted for more as war became a more costly, elaborate, and expert activity, during and following the sixteenth century; and, with the advent of "modern" total war in the mid-nineteenth century, the link between military success and political and economic resources tightened further. Victory went to the regime that could best mobilize men (and later women) as well as goods and services. Total war, as Arthur Marwick (1974) notes, thus represents the supreme test of a regime, of its legitimacy, authority, and capacity. Failure in war could, therefore, represent domestic failure; ostensibly, war-induced regime change could be as much endogenous (caused by internal regime failure) as exogenous (thrust upon a successful regime by the ineluctable fortunes of war).[4] In this context, it is important to recall the many regimes that withstand not just temporary reverses but even serious ("delegitimizing") defeats: Britain and the American Revolution; Mexico and the Mexican-American War of the 1840s; the United States and Vietnam; Iraq's Ba'athist regime after 1990. Each of these events engendered a mood of crisis, but a crisis mood did not guarantee a regime transformation.

Why not? An easy, but clearly erroneous, answer would be that the crises—or defeats—were not sufficiently severe. Of course, this might be true in some cases. (We might expect that overseas reverses, suffered by imperialist powers, might be less "critical" and destabilizing than defeats suffered on domestic soil;[5] but we should note, in contrast, the survival of invaded, battered, and beleaguered regimes like Mexico's in the 1840s or Iraq's in the 1990s.) However, outcomes clearly depend a great deal on the capacity of the regime as well as the severity of the crisis; indeed, given the importance of subjective factors, mentioned above, the very perception of "crisis" will reflect the regime's capacity—its legitimacy, efficiency, even its public relations. Thus, it would be clearly wrong to calibrate a crisis purely (or even primarily) on the basis of its outcome, that is, to assert that a crisis that toppled regime

A must have been more severe than a crisis that did not topple regime B. A frail regime (even if its frailties are not obvious) may be felled by a single punch; a strong regime (however frail it may appear) can survive a flurry of blows. We need, as I have said, to try to calibrate the severity of crises, distinguishing between objective and subjective elements, exogenous and endogenous factors. But we cannot derive the severity of crisis simply from the severity of outcome.

Wars offer good examples of crisis-inducing situations and hence of the interplay between objective and subjective, between external and internal, and between short-term critical conjunctures and longer-term processes of change. So, too, do economic shocks, which have been held responsible for a swath of coups, revolts, and regime changes in Latin America in the 1930s and again in the 1980s. Similar etiological questions apply. Subjective evaluations of stability, competence, and confidence are often crucial: Argentina withstood the "tequila effect" of Mexico's peso collapse in 1995 because Finance Minister Dominingo Cavallo could—just about—reassure the teetering markets. The balance of exogenous and endogenous factors is also highly relevant. Some Latin American countries—genuine victims of outright dependency—are, in effect, reflex economies, highly vulnerable to fluctuations in the global economy, and sometimes to fluctuations in the price of a single product. Take the case of Cuban sugar. While we may criticize Cuban policymakers for allowing sugar monoculuture to take hold (this is a staple critique of the *dependistas*), a point is reached at which monoculture becomes a fact of economic life. It brought bonanza one year (1920), bust in another (1930); but the timing and severity of these economic crises were essentially exogenous. There was little Cuban governments could do, save to try to protect market share and cushion the domestic impact of depression. Exogenous economic crisis was, therefore, a standing threat to Cuban regimes, of whatever political complexion.[6] But like wars, exogenous economic crises are filtered through domestic screens, subjective and objective. A resilient regime, seen as the "only game in town," can withstand such crises: democracy survived the Great Depression in Britain, France, and the United States while it foundered in Germany, Argentina, and Brazil.[7] The oil-and-debt crisis of the 1980s—a heavily though not wholly exogenous shock[8]—helped transform (i.e., democratize) several Latin American regimes, but others—in Costa Rica, Colombia, Venezuela, and, as I suggest in chapter 4, Mexico—survived roughly intact.

Again, in reviewing these cases we would have to calibrate the severity of the crisis (economic crises are, of course, more amenable to quantitative analysis) and set this against the strengths and weaknesses of respective regimes. Some regimes, perhaps, are more susceptible to military defeat, some to economic crisis. The degree of endogenous as against exogenous causality can also be considered. I have noted that regimes that deliberately provoke wars in order to bolster their flagging legitimacy, and then proceed to lose them, cannot plead the excuse of arbitrary *fortuna;* discerning mass publics will hold them to account. So, too, economic crises may be more or less self-inflicted. When governments irresponsibly run up foreign debt, seeking to buy domestic support (as many did during the petrodollar boom of the late 1970s and early 1980s), the ensuing debt crisis is, at least in part, their own responsibility, for which they, too, may be held to account. Colombia's democratic regime remained intact, despite severe ("implosive") challenges, not only because of the strength of civilian parties but also because successive administrations had pursued relatively consistent and effective (nonpopulist) macroeconomic policies (Urrutia, 1991).

In general, I would argue, the fashionable stress on exogenous factors—at least for the explanation of social revolutions, perhaps for regime transformations in general—is somewhat overdone, at least in the modern Latin American context. To put it differently, Latin American regimes enjoy greater autonomy vis-à-vis their external environment than often imagined,[9] and crises tend to be endogenously generated. In part, this is because interstate warfare in Latin America has been relatively rare, compared with Europe; and those wars that, having been won or lost, did trigger regime transformations have often resulted from ulterior domestic motives: most transparently, Bolivia's provocation of the Chaco War with Paraguay in 1932 and Argentina's seizure of the Falklands fifty years later. External economic shocks are rightly seen as more significant—and clearly linked to Latin America's condition of greater or lesser dependency. But, as I have suggested, recent economic shocks were not random acts of God; they depended in good measure on prior economic policies, autonomously chosen, often with an eye to domestic political advantage. Profligate economic populism, engendered by domestic political pressures, left several Latin American countries highly vulnerable, but it was a vulnerability of their own choosing and making. Only the United States enjoys—up to a point—the luxury of running hefty trade and government deficits without facing swift retribution.

Indeed, one of the most fertile theories of regime transformation in Latin America—a theory propounded by Guillermo O'Donnell to account for the turn to authoritarianism in the 1960s and 1970s—was highly endogenous in its emphases, stressing the exhaustion of the old import-substitution model of industrialization and the ensuing need for capital accumulation under authoritarian auspices (O'Donnell,

1973). The demise of democracy in Argentina, Brazil, Chile, and Uruguay, therefore, followed domestic, endogenous causes. There was no external war, no economic shock on which to base an exogenous explanation: the Cuban Revolution and global inflation may have played a part, but it was a bit part, not the leading role. Furthermore, while critics of O'Donnell make some telling points, they, too, stress domestic factors—class antagonisms, the mobilization of the Left and the rural sector, the politics of competitive distribution, alias populism (Collier, 1979).

By stressing domestic factors and the contrasting capacities of regimes to withstand external shocks, we shift the focus away from the asteroidal "crisis" and toward the putative victims of crisis: the dinosaurs, who perished, or the small woolly mammals, who survived and prospered. In this volume's terminology, we must turn to domestic collective actors: elites and mass publics. Our working definition of elites is relatively clear and—no less important—well-honed by scholarly usage.[10] However, there are some problems in the application of the elite concept, apart from the risk of tautology that I raised earlier. First, there is a sense in which the elite approach is least appropriate precisely at times of social and political upheaval. It is no coincidence that the great proponent of elite political history (prosopography), Sir Lewis Namier, should have focused on the long-term, structural features of a particularly stable era in British politics: the Whig oligarchy of the eighteenth century. Nor is it surprising that attempts to generate "Namerite" (prosopographical) explanations of the Long Parliament—a time of political upheaval, ideological polarization, and armed confrontation (in short, a "crisis")—should have proved unsuccessful (Namier, 1957; Brunton and Pennington, 1954). Precisely in times of crisis, elites become more fluid, open, and unpredictable (Hill, 1990). Indeed, this is a diagnostic feature of revolution and perhaps of crisis more generally. New elites suddenly surface, old elites find they can no longer command allegiance; ergo, they lose elite status.

On January 1, 1994, Subcommandante Marcos, leader of an Indian uprising in Chiapas, suddenly joined the ranks of the Mexican elite, where, arguably, he has remained ever since. Yet, needless to say, he did not figure in standard prosopographical works of reference (the Mexican *Who's Who?*), which rely on conventional criteria of elite status based on decades of prior political stability. This is a way of saying that elite theory may not be the ideal analytical tool for grasping the essence of crisis, still less of social revolution. For one of the key features of elites—one of the features that makes them elites—is their capacity to exert power, predictably and confidently, over time. This is, for most class societies, the norm. Indeed, it would be hard to imagine a class society in which elite turnover is constant and incessant; and, if such a society—of permanent revolution or persistent implosion—existed, Pareto and Mosca would not be its ideal social interpreters. In sum, the more stable the elites, the more useful elite theory (or Namer-ite history); the more unstable the elite establishment, the more we should seek theoretical illumination elsewhere: in Hobbes, Marx, and the "new social history."

Elites

This consideration invites us to ponder the bases of elite power, and thus of elite status, and it leads us to two necessary focuses: historical context and, more important, elite autonomy. As Dogan and Higley recognize, elites operate in circumstances that combine the conjunct-ural (which may be amenable to elite control) and the structural (which usually is not). The Cuban and Argentine elites of the 1930s could not wrench their countries away from dependency on certain export sta-ples and foreign markets; at best, they could cut deals with major trad-ing partners and try to limit the domestic political fallout. Demographic variables (population collapse in fourteenth-century Eu-rope; rapid population growth, which eats into per capital GNP, in the modern Third World) have set compelling limits to the action of elites.[11] In contemporary Mexico, certain trends are more or less given: grow-ing population, urbanization, rising literacy. Such inexorable trends affect the very makeup, as well as the decisionmaking, of Mexican elites, as I discuss in chapter 4. Some experts, in and out of govern-ment, now regard neoliberal economics as a similar given. Indeed, one of the successes of neoliberal technocrats around the world has been to "naturalize" their nostrums, to proclaim, often convincingly, "There is no alternative." Constraints on elites are therefore important; some-times they are genuinely set by "grand impersonal forces" ("etic" con-straints); sometimes their inexorability is man-made ("emic" constraints).

Constraints on elites, as well as opportunities for elites, relate not only to inexorable forces but also to the more mutable allegiances of mass publics, whom elites lead, represent, or betray. Without elite leadership, Dogan and Higley assert, mass publics cannot unseat gov-ernments or, presumably, achieve other purposive collective goals. This proposition is open to question.[12] Indeed, it is particularly at times of crisis—classically times of revolution—that mass publics achieve le-verage, putting elite power and status at a discount. Peasant revolts and urban insurrections do sometimes proceed in the relative absence of "elite" leadership. (Take, for example, dramatic and certainly "critical" city uprisings during the twentieth century: Barcelona, 1909; Buenos Aires, 1919; the Bogotazo, 1948.) It is for this reason that the authorities often sweat in vain to find "leaders" who scarcely exist (Taylor, 1979). When it comes to the broad category of political crisis (which includes but is not confined to revolution), the Dogan and Higley assertion can be somewhat salvaged by their definition of elites as those who lead significant movements capable of affecting national outcomes. The Bogotazo certainly affected the national outcome in Colombia—it started the Violencia!—yet it was a leaderless phenomenon. As Herbert Braun observes, "Its anonymity was total . . . . The Conservatives' . . . initial response was prompted by images of conspiracy, for they were unable to conceive of individuals who were strangers to one another acting coherently" (Braun, 1985, 150–51, 157). More often, it is true, affecting national outcomes requires greater organization over time (and maybe space). If organization means leadership, elites, by definition, leap into place. Then we find we are suddenly baptizing popular leaders as members of the elite—for example, Subcommandante Marcos. The key question that emerges, therefore, is not whether significant political movements are leaderless; probably, any successful, purposive political movement eventually needs, or acquires, leaders, ergo elites. The key question, rather, relates to the character of leadership and its relationship to its "mass public."

For it is overly schematic and misleading to lump together all elites. Elites may vary as much as regimes.[13] Old elites (the entries in *Who's Who?*) are inherently different from new elites—by virtue of being old, entrenched, and probably recruited according to different criteria compared with their upstart rivals. In particular, the basis of their legitimacy—their means of eliciting obedience—is likely to differ significantly as regards both character and efficacy. For, if mass publics without elite leaders are, as Dogan and Higley suggest, ineffectual—at best capable of running around like headless chickens—it is also true that elite leaders without mass publics (decapitated chickens' heads, we might call them) are equally ineffectual; indeed, they are probably no longer "elites" at all. Some elites, of course, have unconditional followers, equivalent to the Ottoman sultan's janissaries. More often, even in authoritarian systems, there is some element of conditionality and reciprocity, of give-and-take—especially in times of crisis, when, by definition, elites' roles are in flux and authority is questioned. In extreme cases (social revolutions; some revolts and "implosions"), army officers now find their troops mutinying, landlords are strung up, factories are occupied by their workers. Briefly, the old charivari of "the world turned upside down" is politically enacted. More usually, of course, elites strive and contrive to avoid such outcomes: but, again particularly in times of crisis, this involves negotiation, whether explicit or (more likely) implicit. Given this degree of contingency, elites do not enjoy untrammeled power and have to ponder the attitude of their "mass publics." This applies to authoritarian as well as democratic systems: Roman emperors could not count unconditionally on the praetorian guard; Hitler was preoccupied with German public opinion and morale.

We may, therefore, borrow the familiar notion of the relative autonomy of the state and amend it to denote the relative autonomy of elites—the capacity of elites to elicit support and obedience from their mass publics with some confidence. At one extreme, for example, would stand the Ottoman sultan, enjoying extreme autonomous power over his janissaries; at the other extreme, perhaps, we have Subcommandante Marcos, submitting policy decisions to local debate and plebiscite—or even his forerunner, Emiliano Zapata, who, in John Womack's (generally convincing) portrait, appears as a leader constantly haunted and inhibited by his fear of betraying his *suriano* supporters (Womack, 1968). Indeed, in the Mexican context, the idea of relative elite autonomy fits well with recent historiographical debates, which have revolved around the relative roles of elites and masses: hence the relative merits of top-down and bottom-up interpretations of history. Modern Argentine social and political histories display similar trends (James, 1988). Relative elite autonomy is not peculiar to Latin America, nor is it confined to modern mass democracies (as the term "mass publics" might seem to suggest). Medieval kings were constrained by their constituencies (recall the famous Aragonese oath of allegiance[14]), while, conversely, modern elites may enjoy relatively high levels of autonomy—not only under authoritarian systems (e.g., Stalinism) but also under "elected (parliamentary) dictatorships."

The greater relative elite autonomy, the more important elite decisionmaking is, and the more we are justified in focusing on elite activities: pacts, negotiations, settlements. The less that autonomy, that is, the greater elite dependence on mass publics, the less merit is to be found in elite analysis. The danger is that we convert elites (who are known, named, easier to research, and like to convey an impression of autonomy) into the undisputed kingpins of history, which—particularly in times of crisis—they may not be. This danger exists because elite negotiation with mass publics is not necessarily overt and obvious; few leaders have attempted Subcommandante Marcos's plebiscitarian consultations. Some outstanding examples of elites following mass publics exist—such as Marshall Michel Ney reneging on his newfound royalism in order to follow his mutinous troops in support of

Napoleon in 1815. But more usually, elite dependence (or limited autonomy) is a matter of taking soundings, of avoiding unpopular decisions, of operating within safe, and therefore limited, guidelines and not outrunning popular (mass public) tolerance. It is, in other words, proactive more than reactive; hence, somewhat disguised but nonetheless important.

Such proactive politics are not, as I have said, confined to the psephological fixations of American politicians. Brazilian populism, Adhemar de Barros testified, was premised on the notion of "making the revolution before the people did"—that is, outrunning and thereby controlling popular demands (quoted in Conniff, 1982). A whole tradition of British Whig and Tory reform followed a similar rationale. But it would be a mistake to see British political elites, for all their apparent Olympian detachment and farsighted perspicacity, acting autonomously, unaffected by mass publics. Electoral and later social reform emerged from an interaction—sometimes conflictual, sometimes negotiated—between elites and mass publics; and the latter, however dispersed and anonymous, helped set the scene and write the plot. Whig, Tory and Liberal reformers—the elite architects of British democracy— are inconceivable without John Wilkes, the Corresponding Societies, Chartism, the early unions, the suffragettes.[15] A similar interpretation, *mutatis mutandis,* applies to the processes of reform and state building in modern Mexico (Joseph and Nugent, 1994).

Even if we concede (probably wrongly) that mass publics without elite leadership are invariably ineffectual, we must also recognize that elites need mass publics and are, to varying degrees, constrained by their demands. Furthermore, it is precisely in times of crisis that elite authority wavers and elite autonomy constricts. Such trends and relationships, however, can only be unraveled in specific historical situations. In chapter 4, therefore, I try to apply some of these theoretical notions in a specific historical context: that of modern Latin America, especially Mexico.

Notes

1. The definition is Dahl's (1971), and, by virtue of stressing procedural rules rather than substantive outcomes, it is fairly specific and useful for comparative purposes; hence, it seems to represent a rough consensus. It runs the risk, however, of exaggerating the importance of elections *tout court* (Mainwaring, 1992, 296–98).

2. A recent symposium (Dunn, 1995), which usefully debates the "contemporary crisis of the nation state," tends to take "crisis" for granted; an excep-

tion is Istvan Hont's contribution (Hont, 1995, 167–70), which grapples with—but fails to elucidate—the meaning of the term.

3. It was exogenous in the sense that the dinosaurs were doing fine and had "ruled the world" for some sixty million years; the asteroid did not deliver the coup de grace to a decadent species. Whether the same is true of political dinosaurs in regimes like that in Mexico is another matter.

4. War-induced regime change would be additionally "endogenous" if it could be shown that the outgoing regime ventured into war in the hope of saving its political skin: as, for example, Bolivia's president Daniel Salamanca did in provoking the Chaco War with Paraguay (1932–35); as, perhaps, both the Kaiserreich and the Third Reich did in 1914 and 1939, respectively.

5. This raises the interesting question of how the Argentine invasion of the Falkland (Malvinas) Islands should be defined.

6. Sugar dependency continued after the Castro revolution and the turn to communism, despite ambitious efforts to industrialize. This would seem to confirm the deeply rooted character of Cuban monoculture, the limits of Cuban elite autonomy within the global economy, and the highly exogenous nature of crises stemming from ups and downs in the sugar markets.

7. Of course, the depression spurred political changes, most obviously the New Deal; but I assume that the New Deal does not equate to a "regime transformation," according to the terminology used in this volume. This, obviously, suggests some of the terminology's limitations.

8. As I note in chapter 4, the impact of the oil-and-debt crisis obviously depended on prior policies: governments that had encouraged heavy reliance on oil exports or had run up large foreign debts were more vulnerable, more prone to crisis.

9. This, I admit, is a feeble, highly impressionistic statement. It is tossed out as a rhetorical rejoinder (1) to the old *dependista*/world-system school and (2) to the newer school of international state-system theorists whose stress on exogenous politicomilitary causation—however valid it might be for Europe— seems deficient in the Latin American context.

10. "Elite" studies are a recognizable corpus of knowledge in a way that, as far as I know, "crisis" studies are not.

11. Demographic variables are a particularly good example of elites' incapacity to control their own structural environments. For much of history, elites have exercised some control over death rates, but very little over birth rates; demographic changes have usually responded to "grand impersonal forces" rather than to purposive decisionmaking; and official attempts to either promote or curtail population have, even in the twentieth century, proved of limited success.

12. Since most historical societies have been class societies, possessed of elites, it follows that most purposive collective action in history involved elites. That does not prove that elites are essential to such action. For most of human prehistory (e.g., in hunter-and-gatherer societies or early farming communities), classes and elites were absent; yet purposive collective action was possible—some of it (e.g., the building of western European megaliths) quite sustained and sophisticated.

13. Dogan and Higley offer a useful typology of elites (consensual, ideo-cratic, disunited). These distinctions, however, hinge upon elites' relations with other elites. I am proposing a different typology, based on elites' relations to mass publics, which I see as similarly variant.

14. The Aragonese nobility allegedly swore allegiance to the Crown thus: "We who are as good as you swear to you who are no better than we to accept you as our king . . . provided you observe all our liberties and laws; but if not, not." (quoted in Anderson, 1974, 65).

15. Of course, the Corresponding Societies, Chartism, and the unions all had their elites as we are defining them. My argument would be that these elites were differently constituted, in terms of their selection, goals, and relation to their mass publics—compared, say, with kings, generals, and prime ministers. In some cases, indeed, the differences are so marked—the elites so anonymous and "dependent"—that subsuming all these notional elites under the same label is potentially misleading.

References

Anderson, Perry. 1974. *Lineages of the Absolutist State.* London: Verso.

Braun, Herbert. 1985. *The Assassination of Gaitan.* Madison: Univ. of Wisconsin Press.

Brunton, David and D.H. Pennington. 1954. *Members of the Long Parliament.* Cambridge: Harvard Univ. Press.

Carr, Ernest Hallett. 1939. *The Twenty Years' Crisis, 1919–1939.* London: Mac-Millan.

Collier, David, ed. 1979.*The New Authoritarianism in Latin America.* Pittsburgh: Univ. of Pittsburgh Press.

Conniff, Michael L. 1982. *Latin American Populism in Comparative Perspective.* Albuquerque: Univ. of New Mexico Press.

Dahl, Robert A. 1971. *Polyarchy: Participation and Opposition.* New Haven: Yale Univ. Press.

Dunn, John. 1995. *Contemporary Crisis of the Nation State.* Oxford: Blackwell.

Grindle, Merilee S. 1996. *Challenging the State: Crisis and Innovation in Latin America and Africa.* Cambridge: Cambridge Univ. Press.

Harris, Marvin. 1979. *Cultural Materialism.* New York: Random House.

Hill, Christopher. 1990. *Puritanism and Revolution.* Hammondsworth, Eng.: Penguin.

Hont, Istvan. 1995. "The Permanent Crisis of a Divided Mankind: 'Contemporary Crisis of the Nation State' in Historical Perspective." In *Contemporary Crisis of the Nation State?*, ed. John Dunn. Oxford: Blackwell.

James, Daniel. 1988. *Resistance and Integration: Peronism and the Argentine Working Class 1946–1976.* New York: Cambridge University Press.

Joseph, Gilbert, and Daniel Nugent, eds. 1994. *Everyday Forms of State Formation.* Durham: Duke Univ. Press.

Mainwaring, Scott. 1992. "Transitions to Democracy and Democratic

Consolidation: Theoretical and Comparative Issues." In *Issues in Democratic Consolidation*, ed. S. Mainwaring, G. O'Dopnnell, and S.J. Valenzuela. South Bend: Univ. of Notre Dame Press.

Marwick, Arthur. 1974. *War and Social Change in the Twentieth Century*. London: Macmillan.

Namier, Lewis. 1957. *The Structure of Politics at the Accession of George III*. London: Macmillan.

O'Donnell, Guillermo. 1973. *Modernization and Bureaucratic Authoritarianism*. Berkeley, Calif.: Inst. of International Studies.

Parker, Geoffrey and Leslie M. Smith. 1978. *The General Crisis of the Seventeenth Century*. London: Routledge and Kegan Paul.

Skocpol, Theda. *States and Social Revolution*. New York: Cambridge Univ. Press, 1979.

Taylor, William. 1979. *Drinking, Homicide and Rebellion in Colonial Mexican Villages*. Palo Alto, Calif.: Stanford Univ. Press.

Urrutia, Miguel. 1991. "On the Absence of Economic Populism in Colombia." In *The Macroeconomics of Populism in Latin America*, eds. R. Dornbusch and S. Edwards. Chicago: Univ. of Chicago Press.

Womack, John. 1968. *Zapata and the Mexican Revolution*. New York: Knopf.

3

Political Crises and Elite Settlements

Michael Burton and John Higley

Possibly the most basic questions in comparative politics and political sociology are why and how politics in some countries are "tamed" so that political competitions cease being deadly, warlike affairs (Sartori, 1995). One key way this taming occurs is through elite settlements: sudden and deliberate compromises of core disputes among political elites (Burton and Higley, 1987). Prior to settlements, elites disagree about the legitimacy of government institutions, engage in unchecked fights for dominance, and view politics as winner-takes-all. After settlements, elite persons and groups continue to be affiliated with conflicting parties, movements, and beliefs, but they share a consensus about the worth of institutions and the codes and rules of political competition. Settlements tame politics, in other words, by generating tacitly accommodative and overtly restrained practices among competing political elites.

More concretely, settlements tame politics by establishing relatively inclusive elite cartels. Elites become connected to one another through a web of power and influence networks that facilitate power sharing (Higley et al., 1991); they increasingly recognize boundaries and horizontal accountabilities between the organizations and institutions they head; and they come to expect that sanctions will be applied if boundaries and accountabilities are violated. Elites become accustomed, in other words, to respecting one another's basic organizational and sectoral interests while engaging in essentially peaceful and restrained competitions for government power that involve appeals for the electoral support of somewhat conflicting mass interests and categories.

For quite some time, the elite cartels and restrained competitions emanating from settlements may stop short of the differentiated elite polyarchies and freely contested, fully participatory elections that mark well-established democratic regimes like those in the United States, Britain, or Sweden today. Several scholars have speculated that democratization is in fact retarded by settlements and their aftermaths (e.g., Karl, 1987; Knight, 1992). Nevertheless, there is substantial evidence that by taming and stabilizing political competitions along broadly representative lines, elite settlements unleash a political dynamic that over time disperses cartels and fosters the adoption of modern democracy's procedural features.

Democratization certainly occurs without settlements and the basic elite reorganizations they produce. But where this happens, political competitions, though centered in the electoral process, usually remain quite unchecked and zero-sum in character. As in Russia during the past few years, electoral contests are desperate struggles involving many fraudulent practices and the distinct possibility of democratic breakdown. Nor are elite settlements the only origin of accommodative elites and restrained democratic competitions. Even where no settlement has occurred, the electoral contests that unfold in unstable democracies may contribute to a gradual convergence of disunited elites. French political elites during the twenty-five years following the Fifth Republic's founding in 1958 are one example; Italian elites between the time of the "opening to the left" in 1963 and the stabilization of Italy's democratic regime in the early 1980s are another (Burton, Gunther and Higley, 1992; Cotta, 1992). In still other countries, such as Australia, Canada, India, New Zealand, and the United States, the patterns of elite accommodation and tacit cooperation that underpin stable democracy originated in long experiences with representative politics under colonial rule, augmented by unifying elite struggles for national independence (Weiner, 1987). However, with this colonial route to accommodative elites and stable democracy now historically closed, it is likely that countries that lack stable democracy will achieve it only if their elites fashion settlements or undergo gradual convergences.

Profound political crises figure prominently in both the initiation and consolidation of elite settlements. The evidence is compelling that such crises are a necessary trigger for settlements and that further crises often motivate elites to cement initial accommodations and understandings. The connection between political crises, elite settlements, and democratic stabilization is thus a cardinal illustration of this book's more general claims about the relation between elites, crises, and the origins of regimes.

Settlement Circumstances and Triggering Crises

Table 3.1 summarizes the main components of twelve elite settlements that have been investigated by ourselves and other scholars. The table

excludes a half dozen additional cases that might plausibly be regarded as settlements: the establishment in Austria in 1945 of a lasting
grand-coalition government with an elaborate elite power-sharing (*pro-
porz*) arrangement as the seminal political step in postwar reconstruction (Steiner, 1972); Chile's complicated two-stage negotiations to form
a center-left elite coalition in 1988 and to then reach understandings
with right-of-center elites in 1989 (Cavarozzi, 1992); the Dominican Republic's electoral crisis of 1978, in which the two main contending
elites indemnified each other by sharing congressional power (Sanchez, 1992); Czechoslovakia's hasty, behind-the-scenes negotiations between communist and anticommunist elites in November-December
1989 to share power until free elections could be held six months later
(Higley and Pakulski, 1995); the significant elite negotiations and understandings reached in Guatemala among party, military, business,
trade union, and popular movement leaders through the Instancia
Nacional de Consenso during the two weeks following president Jorge
Serrano's failed *autogolpe* in May 1993 (McCleary, 1997); and Taiwan's
National Affairs and National Development Conferences in 1990 and
1996, which involved important compromises between ruling Kuomin-
tang and opposing Democratic Progressive Party elites. Further research into these cases may show that they were, indeed, elite
settlements. For example, research completed after this chapter was
written has uncovered strong evidence that the two elite conclaves in
Taiwan during the 1990s constituted a settlement (Higley, Huang, and
Lin, 1998).

This is not the place to rehearse accounts of the twelve settlements
listed in table 3.1, which have been published elsewhere. (For England
and Sweden, see Burton and Higley, 1987; for Spain, see Gunther, 1992;
for Costa Rica, Colombia, and Venezuela, see Peeler, 1992, and Peeler,
1995, on Costa Rica; for Mexico, see Knight, 1992, and chapter 4 in this
volume; for Uruguay, see Gillespie, 1992; for Poland and Hungary, see
Higley and Pakulski, 1995; for Korea, see Burton and Ryu, 1997; for
South Africa, see Friedman, 1994, 1995, and Kotze in this volume, chapter 10). We instead compare their circumstances, processes, and consolidations, paying particular attention to the role of crises in triggering
the settlements and in then spawning new and usually more democratic regimes.

It is essential to consider first the broader circumstances in which
settlement-triggering crises occur. Two sets of circumstances appear to
be critical: (1) a background of intense, costly, but inconclusive conflict
between deeply disunited political elites; and (2) an aggregation of
elites into two or three distinct and antagonistic camps, each of relatively long duration with well-articulated organization and leadership
and thus having the capacity to cause widespread disruption and in-

TABLE 3.1
Cases and Components of Elite Settlements

	Settlement Circumstances		Settlement Processes
Country/Date	Elite Alignments	Triggering Crisis	Concerted Actions
England 1688–89	Civil wars 1640s w/o clear victor; Tory-Whig rivalries/plots 1660–85	James II's pro-Catholic policies; prospect of Catholic succession w/birth of James's son in 1688	Whig-Tory ldrs. invite William's invasion of Nov 1688; mil. officer desertions; James driven out
Sweden 1808–09	Hat-Cap rivalries from 1720s, standoff from 1760s; Gustav III assassinated 1792	Loss of Finland, foreign invasion, econ. disarray 1808	Hat & Cap ldrs. depose Gustav IV Mar 1809
Mexico 1928–29	Revolution with no clear victor 1910–20; power struggles, assassinations, revolts in 1920s	Pres.-elect Obregon assassinated July 1928; renewed fighting impends	Caucusing of key revol. ldrs. Aug 1928; Calles appeals to Congress for order and peace, Sep 1928
Costa Rica 1948	Polarization of Calderonistas, Social Dems. & Conservatives 1940–48	Calderonistas annul election of unified opposition pres. cand. Ulate	Jose Figueres forces ouster of Calderonistas in brief civil war
Colombia 1957–58	Long hist. of bitter, inconclusive Lib-Con struggles leading to "La Violencia" 1948–53 & Rojas Pinilla coup 1953	Rojas's *continuismo* and econ. crisis 1956–57	Lib-Con coalition forms via Gomez-Lleras Pacts of Benidorm & Sitges; Rojas ousted May 1957
Venezuela 1958	Unbroken hist. of dictatorships until AD's "Triennio" from 1945, overthrown 1948 by Perez Jimenez	Jimenez corruption & *continuismo,* econ. crisis, mass protests 1956–57	New York City meeting of 5 AD/COPEI/URD/busns. ldrs. Dec 1957; Jimenez ousted Jan 1958
Spain 1977–78	Civil war 1936–39; Author. regime 1939–75	Franco's death 1975, efforts of Franquists to perpetuate author. regime, mounting strikes	King Juan Carolos appoints Adolfo Suarez PM 1976; Suarez persuades Franco-formed Cortes to give way to newly elected Cortes to enact pol. reforms
Uruguay 1984	Protracted Blanco-Colorado rivalries + emergence of Tupamaro urban revol. movement in 1960s–70s; military takeover after 1973	Military's constit. rejected Nov 1980; pol. impasse 1983 w/increasing mass protests, arrest of Blanco ldr. Wilson Ferreiria Jun 1984	Naval Club talks betw. military, Colorado, Broad Left ldrs., boycotted by Blanco ldrs. 1983–84
Korea 1987	Author. regimes 1948–87; strong dem. mvmt. w/veteran ldrs. by mid-1980s; Park assassin., Chun coup 1979–80; strong opposition showing in 1985 legis. election	Jan–Jul 1987: Pres. Chun halts constit. talks, arrests opp. ldrs., sweeping mass protests; Jun 1987, Roh Tae Woo chosen as DJP pres. cand., protests massive	W/backing of DJP moderates, Roh accepts all opp. demands for dem. reform on Jun 29
Poland 1989	Significant anti-comm. camp from mid-1950s; repeated protests/strikes; KOR & Solidarity formed 1980–81; standoff crisis forcing martial law Dec 1981	Strike wave Apr–Aug 1988 & ambig. Soviet support for regime	Secret talks betw. govt & Walesa, summer/fall 1988 agreeing Rountable betw. govt., Solidarity, Church ldrs., Feb–Apr 1989
Hungary 1989	1956 revolt; gradual emerg. of cautious reform factions from 1968; reformers dominant in comm. party conf. May 1988	Mass demonstrations Mar–Jun 1989; dismantling of border w/ Austria; comm. party split into two wings	Nat'l Rountable Jun–Sep 1989 involving 50 main delegates, 1,000 documented meetings/ talks
S. Africa 1992–93	Afrikaner-imposed apartheid regime beseiged by ANC-led insurgency; declining support of business, church & other white elites + internt'l sanctions, 1980s	Prolonged crisis late 1980s/early 1990s w/Nat'l Party (NP) ldrs. concluding liberalization is unavoidable; ANC ldrs. concluding insurgency is unwinnable	Secret govt.-Mandela talks 1985–90; Mandela & other ANC ldrs. freed 1990; CODESA talks break down Jun 1992

Settlement Processes	Settlement Consolidations	
Negotiations/Compromises	Power Sharing/Political Restraint	Other Stabilizing Developments
Jan–Feb 1689, 3-wk. Parl. Convention produces Declaration of Rights, accepted by Wm. & Mary as condition for taking the throne; Parl. passes Toleration Act, May 1689, Bill of Rights, Dec 1689	1689–1703: William serves as const. monarch, gives offices to Tories and Whigs alike; Jacobites defeated peaceful removal of Dutch troops; Anne's succession engineered	Settlement Act of 1701 established Hanoverian succession, further specifies powers of Parliament and monarch
16-man cttee + Estates agree a const. monarchy and Diet elects king regent, spring 1809	Royalist countercoup foiled, Diet recruits/elects Crown Prince Bernadotte 1810 who steers evenly between Hats & Caps, rescuing Sweden from crisis	Peaceful accession of Bernadotte as constitutional monarch, 1818
Calles meets w/major rev. factions Sep–Oct 1928, engineers pres. succession; Omnibus PNR (PRI) created as vehicle for limiting competitions and distributing benefits Feb–Mar 1929	Failed Obregonista mil. revolt Mar–Apr 1929; Cardenas displaces Calles 1934 & rules moderately	Gradual incorporation of excluded labor, business, church factions
Soc. Dem. & Conserv. elites agree on 18-mon. junta and reforms to be followed by Conserv.-led government	Calderon insurgency defeated 1955; further reforms by Figueres implemented peacefully 1953–58	Calderon allowed to re-enter political competitions 1958, communists & other left parties enter in 1970
National Front agreed Jul–Oct 1957; Dec 1957 plebiscite approves Nat'l Front; 1958 Lib-Conserv. agree on Lib. as 1st pres., Cong. enacts constit. amend. on 16-yr power-sharing 1958	50/50 split of all positions 1958–74; attempted coups by Rojas faction defeated	Gradual reduction of civil warfare; open elections after 1974
Worker-employer pact April 1958; Pact of Punto Fijo Oct 1958; Statement of Principles & Minimum Govt. Program Dec 1958; coalition govt. to be formed regardless of electoral outcome	Betancourt coalition govt. & new constitution 1958–63	Cuban-sponsored revol. groups attenuate, elections opened to all parties in late 1960s
8 UCD & PSOE ldrs. agree key religious, labor, const. issues 22–23 May 1978; limited autonomy for Catalan & Basque regions; Moncloa Pacts, new constitution 1977–79	Abortive civil guard coup condemned by all factions 1981; PSOE peacefully elected 1982	4 cycles of open & honest elections 1982–96 w/continuing efforts to settle Basque separatist question
Naval Club Accord reached Jul–Aug 1984 spells out return to civilian rule, indemnifies military against reprisals	Colorados win open elections Nov 1984, all pol prisoners freed, parties legalized during 1985; amnesty for military officers in 1986, sustained in 1989 plebiscite	Blanco-Colorado coalition govt. 1990–93
8 DJP & opp. reps. agree new const. in Aug. approved overwhelmingly by nat'l assemb. and plebiscite in Sept–Oct	Opp. split enables Roh/DJP to win Dec. 1987 elections; Roh commits mil. to civilian control; 3 parties merge to create DLP in 1990	Kim Young Sam elected pres. 1992, purges old regime holdovers, launches pol. reforms; indictment of Chun for 1979–80 misdeeds avoided 1994; Chun & Roh arrested/jailed late 1995
Gradual regime opening based on power-sharing, legaliz. of Solidarity, pol. reforms, incl. open elections w/some Sejm seats reserved for communists + econ. liberaliz. measures; subseq. deal to re-elect Jaruszelski pres. but w/Solidarity-dominated cabinet	Solidarity-led coalition govt., with communists, Sep 1989–Dec 90; Walesa elected pres. Dec 1990; series of reform cabinets; peaceful election of ex-communist SLD/Peasant coalition govt. Sep 1993 and SLD ldr. Kwasniewski as pres. Dec 1995	Peaceful/legal handling of "Olesky spy affair" early 1996
Immed. dem. trans. w/o power-sharing; terms of transition, election specifics, major legis. agenda agreed	Parliament elected 1990 serves full term; ultra-nationalist Czurka faction contained; peaceful Socialist election victory 1994	Electorally unnecessary Socialist-Free Democrat coalition govt. to allay fears, promote reforms 1994–?
Mandela & de Klerk sign "Record of Understanding" committing to a settlement, Sep 1992; multi-party negotiations agree interim const. w/power-sharing provisions Nov 1993	Despite irregs, in Apr 1994 elections, NP & ANC ldrs. agree secretly to accept results; Mandela becomes pres. with de Klerk dep. pres.; coalition ANC/NP/Inkatha cabinet formed	Despite ANC/Inkatha fighting in KwaZulu/Natal, coalition cabinet holds together 1994–96 and moderate forces prevail in local elections Oct 1995

flict serious harm to its opponents. Let us briefly inspect the dozen settlement cases in both regards.

At least four of the countries had experienced bloody civil wars in their recent history: England in the 1640s, Mexico during 1910–20, Colombia during 1948–53, and Spain from 1936 to 1939. In each country, the main factions in the civil wars survived, and most of the issues they fought over remained unresolved, frequently erupting again in mass actions, rebellions, and plots as well as executions, mass arrests, and other repressions. In Costa Rica, Venezuela, Korea, and Poland there had been protracted struggles by increasingly powerful democratic movements against authoritarian regimes, involving substantial mass actions and often brutal suppressions. In Sweden, battles between the Hat and Cap elite factions had waxed and waned for more than a century, creating an opening for a peasant uprising and march on Stockholm in 1743 and figuring in the conspiratorial assassination of King Gustav III in 1792. In Uruguay, interparty and intraparty factional rivalries, coupled with the emergence of the powerful Tupamaro urban revolutionary movement and its brutal repression by the military, resulted in the breakdown of democracy and a military dictatorship after 1973, followed by growing public support in the late 1970s and early 1980s for a return to democracy. In Hungary, memories of the bloody crushing of the 1956 revolt against the communist regime remained vivid, and the strength of reformist forces had grown steadily from the 1960s into the 1980s. In South Africa, the Afrikaner-imposed apartheid regime was increasingly besieged by the ANC-led insurgency, with the specter of a full-scale black uprising looming.

In most of the cases, elites were aggregated into two or three distinct and warring camps during the periods just prior to the settlement-triggering crises: the Tory/Whig, Hat/Cap, Conservative/Liberal oppositions in England, Sweden, and Colombia, respectively; regime and antiregime camps in Korea, Poland, and, more ambiguously, Hungary; and right-wing, centrist, and left-wing camps in Costa Rica, Venezuela, and Uruguay. In Spain and South Africa, however, elite alignments were more complex because of multiple ethnoterritorial or racial cleavages, while in Mexico alignments were quite inchoate due to the chaotic 1910–20 civil war and subsequent assassinations and uprisings.

Prior to at least five settlements—England, Sweden, Colombia, Poland, and South Africa—the main elite camps had fought each other to a standstill, and prior to at least six settlements the main camps were jointly under the heel of a more or less incompetent, corrupt, and despised autocrat or military regime: Tories and Whigs under James II, Hats and Caps under Gustav IV, Conservatives and Liberals under the Colombian dictator Rojas Pinilla, Costa Rica's Conservatives and Social

Democrats under the authoritarian presidency of Rafael Calderon, Venezuela's Democratic Action, Social-Christian, and Democratic Republican elite camps under the Perez Jimenez dictatorship, and Uruguay's Colorado, Blanco, and Broad Front forces under its military regime. In Spain, Korea, Poland, and Hungary, by contrast, elites were divided into camps supporting or opposing a military or one-party regime. Overall, autocrats or authoritarian regimes held sway in ten of the twelve countries immediately before their elite settlements. Only in Mexico and South Africa were "democratically" elected regimes in power on the eve of settlements; but the Mexican regime was of very recent vintage (1920) and highly unstable, while the white South African regime, though of long duration, was sharply exclusionary, besieged, and engaged in a variety of extralegal and strongly repressive measures. Finally, although elites in each of the twelve countries were about to fashion settlements that would have democratizing consequences, in seven cases they had little or no previous experience of democratic politics (England, Sweden, Mexico, Venezuela, Korea, Poland, and Hungary), in one there had been a relatively short-lived democratic regime (Spain between 1930 and 1936), while in four countries most key elites had considerable, if distorted, democratic experience (Costa Rica, Colombia, Uruguay, and South Africa).

These were the main political circumstances in the twelve countries during the years immediately preceding their settlements. However, elites in many countries have had similar histories of intense conflict and have been similarly clustered into two or three distinct and well-articulated camps without then going on to settle their basic differences. A sharp and profoundly dangerous triggering crisis, therefore, also appears to be necessary for a settlement to occur. Let us recall key elements of the triggering crises in the cases under discussion. In England elite antagonism toward James II over his use of monarchical powers, his aggressive attempts to promote the Catholic religion, and his close relationship with France's Louis XIV was brought to a boil by the birth of James's son in 1688. This virtually guaranteed a Catholic succession in a predominantly Protestant country, with all that it would entail for still raging religious conflicts. The crisis in Sweden involved the loss of Finland to Russia in 1808, impending Russian and Danish-French invasions, and economic disarray, all of which were viewed by Hat and Cap leaders as consequences of Gustav IV's ill-considered policies and personal failings. Mexico's triggering crisis grew out of the assassination of president-elect Alvaro Obregón by a religious fanatic in July 1928, which created the very real prospect of renewed civil war. In Costa Rica the triggering crisis was the actual outbreak of civil war brought about by the Calderonistas' annulment of the 1948 presidential election, which had been won by Otilio Ulate, the candidate of a newly unified opposition. The crises in Colombia and Venezuela during 1956–57 involved sharp economic downturns accompanied by the efforts of dictators Rojas Pinilla and Perez Jimenez, respectively, to expand their powers and prolong their presidential tenures; the crisis in Colombia was made particularly acute by continuing civil strife, and mass unrest was spreading in Venezuela, as well.

In Spain the death of Francisco Franco in 1975 encouraged his regime's long-suppressed opponents to mobilize against efforts to perpetuate the authoritarian regime, creating widespread fears of a new civil war. The Uruguayan crisis was more protracted and less palpable than most, but it can be seen as entailing the rejection of the military's proposed constitution by a 1980 plebiscite, a political impasse among the main elite factions during 1983–84, an economic downturn, and intensifying mass protests against the military regime. In Korea a long-simmering and often violent confrontation between the military regime and its democratic opponents was inflamed between January and June 1987 by President Chun Doo Hwan's abrupt cessation of constitutional negotiations, the death of a student protester at police hands, arrests of opposition leaders, mounting protest demonstrations, fears that the 1988 Seoul Olympics would be canceled, and the announcement in June that the ruling party's presidential candidate would be General Roh Tae Woo, Chun's right-hand man, which sparked demonstrations of unprecedented magnitude. In Poland and Hungary, Mikhail Gorbachev's "Sinatra Doctrine" left the communist regimes to fend for themselves against growing opposition movements, most notably manifest in a wave of strikes in Poland during April-August 1988 and mass demonstrations in Hungary during March-June 1989. Finally, as Hennie Kotzé recounts in chapter 10, the crisis triggering a settlement in South Africa became most acute when constitutional negotiations between the government and a wide range of opposing party and movement elites broke down in June 1992, and there immediately followed a violent test of strength involving several massacres during the next three months.

Several observations about these triggering crises need to be made. First, they obviously involved historical accidents. Just to mention a few: James II's ardent Catholicism and his long-barren wife's sudden pregnancy and birth of a son; Gustav IV's gross incompetence; the assassination of Alvaro Obregón by a religious fanatic; the hunger for power and political miscalculations of Rojas Pinilla and Perez Jimenez; the long-expected but still jolting death of Francisco Franco; the upheavals in Gorbachev's Moscow, which greatly and immediately undermined the communist regimes in Budapest and Warsaw; the decision by Blanco leaders in Uruguay to boycott and thereby simplify talks between military and other party leaders; and a stroke suffered by South Africa's intransigent P. W. Botha, which opened the way to the much more conciliatory presidency of F. W. de Klerk.

Second, in most instances triggering crises grew out of what Latin Americans call *continuismo*—efforts by those holding government power to perpetuate their rule indefinitely. In England and Sweden, this involved attempts to maintain absolutist monarchies. In Costa Rica, Rafael Calderon and his followers attempted to hold onto power by annulling an election they had lost. In Colombia and Venezuela, the dictatorial Rojas Pinilla and Perez Jimenez violated understandings that they would step down or hold elections within a specified time period. In Spain, Franquists tried to preserve their power bases within the authoritarian structures created under Franco. In Korea, Chun Doo Hwan and his supporters in the ruling party and the military appeared to be unwavering in their commitment to the authoritarian Yushin constitution.

Third, while elites were the main actors in the triggering crises, mass publics frequently played strong supporting roles. In at least six cases—Venezuela, Uruguay, Korea, Poland, Hungary, and South Africa—mass mobilizations stemming from economic or political discontents were ominous aspects of the crises. In two of these countries, "stunning elections" (Huntington, 1991) helped bring on crises: defeat of the military's proposed constitution in Uruguay's 1980 plebiscite and sharp gains for antiregime parties in Korea's 1985 congressional elections. In all of the countries being considered, fears of crippling strikes or mass unrest getting out of hand lent urgency to elite negotiations.

Settlement Processes

The processes through which settlements are accomplished unfold principally among a small circle of leaders, and they manifest some common features, all of which reflect the atmosphere of crisis. First, settlements are accomplished with considerable speed, seldom taking more than a few weeks or months; the longer the process takes, the more likely it becomes that blocking actions by elites outside the small circle will be effective. Second, settlements entail face-to-face and secret meetings and consultations, which are so frequent and intensive that they often spawn a conspiratorial camaraderie among sworn enemies. Third, some formal document (a signed pact, a new constitution) embodying informal and tacit understandings that have been reached is normally part of a settlement. Fourth, settlements are typically and primarily the handiwork of established, experienced, and skilled leaders who have painful personal memories of past conflicts and deep knowledge of political levers that can be pulled within and between their camps and who possess enough authority to bring recalcitrant allies and followers along. Fifth, considerable elite autonomy from cadre and mass pressures appears to be necessary, because in settlements elites, in effect, agree on the principle that their competitions will no longer be governed by principles (Mansfield, 1964); this is often a change so shocking to followers that it can be accomplished only if key elite persons are relatively free to strike heretical bargains.

Settlements begin with concerted elite actions that prepare the way for negotiations and compromises. In five countries—England, Sweden, Costa Rica, Colombia, and Venezuela—a handful of key leaders from opposing elite camps jointly planned and, with the help of military allies, executed overthrows of autocrats and their entourages. In two other countries, Spain and Hungary, settlements began when elites in power first liberalized authoritarian regimes and then moved toward negotiated rapprochements with opposition elites. In the remaining five cases—Mexico, Uruguay, Korea, Poland, and South Africa—settlements occurred after overtures between regime and opposition leaders paved the way for negotiating a reconstitution of the existing regime, in the Mexican case to achieve stability behind a democratic facade but in the other cases to initiate fully democratic competitions.

We have already noted that accidental events and actions of individual leaders played a large role in all twelve elite settlements, but this is a point so important that it deserves further illustration. In the English case, for example, William's invasion of England, secretly invited by top Tory and Whig leaders in June 1688, would not have been approved by the Dutch States-General, to which William was accountable, had Louis XIV not recently made threatening gestures toward the Dutch provinces. Once approved, William's invasion in November 1688 hinged on the "Protestant wind" that sped his fleet to its landing site at Torbay while confining James's defending Channel Fleet to the Thames estuary—a "gift from God" helped along by chaos in the Channel Fleet due to officer desertions orchestrated by John Churchill and a few other key military leaders (Webb, 1995, 271–86). In the immediate wake of Alvaro Obregón's assassination in Mexico in mid-1928, the incumbent president Plutarco Calles exercised remarkable skill in getting leaders of groups making up the "revolutionary family" to agree on an interim president and, during the ensuing months, in promoting the March 1929 formation of the omnibus Party of National Revolution (forerunner of the PRI). Calles' actions began a shift from *caudillismo* to institutionalized rule in Mexico (Knight, 1992). In the Colombian situation, the previously intransigent Conservative former president, Laureano Gomez, unexpectedly entered secret negotiations in Spain with his principal enemy, Liberal former president Alberto Lleras, to produce several pacts that initiated a Liberal-Conservative plot to oust Rojas Pinilla and then outlined the elaborate National Front power-sharing arrangement elites negotiated after Rojas's ouster (Peeler, 1992). In Spain, the surprisingly swift and sagacious action by King Juan Carlos in appointing Adolfo Suarez prime minister, and then Suarez's skill in convincing the Franquist Cortes to give way to a freely elected Cortes that would serve as a constituent assembly, set the stage for the settlement negotiations and compromises (Gunther, 1992; see also Linz and Stepan, 1996). Finally, in Korea, Roh Tae Woo, chosen by Chun Doo Hwan as the military regime's presidential candidate, startled everyone, except perhaps a few close associates, with his acceptance of all key opposition demands on June 29, 1987 (Burton and Ryu, 1997).

Once they were under way, negotiations at the core of the twelve settlements had important uniformities. First, the negotiations were conducted by relative handfuls of political leaders: William and about a dozen Tory and Whig parliamentary leaders in England; party leaders themselves in Costa Rica, Colombia, and Venezuela; military and party leaders in Uruguay; and small officially designated and politically representative negotiating committees in Sweden, Spain, and Korea. In the two communist countries, negotiations were centered in the famous "national roundtables," around which, in Hungary, sat some fifty main participants (Welsh, 1994; Tokes, 1996). Reflecting the more diffuse elite alignments noted above, negotiations in Mexico and South Africa occurred among larger circles of leaders—in Mexico between Calles and various generals, governors, and congressional delegations, and in South Africa initially within the Convention for a Democratic South Africa (CODESA), which involved leaders and aides from twenty-six parties, and later within the so-called Multi-Party Negotiating Process (MPNP), which was made possible, however, by a "record of understanding" reached by the two paramount leaders, de Klerk and Nelson Mandela, in September 1992. Second, except in South Africa and the two communist countries, negotiations were everywhere confidential. Third, they unfolded rapidly, requiring in all but the South African case no more than six months and being completed in no more than three months in England, Sweden, Costa Rica, Uruguay, Korea, Poland, and Hungary.

Some settlements involved more fundamental compromises than others. Overthrowing James II in England and Gustav IV in Sweden and replacing them with "elected" monarchs whose powers were limited by representative parliaments involved "unprincipled" actions by elites that had long insisted on monarchical prerogatives. Also at stake in England were questions of "right" religious belief and practice, so that adopting a religious tolerance act permitting each person to worship more or less as she or he pleased while allowing continued discrimination against non-Anglicans in education, employment, and office holding was a basic compromise of everyone's principles. Compromises reached in South Africa and the two communist countries were similarly fundamental. They involved greatly altering or dismantling whole structures of power through which one set of elites and its followers had dominated all other elites and population segments, as well as the latter elites' acceptance that sharing power with their former oppressors or allowing them to regain power through electoral contests was unavoidable. Because they also involved power sharing among elites who had long been at one anothers' throats, the settlements in Mexico, Colombia, Venezuela, and Spain were nearly as fundamental. By contrast, the three remaining settlements—in Costa Rica, Uruguay, and Korea—were mainly concerned with engineering transitions to fully democratic regimes. But enmities between elites were nevertheless deep in these countries, too, and, except perhaps in Costa Rica, memories of horrors perpetrated by one or more camps were fresh, including the Tupamaro guerrilla insurgency and the brutal military retributions it unleashed in Uruguay, and the 1980 Kwangju massacre and assorted other crimes and corruptions of the Korean military regime. Thus, while these last three settlements appear to have involved fewer compromises of principles, the efforts by elites to overcome legacies of bitter conflict and bloodshed were still impressive. In Korea, for example, the very act of compromise was alien to Confucian doctrine (Han, 1990, 332).

Finally, it needs to be emphasized that all of the settlements were first and foremost political expedients that enabled former enemies to live and compete peacefully. Rarely did they "solve" conflicts. Instead, elites committed themselves to expressing and adjudicating old and new conflicts in restrained, nonviolent ways. Especially for the most recent settlements, these commitments are still being tested, but even where settlements occurred scores or hundreds of years ago, norms of political restraint and accommodation have had to be regularly reaffirmed and policed by the elites.

Consolidation Processes: Power Sharing and Crisis Management

It is important to distinguish between an initial elite settlement and its subsequent consolidation. While the crucial result of a settlement is elite power sharing, this takes time to jell. Settlements always exclude some individuals and groups, notably autocrats and their entourages who are usually the immediate target. These elites seldom go quietly, often launching countercoups or trying to subvert the nascent power-sharing arrangement. Moreover, there are certain to be elite groups whose ideological, religious, ethnic, or regional commitments keep them from participating: old hatreds and distrusts die hard, while new patterns of cooperation, trust, and restraint solidify slowly, and their payoffs—peaceful elite competitions and enhanced elite security—unfold gradually. For these reasons, the consolidation of elite settlements takes years, perhaps a generation, during which conciliation and forbearance by persons holding the most central political positions are essential. Two processes appear especially important to consolidation: power sharing in the aftermath of the settlement and the effective handling of new crises.

Power sharing during the months and years following a settlement is an important ingredient of consolidation; it occurred formally or informally in at least nine of the twelve cases considered here. Colombia and South Africa are instances of elaborately formal power-sharing arrangements: an even division of all government offices and the strict alternation of Liberals and Conservatives in the presidency for sixteen years following the Colombian settlement, and allocation of a deputy president post to any party securing more than 15 percent of votes, as well as provision for a grand-coalition cabinet, under South Africa's interim constitution of 1994–96. Similarly, in Poland and Hungary, government power was shared formally by communists and their opponents between the conclusion of roundtable negotiations and the holding of freely contested elections about six months later. In Venezuela, coalition cabinets consisting of representatives from the main parties followed the first postsettlement elections.

In England and Sweden, power sharing occurred more informally through balanced appointments of Tory and Whig and Hat and Cap leaders by William and by the interim Charles XIII (uncle of Gustav IV), respectively, to important posts. And in Mexico, the main rationale for creating the PNR early in 1929 was to give groups in the revolutionary family shared access to government power, a mechanism that proved long lasting in the subsequent PRI-dominated regime. By contrast, in Costa Rica a temporary junta led by the Social Democrat, Jose Figueres, monopolized power, albeit with clear understandings about its reform agenda, its maximum eighteen-month duration, and the eventual replacement of Figueres by the Conservative leader, Otilio Ulate. In Spain, Uruguay, and Korea, there were prompt moves to competitive elections, through which the most important opposition groups soon won government power (Spain and Uruguay) or made gains large enough to deprive government parties of a reliable legislative majority (Korea). In Uruguay and Korea, more overt power sharing came later: the Blanco-Colorado coalition government of 1990–93 and formation of the semi-omnibus Democratic Liberal Party in Korea during 1990, which carried Kim Young Sam into the presidency in 1992.

The effective handling of new crises, made possible in considerable part by power sharing, is crucial for the consolidation of elite settlements. This involves formerly opposed elites standing together to defeat violent challenges by groups displaced by or excluded from settlements or to confront wholly new problems. Surmounting such crises cements commitments to the new cooperative arrangements by motivating elites to defend them. In about half the cases, new crises took the form of countercoups or insurgencies that newly accommodative elites managed to defeat: attempted invasions of England by Jacobites in Ireland during 1690–91, an attempted royalist coup in Sweden in 1810, the Obregonista revolt during March and April 1929 in Mexico, insurgencies in Costa Rica launched by Calderonistas exiled in adjacent Nicaragua during the 1950s, revolutionary, mainly rural, insurgencies in Colombia and Venezuela in the 1960s (which have continued in Colombia), and the dramatic, televised capture of Spain's Congress of Deputies chamber by disgruntled Civil Guard troops in February 1981.

In the other cases, new crises involved challenges to components of the settlements or confrontations with military or other adherents of the presettlement regimes. In Uruguay, agitation to rescind the amnesty granted to military officers as part of the 1984 Naval Club Accord peaked in a 1989 referendum that was intensely fought but finally won by the elites who struck the deal. In Poland and Hungary, elite cooperation and restraint survived the electoral victories of former communists and their return to power during 1993 and 1994, respectively. Polish elites then managed to contain a serious crisis at the end of 1995 and early 1996 when, in the wake of former communist Aleksander Kwasniewski's election victory over Lech Walesa for the presidency, Jozef Oleksy, the prime minister allied with Kwasniewski, was forced to resign over allegations that he shared state secrets with Russian spies. In Korea, the late-1995 decision to arrest and prosecute the two former presidents of the military regime, Chun Doo Hwan and Roh Tae Woo, for their actions in the 1979 coup and 1980 Kwangju massacre tested military acceptance of the new democratic regime; but the two leaders were jailed, convicted, and sentenced without an explosion. Finally, in South Africa, it remains to be seen whether serious problems involving the status and control of KwaZulu/Natal, the departure of de Klerk's National Party in mid-1996 from the interim grand-coalition government, and the profound racial and economic divisions within the population will erupt in crises that rupture or strengthen the still embryonic settlement consolidation.

There is much evidence that the effective handling of still further crises has been important for solidifying elite commitments to norms of political cooperation and restraint and to structures of power sharing that settlements produced. For example, in addition to defeating the Jacobite Rebellion in 1690 and recapturing Ireland in 1691, English elites had to deal with numerous other crises during the first several decades following the settlement of 1688–89: war with the French in the 1690s, removal of the large Dutch army that Prince William had brought onto English soil in order to depose James II, the need to secure parliamentary authority against William's headstrong proclivities in financial and foreign policy matters, the need to formulate clear succession rules that would permanently exclude the Stuart (Catholic) line, and another Jacobite uprising in 1715. That elite cooperation in containing these and still other postsettlement crises served to solidify commitments to a tamed politics is indicated by Britain's subsequent long record of regime stability. By the time British elites confronted the crisis of military defeat in the American colonies, for example, pacific elite competitions were sufficiently entrenched to withstand that debacle. Notable crises of the nineteenth and twentieth centuries surmounted peacefully by British elites include the Chartist rebellion, the rise of an initially hostile and powerful labor movement, struggles by this and other groups for suffrage, two world wars, and the delicate dismantling of a far-flung empire.

Observations about Crises, Elite Settlements, and Regime Change

We want to be clear about what we are and are not saying. We are saying that a severe political crisis appears to be a *necessary* condition for an elite settlement; at least, we know of no instance in which a settlement occurred in the absence of a crisis. We are not saying, however, that a crisis is a *sufficient* condition for an elite settlement. No matter how severe they are, most crises do not give rise to settlements. Some result in revolutions and major regime changes (the French Revolution), some launch civil wars or other massive blood-lettings but produce no basic regime change (Nigeria's civil war between 1966 and 1969; the recent and horrifying Tutsi and Hutu massacres in Rwanda), while some crises, which occur where elites have already achieved a tamed politics, are managed peacefully with no regime change (the Anglo-American and Scandinavian countries during the Great Depression).

Second, we must admit that many of the crises that have triggered elite settlements do not fit easily into the rough inventory offered by Dogan and Higley in chapter 1. Withdrawal of foreign support by the Soviet Union was an important aspect of the crises that led to the Hungarian and Polish settlements. Economic disaster—though the term may in some cases be too strong—figured in the triggering crises in Sweden, Colombia, Venezuela, and Uruguay, while defeat in international warfare was also part of the Swedish crisis. However, by far the most common feature of triggering crises was the prospect of internal warfare. The specter of civil war, or of some other major confrontation between powerful groups able to seriously harm each other and society, was what drove settlements forward in England, Sweden, Mexico, Colombia, Venezuela, Spain, Uruguay, Korea, and South Africa. The Dogan-Higley inventory should incorporate this dimension of some crises more clearly.

While a systematic connection between the different kinds of crises outlined in chapter 1 and the occurrence or nonoccurrence of elite settlements is difficult to find, it is still worth asking why and how some crises trigger settlements while most do not. Do they present elites with a virtually unique decision-making environment? For example, do these crises but not others contain exceptional latitudes for elite maneuvering? Alternatively, are they distinctive because they close off most possibilities for action and leave only one or two open? In line with Alan Knight's distinctions in the preceding chapter, are triggering crises objectively experienced or subjectively perceived to be of surpassing severity? Are they, perhaps, distinguished by external pressures and interventions that have not been sufficiently investigated? Although we cannot give firm answers, we suspect that more important than the specific properties of crises are the combinations of elite orientations and abilities that happen to exist at the time crises occur.

It is also important to investigate, though we have not done so in this chapter, how triggering crises are related to changes and continuities in elite composition. Settlements appear to involve exceptionally small amounts of elite circulation. Primarily, only those elites holding the highest government offices during the period immediately preceding a settlement are displaced, and then not always permanently. This essential continuity in elite makeup accords with the very nature of settlements, because through them existing elites reorganize their relations so as to make their previously insecure positions more secure.

Why do political crises appear to be a necessary condition for elite settlements? Unchecked political competitions constitute the modal "game" played by elites in most countries throughout history: vicious, zero-sum struggles for power are repeated endlessly. In this modal game, the only way for elites to gain a modicum of security is by dominating or liquidating their opponents; cooperation that might benefit opponents is more or less unthinkable. Using game-theoretic concepts, both Robert Putnam (1993) and Barry Weingast (1997) have described the modal game as an "equilibrium situation." To break out of the equilibrium, elites must see that the next round of conflict is likely to visit disaster on all sides. Only in the face of an abrupt and profound political crisis is this grim prospect likely to be widely recognized and keenly felt. And only then does cooperation and compromise with one's enemies (what game theorists call a solution to the "coordination dilemma"), even to the extent of sacrificing cherished principles and interests, become conceivable.

Is it nevertheless possible that the occurrence of elite settlements is becoming less dependent on abrupt and profound political crises? The fact that in Uruguay, Korea, Hungary, and Poland no civil war or other catastrophe clearly impended lends credence to this speculation. It may be that the spreading acceptance of democracy as the only viable regime in today's world increases the likelihood that disunited elites will resort to settlement-like compromises without there first having to be a dire crisis. But at present, the evidence for this possibility is weak, while that for a close connection between crises, elite settlements, and regime change is strong.

Criticisms of the Settlement Concept

In chapter 2, Alan Knight raises seemingly fundamental doubts about our focus on the connections between crises and elite settlements. He suggests that "there is a sense in which the elite approach is least appropriate precisely at times of social and political upheaval"; that "the more unstable [elites are], the more we should seek theoretical illumination elsewhere: in Hobbes, Marx, the 'new social history' "; and that "it is precisely in times of crisis that elite authority wavers and elite autonomy constricts." Knight backs his doubts with a disparate mix of general and specific examples of crises in which elites lacked control. These range from elites confronting exogenous forces, such as Third World population explosions or the structural economic dependency confronted by Cuban and Argentine elites during the 1930s, to situations in which elites lost control of or were greatly constrained by autonomous actions of mass publics, such as revolutions in general or Colombia's 1948 Bogotazo uprising in particular.

While we accept that Knight has identified situations in which elite control was limited or absent, we argue that such examples, in fact, buttress our position: that elites shape the outcomes of severe crises only when they forge some basic accommodation in the midst of such crises. In virtually all of Knight's examples, elites lacked control because they were *and remained* deeply disunited, a configuration that precludes a coherent response to "grand impersonal forces" and one that invites unchecked mass actions (though such actions are more often led by disaffected elites than Knight admits). Significantly, none of his examples presents a crisis that provoked an elite settlement; thus, they mainly illustrate what can happen when elites *fail* to settle their differences. By contrast, the twelve settlement cases examined here powerfully demonstrate the potential for elite control in crisis situations.

Our analysis shows that it is primarily elites who orchestrate challenges to presettlement regimes. This orchestration often includes deliberate mobilizations, but sometimes also deliberate demobilizations, of mass publics. Moreover, it is elites who conduct secret meetings, fashion compromises, write constitutions, get them adopted and implemented, and see to their enforcement. Elite autonomy and control are also demonstrated by the ability of elites to rally their followers in support of controversial compromises they make. If, as Knight suggests, revolutions are at one end of a continuum, constituting crises when elites are least in control, settlement-triggering crises must be situated near the continuum's other end. His assertion that elites have the least control in times of crisis is thus clearly wrong as regards crises that trigger settlements.

Nor will the occurrence of elite settlements be illuminated theoretically by turning to Hobbes, Marx, or the "new social history." Knight is not the first scholar to speculate that elite settlements are largely epiphenomenal outcomes of structural class struggles or perhaps of cultural evolutions. Because it is frequently voiced, let us consider this alternative "structural" explanation more closely.

From the class-centered perspective, elite settlements mainly reflect the earlier resolution of class struggles. For example, Marxist interpretations of political change in England during the seventeenth century have focused on the civil wars of the 1640s, arguing that the landed upper class emerged victorious from those wars and thereby secured its dominance of British politics and society (e.g., Moore, 1966; Cammack, 1990). The elite settlement of 1689 is thus seen, if it is mentioned at all, as simply ratifying rule by the landed upper class. Even Theda Skocpol (1979, esp. 144), in her effort to combine class and political variables to explain revolutions, glosses over the 1689 settlement, observing that when King James II "forgot" that landed upper-class dominance through parliament had been secured, he was quickly replaced "with very little fuss." Aside from facile maneuvers such as relegating William's elite-invited invasion and expulsion of James II to the status of a minor event hardly worth mentioning, a key difficulty with class-based interpretations is that class divisions comparable to those in England prevailed throughout western Europe during the seventeenth century, yet elite settlements were elsewhere nonexistent: if in England, why not in Denmark or France or Spain or Sweden in the same period? Additionally, the intense struggles between Tories and Whigs in the period leading up to 1688–89 are a problem for class-centered explanations: if a new ruling class was forged in the civil wars, why were its main components at each others' throats during the next four decades? While answers consistent with a class-centered framework can doubtless be devised, the thesis that because of a unique political crisis English elites alone reached a settlement during the early modern period is more parsimonious, less disembodied, and it accords better with the conclusions of historians who have studied the period closely (e.g., Jones, 1972; Schwoerer, 1981; Speck, 1988; Webb, 1995).

Application of the settlement thesis to Venezuela has been challenged on similar grounds. Kevin Neuhouser (1992) argues that the rise of leftist parties and revolutionary movements during the 1960s showed that no elite settlement occurred in 1957–58; there was, instead, only a temporary "class compromise" during the 1970s, made possible by the OPEC-induced inflow of petrodollars. When that inflow ceased a few years later, so also did the ability of Venezuelan capitalists and "state managers" to contain class conflict, which promptly resumed. Prior to the petrodollar inflow, Neuhouser claims, the Venezuelan state was in essentially the same degenerate condition as the Brazilian and Chilean states before their military overthrows in 1964 and 1973, respectively. Thus, had it not been for petrodollars Venezuela would presumably have suffered the same fate.

Neuhouser's claim that because there was a resurgence of leftist parties and movements in Venezuela during the 1960s (not to mention the drumbeat of such uprisings in Colombia throughout the past forty years) there could not have been an earlier settlement misunderstands what settlements accomplish. Settlements tame politics by establishing a basis for restrained and peaceful political competitions between major elite camps. This was the main consequence of the Venezuelan settlement: an unbroken string of peaceful and binding electoral contests, in a country that had almost no prior experience of such contests, since the first postsettlement election in December 1958. It is significant that most students of Venezuelan politics recognize the watershed character of the 1958 events (e.g., Blank, 1973; Levine, 1978; Karl, 1987; Peeler, 1992, 1995). Second, no one has said that settlements preclude a resurgence of radical political forces. Rather, settlements make it likely that the main elite camps that have forged them will cooperate to defeat or stifle resurgent radical forces. This is what happened in Venezuela during the 1960s and what clearly did not happen in Brazil under Joao Goulart's government between 1961 and 1964 or in Chile before and during Salvador Allende's ill-fated government of 1970–73. In Venezuela, governments dominated by the Democratic Action Party (AD) between 1959 and 1969—despite internal AD splits and the loss of supporters to other centrist and center-right groups and parties— successfully resisted and increasingly marginalized Cuban-supported guerrilla movements, in large measure because AD had strong support from most business, trade union, and peasant elites and organizations. This enabled the Social Christian-dominated government after 1969 to legalize the Communist Party and induce most guerrillas to lay down their arms.

A general shortcoming of class-centered structural frameworks is that classes and other large collectivities are never actors; nor, for that matter, are "states." Various organizationally based elites may purport to speak for a class, ethnic category, geographic region, or religious community, and they may successfully mobilize various segments of it. But these elites are almost always at odds with one another: on most issues most of the time, classes and similar collectivities are to this extent disunited, and they never "act" (Etzioni-Halevy, 1993, 34–50). Similarly, state managers do not simply register whatever balance there might be between classes or other collectivities; elites and leaders in charge of states have their own interests and varying degrees of autonomy. Thus, a "class compromise" orchestrated by state managers is nothing more than some policy strategy on which elites representing diverse and powerful interests for the moment agree. In Venezuela, once petrodollars began to flow in (mainly during 1974, after the "class compromise" made possible by that in-flow allegedly occurred), the main political, business, labor, and state administrative elites concluded that using them to expand accumulation and consumption simultaneously was a low-cost policy strategy, albeit one that could not, it turned out, be sustained or easily abandoned. Throughout the third quarter of the twentieth century, Venezuela's petroleum-based economy was virtually unique in Latin America; but while this may well have made a settlement easier to effect in 1957–58 (Karl, 1987), it sheds no light on why settlements were also effected in petroleum-poor Mexico thirty years before, Costa Rica in 1948, or Colombia at the same time.

Another influential line of thought implies that elite settlements mainly articulate value orientations of compromise and accommodation that have come to prevail culturally among elites and masses (e.g., Putnam, 1993; Diamond, 1994). We do not think this interpretation fits well with the situations in our twelve countries during the periods encompassing the settlements and their immediate aftermaths. What stands out for us is substantial conflict among groups holding mutually exclusive value orientations. In the settlements, these groups began to devise ways to live together and compete peacefully for political influence. We would suggest, therefore, that elite settlements represent high moments of "cultural creation": almost overnight, a narrow circle of elites agree to cast aside a culturally embedded practice of unchecked power struggles, putting in its place norms of political compromise, accommodation, and restraint. Typically, these aspects of a new and radically different political culture are not widely understood or accepted in the general population, and some elites also remain hostile to them. Elite and mass commitments to the norms of a suddenly tamed politics gradually spread when their payoffs in enhanced elite security and peaceful alternations in government office become clear. Over time, these commitments become deeply cemented in laws, political conventions, and in many cultural symbols and rituals—the process Dankwart Rustow (1970) aptly terms "habituation." In short, cultural analysts stand to gain much explanatory mileage by examining how elite settlements transform, rather than reflect, political cultures.

In stressing the impacts of elite settlements on political cultures, it is also important to recognize their often mixed consequences. The political culture that grew out of Mexico's 1928–29 settlement is perhaps the most extreme example. As Alan Knight describes in chapter 4, the myth of an institutionalized "revolutionary" elite and regime that crystallized around the PNR/PRI served to legitimate the PRI's dominance of Mexican politics through clientelism, force, and fraud. Yet within the PRI, norms of elite cooperation, power-sharing, restrained competitions, and "careers open to talents" became strongly entrenched. Elite commitment to the sexennial presidential cycle resolved the problem of executive *continuismo*, which has brought so many regimes down, yet it was coupled to a norm of executive discretion that has sharply limited elite access to central decision-making processes. As recounted by Knight, these elements of Mexican political culture have contributed to the effective management of eight serious crises since the 1930s, indicating the regime's "Whiggish resilience." The regime's response to most of these crises involved giving a stronger voice to one or more previously excluded elite groups. Gradually, the tight elite cartel created in the 1928–29 settlement has become more dispersed, and despite many twists and turns, Mexican political culture and politics have slowly become more democratic.

The absence of any systematic relation between class or cultural forces and the occurrence of elite settlements points strongly to the conclusion that they are highly contingent events. We have seen that the crises that triggered settlements were largely accidental in nature. Similarly, the processes through which settlements were accomplished depended heavily for their success on accidental combinations of circumstances: the presence of skilled leaders with sufficient political capital, bold and unpredictable elite choices, delicate balances of elite autonomy, and mass pressures. Our conclusion about the contingent character of elite settlements accords with what is becoming apparent about the "third wave" of democratization, which displays, as Karen Remmer (1995, 105) has recently put it, "an extraordinarily wide variety of conjunctural conditions, socioeconomic structures, patterns of state-society relationships, transitional paths, and historical traditions." Of course, most third-wave democratizations occurred in the absence of elite settlements, which goes a long way, we think, toward explaining why so many of today's new democratic regimes remain fragile and incomplete.

References

Blank, David, E. 1973. *Politics in Venezuela.* Boston: Little, Brown.

Burton, Michael G., Richard Gunther, and John Higley. 1992. "Introduction: Elite Transformations and Democratic Regimes." In Higley and Gunther, *Elites and Democratic Consolidation in Latin America and Southern Europe.* New York: Cambridge University Press, 1–37.

Burton, Michael G., and John Higley. 1987. "Elite Settlements." *American Sociological Review* 52 (June): 295–306.

Burton, Michael G., and Jai P. Ryu. 1997. "South Korea's Elite Settlement and Democratic Consolidation." *Journal of Political and Military Sociology* 25 (summer): 1–24.

Cammack, Paul. 1990. "A Critical Assessment of the New Elite Paradigm." *American Sociological Review* 55 (June): 415–20.

Cavarozzi, Marcelo. 1992. "Patterns of Elite Negotiation and Confrontation in Argentina and Chile." In Higley and Gunther, *Elites and Democratic Consolidation*, 208–36.

Cotta, Maurizio. 1992. "Elite unification and democratic consolidation in Italy: a historical overview." In Higley and Gunther, *Elites and Democratic Consolidation*, 146–77.

Diamond, Larry. 1994. "Causes and Effects." In *Political Culture and Democracy in Developing Countries*. ed. L. Diamond, 229–49. Boulder, Colo.: Lynne Rienner.

Etzioni-Halevy, Eva. 1993. *The Elite Connection: Problems and Potential of Western Democracy*. London: Polity Press.

Friedman, Steven. 1996. *Yesterday's Pact: Power Sharing and Legitimate Governance in Post-Settlement South Africa*. Johannesburg: Centre for Policy Studies.

———. 1995. "South Africa: Divided in a Special Way." In *Politics in Developing Countries: Comparing Experiences with Democracy*, ed. Larry Diamond, Juan J. Linz, and Seymour Martin Lipset, 531–82. Boulder, Colo.: Lynne Rienner (2d ed.).

Gillespie, Charles Guy. 1992. "The Role of Civil-Military Pacts in Elite Settlements and Elite Convergence: Democratic Consolidation in Uruguay." In Higley and Gunther, *Elites and Democratic Consolidation*, 178–207.

Gunther, Richard. 1992. "Spain: the Very Model of the Modern Elite Settlement." In Higley and Gunther, *Elites and Democratic Consolidation*, 1992: 38–80.

Han, Sung-Joo. 1990. "South Korean Politics in Transition." In *Politics in Developing Countries: Comparing Experiences with Democracy*, ed. Larry Diamond, Juan J. Linz, and Seymour Martin Lipset, 313–50. Boulder, Colo.: Lynne Rienner.

Higley, John, and Richard Gunther, eds. 1992. *Elites and Democratic Consolidation in Latin America and Southern Europe*. New York: Cambridge University Press.

Higley, John, Ursula Hoffmann-Lange, Charles Kadushin, and Gwen Moore. 1991. "Elite Integration in Stable Democracies: A Reconsideration." *European Sociological Review* 7 (May): 35–53.

Higley, John, Tong-yi Huang, and Tse-min Lin. 1998. "Elite Settlement and Democratic Consolidation in Taiwan." *Journal of Democracy* 9 (April).

Higley, John, and Jan Pakulski. 1995. "Elite Transformation in Central and Eastern Europe." *Australian Journal of Political Science* 30 (October): 415–35.

Huntington, Samuel P. 1991. *The Third Wave: Democratization in the Late Twentieth Century*. Norman: University of Oklahoma Press.

Jones, J. R. 1972. *The Revolution of 1688 in England*. London: Weidenfeld and Nicholson.

Karl, Terry Lynn. 1987. "Petroleum and Political Pacts: The Transition to Democracy in Venezuela." *Latin American Research Review* 22 (June): 63–94.

Knight, Alan. 1992. "Mexico's Elite Settlement." In Higley and Gunther, *Elites and Democratic Consolidation*, 113–45.

Levine, David H. 1978. "Venezuela Since 1958: The Consolidation of Democratic Politics." In *The Breakdown of Democratic Regimes: Latin America*, ed. Juan J. Linz and Alfred Stepan, 82–109. Baltimore: Johns Hopkins University Press.

Linz, Juan J. and Alfred Stepan. 1996. *Problems of Democratic Transition and Consolidation: Southern Europe, South America, and Post-Communist Europe*. Baltimore: Johns Hopkins University Press.

Mansfield, Harvey. 1964. "Party Government and the Settlement of 1688." *American Political Science Review* 58 (June): 933–46.

McCleary, Rachel M. 1997. "Guatemala's Postwar Prospects."*Journal of Democracy* 8 (April): 129–43.

Moore, Barrington. 1966. *The Social Origins of Dictatorship and Democracy*. Boston: Beacon Press.

Neuhouser, Kevin. 1992. "Democratic Stability in Venezuela: Elite Settlement or Class Compromise?" *American Sociological Review* 57 (June): 117–35.

Peeler, John A. 1992. "Colombia, Costa Rica, and Venezuela." In Higley and Gunther, *Elites and Democratic Consolidation*, 81–112.

———. 1995. "Elites and Democracy in Central America." In *Elections and Democracy in Central America*, ed. M. A. Seligson and J. A. Booth, 244–63. Chapel Hill: University of North Carolina Press.

Putnam, Robert D. 1993. *Making Democracy Work*. Princeton: Princeton University Press.

Remmer, Karen L. 1995. "New Theoretical Perspectives on Democratization." *Comparative Politics* 27 (June): 103–22.

Rustow, Dankwart. 1970. "Transitions to Democracy: Toward a Dynamic Model." *Comparative Politics* 2 (September): 337–63.

Sanchez, Peter M. 1992. "The Dominican Case." In Higley and Gunther, *Elites and Democratic Consolidation*, 300–22.

Sartori, Giovanni. 1995. "How Far Can Free Government Travel?" *Journal of Democracy* 6 (July): 101–111.

Schwoerer, Lois G. 1981. *The Declaration of Rights, 1689*. Baltimore: Johns Hopkins University Press.

Skocpol, Theda. 1979. *States and Social Revolutions*. New York: Cambridge University Press.

Speck, William. 1988. *Reluctant Revolutionaries: Englishmen and the Revolution of 1688*. London: Oxford University Press.

Steiner, Kurt. 1972. *Politics in Austria*. Boston: Little, Brown.

Tokes, Rudolf L. 1996. *Hungary's Negotiated Revolution*. New York: Cambridge University Press.

Webb, Stephen Saunders. 1995. *Lord Churchill's Coup: The Anglo-American Empire and the Glorious Revolution Reconsidered*. New York: Knopf.

Weiner, Myron. 1987. "Empirical Democratic Theory." In *Competitive Elections in Developing Countries*, ed. Myon Weiner and Ergun Özbudun, 3–34. Durham: Duke University Press.

Weingast, Barry. 1997. "The Political Foundations of Democracy and the Rule of the Law." *American Political Science Review* 91 (June): 245–63.

Welsh, Helge A. 1994. "Political Transition Processes in Central and Eastern Europe." *Comparative Politics* 26 (October): 379–94.

4

Mexico and Latin America in Comparative Perspective

Alan Knight

Within modern Latin America, where forms of government have been fluid and regime changes frequent (Chalmers, 1977), Mexico stands as something of an exception, at least since the 1920s.[1] Despite major shifts in social structure, as a predominantly illiterate agrarian society gave way to a literate, urban, and industrial one, the Mexican political system, notionally premised on the ideological legacy of the 1910 revolution and the elite settlement of 1928–29, has remained remarkably constant. It is not, of course, an unchanging system (on the contrary, I argue, unoriginally, that maintaining Mexico's political stability has involved constant moderate, incremental change). But certain features have endured through decades of social change: the dominance of a civilian revolutionary party, apparently immune to military coups and, within that party, of a loosely defined revolutionary bloc, or "family," headed by a transient (nonreelectable) president. Here I shall refer to "the PRI" *(Partido Revolucionario Institucional)* to denote not only that party but also the constellation of interests and practices it embodies, of which it is only a part.

As regards Mattei Dogan and John Higley's typology of elites in chapter 1, the Mexican case is again unusual, in that it combines elements of both ideocratically and consensually united elites. The 1928–29 elite settlement forged a degree of revolutionary unity, ending the fratricidal struggles of 1910–28 (Knight, 1992). Within the dark entrails of the party—which served to gather and represent vested interests, without performing the rigorous centralizing role of, say, the Communist Party in the Soviet Union—the dominant (revolutionary) elites, national and provincial, jockeyed, allied, and contested for

71

spoils, displaying that mutual tolerance and respect for (unwritten) rules of the game that characterize consensually united elites. Disaffected elements sometimes broke away and challenged the official leadership—notably in 1940, 1952, and 1988—but during the heyday of the PRI (ca. 1952–68, if not beyond), discipline prevailed, losers took their defeats philosophically, and all meaningful competition for national and state office was confined to the PRI. Three things followed: (1) much of the political conflict that would have occurred in a more pluralist, multiparty regime was channeled through the PRI; (2) the PRI was both ideologically a broad church and politically a *carriere ouverte aux talents;* and (3) since PRI candidates won most political offices, the key battles for office took place within the PRI, prior to the election, following fairly murky and informal procedures.

Outside the PRI there existed dissident forces that had never accepted, or never been admitted to, the party's monopoly of power: political Catholics, fascists, the radical Left, and some dogmatic die-hard liberals. Toward these "out" groups the party—and the system of which it was part—displayed a more ideocratic temper: it was prepared to proscribe, repress, browbeat, and marginalize. Some opposition parties were banned (Mexico's complex, shifting, and somewhat discretionary electoral laws made proscription easy); some were defrauded of legitimate electoral gains; all were confounded by the PRI's monopoly of political resources—patronage, media access, control of elections, public works, and the apparatus of repression. Indeed, using these elements, which underpinned the PRI's hegemony, we can construct a rough model of Mexico's political culture as one in which the central government has jealously guarded its power, intermittently acting as an engine of reform and redistribution, while local politics have remained the preserve of provincial elites and of political machines run by bosses (*caciques*) adept in the use of force, fraud, and the distribution of favors (Knight, 1996). The PRI's role, therefore, resembled more that of the Indian National Congress, the Japanese Liberal Democratic Party, or the Italian Christian Democrats than the "democratic centralist" parties of the U.S.S.R. and communist Eastern Europe. An opposition existed, elections were contested, dissenting opinions could be expressed in the (print) media. But the opposition remained weak and marginal, the dominant party hegemonic, invulnerable not only to opposition challenges but also to the threat of military intervention.

To what extent the PRI's dominance derived from genuine legitimacy—whether, to put to crudely, its massive pluralities in presidential elections were, say, 80 percent "genuine" and 20 percent fraudulent—it is impossible to say. Many would argue that, certainly during its heyday, the PRI would have comfortably won a fair and free election. But this argument is highly speculative, since elections were not fair and free, the playing field was far from level, and the electorate knew it. The normal rules of psephological rationality, therefore, did not hold (and, I suggest, it is a moot point how far they hold today). As regards the nature—as against the strength—of the PRI's apparent legitimacy, I suspect that analyses that stress the ideological legacy of the 1910 revolution are prone to exaggeration; there were always substantial sectors of the population that were indifferent or downright hostile to the revolution; and there were revolutionaries who, after 1940, concluded that the regime had sold out the revolution, anyway.

Hence, PRI legitimacy has been compared to Swiss cheese: full of holes. But, if enthusiastic endorsement was confined to the party *nomenklatura*, their clienteles, and hired claques, the PRI had more tangible assets: money, media access, patronage, and force. These could, at least, ensure a weak legitimacy, premised on the crucial and pervasive perception that there was no realistic alternative to the rule of the PRI (Scott, 1990, 72–77). Again, it is a moot point whether that weak legitimacy is entirely spent.

PRI hegemony also possessed a crucial advantage compared with hegemonic parties in some other countries: it was domestically generated and did not depend on foreign support or Cold War alignments. The PRI did not rule in order to keep the communists out—that was a bonus, rather than a *raison d'etre*. Furthermore, while the Mexican government collaborated closely with the United States after 1940, it was never a pliant partner, and the PRI cultivated a prickly nationalism that at times exasperated Mexico-watchers in the United States (Pastor 1992, 252–55).

I have described the PRI during its heyday—a period that has ended—but one whose expiration date is hard to fix. Certainly, 1968 would be an early candidate; more realistically, we should think in terms of a slow fall from grace, perhaps starting around 1968, accelerating during the 1970s, and palpably evident by the 1980s. During this period, PRI dominance of political office waned and greater pluralism prevailed. In Dogan and Higley's terms, we can discern a weakening—but not a complete disappearance—of ideocratic elite politics and an expansion of the orbit of consensually united elites. Opposition parties have grown in size, numbers, and resources; they began to compete for control of a few cities in the 1960s, acquired a congressional presence (thanks to a new system of proportional representation) during the 1960s and 1970s, benefited from the PRI's sharp loss of popularity during the 1980s, and began to win state governorships in 1989. In the crucial presidential elections, the PRI's vote slid from 80 percent and above to 50 percent in 1988 and 1994 (Molinar Horcasitas, 1991).

Suitably impressed, observers began to hail a genuine democratization, a regime transformation analogous to those taking place in Spain and South America (which exercised a clear demonstration effect, certainly, on Mexican analysts, perhaps on Mexican *politicos*, too). Alternatively, we could see this gradual process as evidence of a shift from an ideocratically to a consensually united elite. While there is no doubt some truth in both views, they have been overemphasized and need to be qualified. Although the opposition has grown in strength, it has not yet won the presidency, the key bastion of Mexico's centralized political system. The PRI still monopolizes Los Pinos (the Mexican White House), dominates Congress (having recovered ground since the 1988 debacle), and holds a majority of other elected offices. It is only compared with its extraordinary heyday, when the PRI's monopoly was almost complete, that its current position seems weak; compared with any other governing party in Europe or Latin America, it remains enviably powerful. The democratizing argument also suffers from a degree of teleology. Change has certainly taken place (I disaggregate its elements shortly), but it does not follow that all change—even change of an ostensibly democratic kind—in fact generates greater pluralism, representation, civil rights, and transparency. In fact, as electoral contestation has increased, respect for civil rights may have deteriorated (Foweraker, 1994); and, certainly, elements of Mexico's old political culture—*caciquismo*, clientelism, and violence—live on as more than mere vestigial remnants.

Indeed, it is now something of a cliché for more skeptical Mexico watchers to cite the Lampedusan epithet, "things have to change so that they can stay the same"—or, to put it in social scientific terms, modest incremental changes are required in order to shore up the greater system, thus preserving its essentials at the expense of certain nonessentials.[2] Since the 1960s, therefore, concessions have been made to the opposition—notably, a series of electoral reforms, offering proportional representation and promising cleaner electoral procedures—concessions that have served to foster a loyal opposition (chiefly the National Action Party, PAN), to defuse extraparliamentary protest,[3] and thus to bolster the legitimacy and prolong the life of the PRI. During the early 1990s, state governorships were allocated to the opposition by means of *concertacesiones*—tacit deals between President Carlos Salinas de Gotari and the PAN which put the PAN in office at the expense both of the provincial PRI and of electoral transparency. Executive discretionary power, a key feature of Mexican presidentialism, was thus reinforced, in political as in economic policymaking (Elizondo, 1992).

The acid test remains the presidency. Until the PRI relinquishes national power, handing over the presidency (and all that goes with it) to a victorious opponent, following a fair and free election, talk of Mexican democracy—or of a thoroughly consensually united elite— remains premature. The 1994 election was the first to be fought in an atmosphere of genuine uncertainty, which is perhaps a sine qua non of genuine democracy (Przeworski 1991, 10); yet, even then, many found it hard to envisage a decorous PRI withdrawal from power or to comprehend the oddly coy campaign mounted by the PAN in its hour of potential triumph.[4] Perhaps it is overly harsh to await a PRI defeat at the polls before pronouncing Mexico as indubitably democratic (or its elites as consensually united). Perhaps the PRI has continued to win—and will continue to win—by virtue of its genuine electoral appeal, outright fraud being a thing of the past.[5] But in this respect, the Mexican system is a prisoner of its own past: until the day dawns— perhaps in November 2000—when the PRI peacefully concedes power to a victorious electoral opponent, it remains moot whether it will ever do so, or whether its ouster from office will require force, protest, internal schism, "implosion," or other departures from transparent democratic procedure.

Despite this record of continuity, the Mexican political system has experienced recurrent crises—although as we review them we inevitably confront the question of "criticality," which I discussed in chapter 2, to wit, how "critical" were these crises? Did the system's survival indicate its own resilience or simply the feebleness of the crises? And, a related point, also discussed in chapter 2, to what extent were these crises exogenous as against endogenous? Were they thrust upon Mexico from outside (what I term the "asteroidal syndrome")? Or were they products of the regime's internal sclerosis—proof that the "dinosaurs" were heading for extinction anyway?[6]

Eight Crises

Mexico-watchers would probably agree in identifying up to eight crises that the system has weathered since the 1930s; and these in turn can be conveniently divided into two series (Camacho Solís, 1978; Basáñez, 1990). The crises of 1940, 1952, 1958–59 and 1968, occurring during the long phase of economic growth, were essentially political crises, involving challenges to the PRI's political tenure and *modus operandi.* Those of 1940 and 1952 followed a standard pattern (reproduced more feebly in 1946—which was not a genuine crisis—and, more surprisingly and "critically," in 1988) whereby a faction bolted the PRI and contested the presidential election under new political auspices. The rather different crisis of 1958–59—whose "criticality" some might question—involved a confrontation between the government and the railroad union, which led to stiff repression. Although economic issues played a part, the 1950s were a decade of rising real wages, and the challenge posed to the PRI was less economic than political, namely, the threat of a leftist challenge, associated with the Communist Party and coinciding with the Cuban Revolution. The end of the PRI's heyday is often dated to 1968, the year of student protest and the Tlatelolco massacre of students—again, a heavy-handed response to a political challenge.

In contrast, the crises that occurred after 1970 reflected the deterioration of the Mexican economy, mounting inflation, and the end of the "miracle." They also involved a rejuvenated electoral opposition, although, as I have already suggested, this opposition should not be seen as unequivocal proof of either democratic advance or of PRI retreat. In 1976, the tensions provoked by President Luis Echeverría's neopopulist project—a project designed to revive "revolutionary" legitimacy and placate the Left after the shock of 1968—boiled over, with land seizures, a dramatic presidential *reparto* in the northwest, and rumors of impending military intervention. Six years later, the slump in oil prices hit an economy that, in a last fling of nationalist *dirigisme,* had incurred hefty foreign debts, a mounting government deficit, and an unhealthy dependence on oil exports. Like his predecessor, President Jose López Portillo left office under a cloud; and the 1982 crisis left a lasting legacy of debt, inflation, and austerity. President Miguel De la Madrid opted—many said he had no choice—for structural adjustment and incipient neoliberal economic reform; the opposition, especially the loosely right-wing, probusiness PAN, made substantial gains, chiefly in the north; and in 1987 the PRI reverted to its bad old ways, splitting on the eve of a presidential campaign.

In the dirty and contentious election of 1988, Carlos Salinas defeated the leader of the breakaway faction, Cuauhtémoc Cárdenas, whose National Democratic Front (soon to be the Party of Democratic Revolution, PRD) mounted a surprisingly strong leftist/nationalist challenge to Salinas's technocratic neoliberalism. As president, Salinas pushed through radical economic reforms, while rhetorically promising political transparency. The PRD was cut down to size and Salinas—and, to a lesser extent, the PRI as well—recovered much of the political ground lost in 1988. Hence, the PRI presidential candidate won handily and relatively fairly in 1994. But the Salinas success story was compromised by growing political violence during 1994 and finally subverted by the economic crisis that was the last of our cycle, at the turn of the year 1994–95.

In one obvious sense, these successive crises indicate a key weakness of the Mexican political system (ergo, they are typically endogenous): they tend to occur at the end of the presidential term, coinciding with the selection and election of a new president. In the 1920s, such climacterics produced military plots and rebellions (1920, 1923, 1927, 1929). In 1940, 1952, 1988, and 1994, they produced political crises, three of which involved splits within the PRI. These crises and splits manifested the tensions associated with choosing the PRI candidate (hence, the next president); throughout the process there is jockeying, lobbying, an orgy of clientelism, and a steady erosion of the outgoing, lame-duck president's power. Such a pattern is inherent in a system where the president's powers are vast, presidential reelection is ruled out, and the president's biggest single decision is the choice of his successor.[7]

If the potential for cyclical (political, endogenous) crisis is something of a constant, the historical pattern is complicated by the shift, over time, from political to economic crises. This, in turn, reflects the increased vulnerability of the Mexican economy as it abandoned the model of "stabilized development"—combining "easy" import-substitution industrialization and relatively stable macroeconomic policy (1954–70)—in favor of, first, a *dirigiste* dash for growth funded by oil and foreign debt (1970–82) and, second, a neoliberal commitment to economic opening, privatization, and free trade (since 1982). Crisis now acquired a sharply economic character; with devaluations in 1976, 1982, and 1994, bank nationalization in 1982, and a sequence of austerity packages along the way. Although this economic vulnerability is not, of course, confined to Mexico (the debt crisis of the 1980s embraced the continent), Mexico has experienced extreme vicissitudes. Under Echeverría it pioneered economic populism; in the late 1970s it flirted with petroleum dependency, Venezuelan-style; like Argentina, but unlike Brazil, it liberalized its economy rapidly and radically—at first with apparent success, now, it seems, with severe consequences.

Elites and Crises

While the commonality of Mexican policy suggests the strength of exogenous factors (the petroleum market; U.S. interest rate policy; the "Washington consensus" of the 1980s), it is important to note that policy also obeyed domestic (endogenous) causes and was, to a significant degree, the work of relatively autonomous Mexican elites. The North American Free Trade Agreement (NAFTA) was not thrust on Mexico; it derived from a Mexican initiative. Mexican structural adjustment packages have gone beyond what the Washington consensus requires. And the disaster of the *tesebonos* in 1994 was largely of the Mexicans' own making.[8] Economic policy also obeyed endogenous causes in that, after 1970, successive administrations broke with the macroeconomic policies of the past and struck out in new directions, at least partly in order to win support and refurbish the faded legitimacy of the PRI. Thus, Echeverría, seeking to woo the Left, advocated "shared development" ("neopopulism," to his critics); López Portillo talked grandiloquently of managing abundance; and Salinas, mouthing a new, distinctive "social liberal" discourse, cast Mexico as a member of the General Agreement on Tariffs and Trade (GATT), NAFTA, and the First World.

All these successive policies, projects, and images involved domestic appeals. Attempts to modernize and relegitimize the aging PRI thus encouraged economic risks.[9] All governments, of course, frame economic policy with an eye toward a balance between long-term legitimacy and short-term popularity. Priming the pump in election years is standard "democratic" practice, so that the events of 1994 are, from a charitable viewpoint, signs of Mexico's gradual democratization and, more certainly, of the ruling elites' desire to use their policy-making monopoly to party advantage.

But the nature of the Mexican system made PRI discretionality (and PRI elite autonomy) unusually extreme. Although the Mexican government has sensitive political antennae, its economic policymaking tends to be highly elitist, even secretive.[10] The "autonomy" of Mexican elites vis-à-vis their domestic publics is, in this area, notorious: the bank nationalization of 1982, the entry into NAFTA, the "reform" of the *ejido* (cooperatively owned land) all resulted from highly closeted elite discussions and scant public debate (Grindle, 1996, 89). Responsibility is not shared; hence, failure instantly delegitimizes the key leaders—López Portillo in 1982, Salinas in 1994. It is not coincidental that, compared with other Latin American countries, Mexico has experienced such violent swings in policy performance: the golden age of the "miracle" (1954–70); the hopes and deceptions of the Echeverría and López Portillo administrations (1970–82); the acclaimed success and final debacle of Salinista neoliberalism (1988–94). The PRI has proved capable of ramming through policy—good or bad—with a fair degree of executive discretion. When it works, it works fast and effectively (e.g., the Mexican conquest of inflation in the late 1980s); when it fails, it fails egregiously.

In simple terms, therefore, the successive economic crises of the last twenty-five years derive from the interaction between narrow, highly autonomous, technocratic elites and a global economic environment that—in terms of oil prices, bank lending, and neoliberal reform—encouraged high-risk strategies that were particularly appealing to those elites. Exogenous economic pressures stimulated crises, in Mexico as elsewhere; but the Mexican system, and the elites who ran it, enhanced Mexican economic vulnerability and greatly exacerbated the "critical" impact.

Elite policymaking also responded to endogenous pressures, in particular, to structural changes over which the PRI had limited control: urbanization, increased literacy, industrialization, and, perhaps, "globalization."[11] It is often argued, or asserted, that these social changes—which some would happily subsume under the rubric of "modernization"—obliged the PRI to democratize, thus demonstrating the functional link between "modernization," development, and democracy proposed by, among others, Seymour Martin Lipset (1960, 45–76). Again, while there may be some truth in this, it is a limited long-term truth, subject to so many qualifications that its utility, especially for the short and medium term, is questionable. The apparent correlation between development and democracy (e.g., in Western Europe and North America, minus Mexico) may be illuminating; but it does not prove that the process of development—or "modernization"-—will, *pari passu,* bring forth democratization. In fact, there is evidence to the contrary. Mexico, for example, has undergone "development" or "modernization" since at least the 1920s, probably the 1880s, perhaps even the 1850s.[12] Modernization Porfirian-style (1880–1910) involved authoritarian developmentalism—a sort of Barrington Moore "revolution from above," which provoked the social revolution of 1910. A second bout of modernization, under the aegis of the new revolutionary elite, resulted in the hegemony of the PRI and its forerunners (1929–68?), which actually consolidated its hold, its (authoritarian) monopoly of power, during forty years of rapid "development."[13] Not until after 1970 does the presumed correlation between development and democratization appear to hold. True believers in the development-democratization thesis may therefore wish to incorporate a 40-, 90-, or 120-year timelag into their model. Democratization was certainly a long time coming: the electoral reforms of the 1960s and 1970s created space for middle-class protest, which had a long tradition, dating back to the opposition movements of 1940, 1929, and 1910.

As that middle class grew in numbers and influence, the PRI —traditionally reliant on mass publics organized in popular corporatist organizations (e.g., *ejidos* and trade unions)—had to take notice. By the

1980s, the decade of debt and depression, a more profound political shift was taking place, in which short-term conjunctural crises (e.g., the 1982 bank nationalization) and long-term structural trends (domestic modernization and international globalization) played mutually reinforcing roles. Middle-class and entrepreneurial opposition grew, to the benefit of the PAN, and the PRI began to shift its appeals to these sectors. After 1982, de la Madrid actively courted the private sector—which had the power not only to bankroll the PAN but also to expatriate capital. Following the electoral shock of 1988, Salinas pitched a broad—and successful—appeal to the urban middle classes and entrepreneurial groups. They, rather than the old PRI stalwarts in the *ejidos* and trade unions, would be the beneficiaries of globalization and "social liberalism." Success was evident in the 1991 and 1994 elections, when the PRI, aided by the media, clawed back much of the ground lost in 1988, especially in the north and the federal capital. Salinas coupled his First World, modernizing, and neoliberal rhetoric with a pitch to the poor, which was the flip (neopopulist) side of Salinista social liberalism. The marginal poor got state benefits via Solidarity, an ambitious revamped form of traditional clientelist politics; the middle class and entrepreneurs benefited from market opening; the necessary and acceptable casualties of this strategy were the old corporate constituencies—*ejidatarlos* and organized labor. Such a strategy fitted not only the structural trends within Mexican—even global—society;[14] it also obeyed conjunctural political logic, since the chief threat to the PRI came from the right-wing, probusiness PAN, while the leftist PRD, which could, in some states, rival the PRI's appeal to the poor, peasants, and labor, was plagued by internal schisms, ideological confusion, and, not least, official harassment.

The most recent crisis, that of 1994–95, derailed Salinas's strategy and undermined the PRI's claim to have led Mexico—with technocratic efficiency and Mosaic vision—into the promised land of the First World. It remains to be seen whether, in the three years before the presidential election of 2000,[15] the current Zedillo administration can repair the considerable damage and hang on to national power—with or without resorting to fraud or force. Expert opinion remains divided; while it is safe to say that this is the deepest political hole the PRI has found itself in during seventy years in power, we should remember that it has climbed out of holes before, and it retains a formidable array of climbing gear—some of it the traditional illicit stuff that has been found in PRI backpacks since the 1930s.

The Lessons of Crises in Mexico

Thus far, the percussive beat of crisis has not drummed the PRI out of office. Indeed, an argument could be made that the system has responded—in Toynbeean fashion—to the challenge of crisis, even endogenous crisis of its own making. Most of the eight crises I have discussed elicited an effective response, usually combining elements of both stick and carrot: electoral reform and a reassuring shift to the right after the contentious 1940 election; constraints on the opposition coupled with a moralization drive after 1952; restrictions on public sector unions but a workers' profit-sharing scheme after the 1959 showdown; Echeverría's overture to the Left after 1968; de la Madrid's conciliation of business after the 1982 bank nationalization; and Solidarity after the 1988 electoral shock. (One cause for PRIista concern following the 1994–95 crisis has been the Zedillo administration's failure to devise an appropriate response, whether substantial or even cosmetic. Does this reflect a failure of individual leadership? Or is it a sign that there are no shots left in the locker?)

Thus, while the recurrence of crisis indicates certain frailties of the system—the sexennial cycle, presidential hubris, executive discretionality—the system's response also suggests a dogged durability, and not, it should be stressed, an adamantine Bourbonic durability but a more pragmatic, Whiggish resilience, captured in the Lampedusan motto cited above. Decades of modernization may produce a democratic Mexico—so that, at the end of the day, a thoroughly modern Mexico will join the ranks of consolidated democracies run by consensually united elites. But, so far, that day resembles a Scandinavian midsummer; and, in the meantime, long phases of modernization, under both Porfirian and revolutionary auspices, have yielded not democratic but authoritarian regimes, albeit of different types. If, since 1970, the presumed correlation between development and democracy looks more positive, we should not rush to convert passing phases into steady states: recall the relapses from "developed" democracy in South America (Chile, Uruguay), not to mention interwar Europe.

Furthermore, crisis in Mexico has not only served as a force for natural selection, compelling the PRI to react, to learn from its (recurrent) mistakes, and to refine its capabilities. Crisis has also scared off potential dissidents, herding them back into the political fold. Although a notionally "revolutionary" society, Mexico has strong currents of conservatism coursing through its body politic. The folk memory of civil strife endures, reinforced by examples in South America and, *a fortiori*, Central America, deterring dissent.[16] The smack of firm government is music to some Mexican ears. Thus, the 1968 massacre of students offended enlightened opinion in Mexico and abroad; but not all Mexicans sympathized with the protesting students or condemned the government's *mano dura*. In 1994 the Zapatista revolt got rave reviews in progressive circles, but "middle Mexico" did not take kindly to uppity young radicals in ski masks who seemed to be introducing the abrasive politics of Central America into a Mexico that had supposedly entered the First World.[17] Later in 1994, PRI presidential candidate Ernesto Zedillo actively and successfully courted the *voto miedo* — the "fear vote." Clearly, the PRI now places more emphasis on the *institucional* than the *revolucionario* in its oxymoronic title.

To be sure, crisis—if sufficiently severe, if "emically" registered as crisis[18]—can prove terminal. But a recurrent dose of manageable crises can, it would seem, keep a regime on its toes and remind voters that, given the alternatives on offer, a grim but familiar status quo may not be all bad. Better the devil you know: political leaps in the dark may be more interesting to scholars than they are attractive to voters.[19] In this respect, the subjective (emic) factor, which I discussed in chapter 2, becomes crucial. A crisis is really only a crisis if enough people so perceive; it becomes a crisis *manqué* (a turning point when history fails to turn) if incumbent elites can reassure their alarmed subjects and preserve the status quo. One key indicator of the severity of crisis, therefore, is the range of possible alternatives. In extreme crisis, such as a social revolution, the sky's the limit; the world is turned upside down; a whole gamut of possibilities—millenarian, Utopian, reformist, reactionary—may open up. In more mundane crises, the range is narrower, but the scope and perception of alternatives are essential factors. However unpopular, regimes become intolerable only when alternatives beckon; conversely, a regime that can "naturalize" itself acquires a stout guarantee of survival.

Prior to 1988, I suspect, very few Mexicans envisaged a demise of the PRI in the short or even medium term.[20] Crises hinged on the degree of change the PRI would permit within the existing system. Briefly, during and after 1988, more radical alternatives seemed possible; and this perception represented a major blow to regime stability. However, with the recuperation of the PRI under Salinas and the rapid decline of Cárdenas's PRD, the options narrowed—as the PRI wanted and had worked to achieve. The chief challenge to the PRI now came from the PAN, a loyal opposition that backed Salinas's economic policy and happily settled for incremental political gains.[21] The complex, stuttering crisis of 1994–95 (Chiapas, political assassinations, financial slump) seemed to reopen the possibility of the PRI's demise; but the force of this perception was and remains mitigated by the strong feeling that no convincing, immediate alternative presents itself. The PAN cannot win national power through the ballot box until 2000; incremental PAN victories will not drastically change the political—still less the economic—map; and, many Mexicans still believe, the PRI remains a political fact of life whose demise, falsely predicted in the past, looks an unlikely proposition.

In Mexico, therefore, we observe a serious objective crisis (marked by opposition gains, dissension in the PRI and, above all, a severe economic recession) that is not matched by an equivalent subjective crisis. It is the reverse of the mass panics of 1789, 1865, and 1919. Popular cynicism and disillusionment, which have a long history and deep roots in Mexican political culture (Knight, 1996), may ultimately prove one of the PRI's greatest assets as it struggles for survival in the short and medium term. Conversely, the PRI could be mortally threatened by the launch of a political movement that catches the popular mood and promises a practical alternative—as Cuauhtémoc Cárdenas came close to doing in 1988. In such a context, the PRI's "weak" legitimacy might crumble overnight—as Porfirio Díaz's did in 1910–11. What such a crisis would lead to—thorough democratization, an authoritarian reaction, "implosion"—is another matter.[22]

Latin American Comparisons

As I said at the outset, Mexico is unusual within Latin America, hence it may not be the most fruitful source of comparative generalizations. Parallels, involving the slow decline—and maybe democratization—of a dominant civilian party within a capitalist society, would be better sought in Italy, Japan, India, or—best of all, perhaps—Taiwan. Nevertheless, the incidence of regime change in Latin America has attracted plenty of scholarly attention, particularly as analysts have explored the collapse, return, and consolidation of democracy in South America (Linz and Stepan, 1978, 1996; O'Donnell, Schmitter, and Whitehead, 1986; Diamond, Linz, and Lipset, 1988–89; Mainwaring, O'Donnell, and Valenzuela, 1992). Here, regime transformation has been relatively clear and dramatic: no need for the endless qualifications that dog Mexican studies and have led Enrique Krauze to appeal for a "democracy without adjectives." In Argentina, Brazil, Chile, and Uruguay, military, (bureaucratic) authoritarian regimes have given way to democratically elected civilian governments. Southern Cone democracy may display many faults—executive discretionality and media bias are familiar complaints in Argentina and Brazil, as in Mexico. But if the democratic playing field, in general, isn't wholly level, Mexico's resembles the slopes of Popocatepetl: steeply cambered to favor the old ruling party and its host of opportunist allies. If Southern Cone democracy is more complete (governments have been changed through free elections), its degree of consolidation may be debated. Experts appear to be confident about Chile and Uruguay, less so about Brazil or Argentina. In other cases—Peru, Guatemala—the democratic deficits are yet greater, the presumed contrasts with "authoritarian" Mexico exaggerated. Even if it is "authoritarian," Mexico remains staunchly civilian, while the tutelary powers of the Peruvian or Guatemalan military eat into the entrails of fragile democracies (Valenzuela, 1992, 62–63). The formal facade of South American democracy, therefore, conceals a host of differences; even if overt relapses to military rule seem unlikely, disguised relapses, partial implosions, and "creeping authoritarianism" are all conceivable.

The impact of crisis on South America also presents contrasts with Mexico. The collapse of previous democratic regimes—Brazil in 1964; Chile and Uruguay in 1973; Argentina in 1976—constituted major crises and regime transformations of the kind that Mexico has not experienced since 1920. Unlike previous "waves" of regime transformation (e.g., that of the 1930s), the "bureaucratic authoritarian" wave responded not to exogenous pressures (war, depression, "demonstration effects") but, rather, to endogenous forces: domestic class, sectoral, and political alignments. In other words, these were self-generated crises. The return to democracy during the 1980s, in contrast, has been less crisis ridden, more gradual, and probably more responsive to exogenous factors. The Brazilian transition, in particular, was protracted, incremental, and partially managed from above. The obvious contrasting example of crisis-driven (or, at least, crisis-associated) transition— Argentina, where the Falklands War undermined the junta—may be misleading, in that the junta was already under severe pressure before the invasion of the islands, which represented a last, desperate, and disastrous effort to bolster a failing regime.

We have, therefore, an apparent pattern that demands some explanation: sudden transitions from democratic to authoritarian rule associated with crisis; gradual, incremental, "acritical" transitions from authoritarian to democratic regimes. In part, the pattern may be accidental: the economic crisis, or crises, of the 1980s, which, most agree, sapped the legitimacy of incumbent regimes (whatever their complexion), happened to occur when several South American countries were languishing under bureaucratic authoritarian rule. Crisis, therefore, prompted—or, more likely, accelerated—a delegitimization of military rule and a return to democracy (*faute de mieux*). Where democracy prevailed (e.g., Venezuela), or civilian authoritarianism (Mexico), democracy and civilian authoritarianism similarly suffered, although in neither case was there a dramatic reversal or regime transformation.[23] The 1980s thus reversed the pattern of the 1930s, when depression tended to compromise civilian, representative regimes.

However, this is only part of the story. It cannot explain why democracies succumbed in the 1960s and 1970s, years of relative economic buoyancy. Nor does it explain why transitions to authoritarian rule should be abrupt and crisis ridden, transitions to democracy more gradual and—at least in Chile, Uruguay, and Brazil—"acritical." First, there is a sense in which authoritarian transitions, involving a relatively narrow elite decisionmaking process, are likely to be more sudden and abrupt. While "creeping" authoritarianism is a recognizable phenomenon (it preceded the Nazi *machtergreifung* in 1930–33), military takeovers are typically sudden and decisive: Brazil in 1964, Chile in 1973, Argentina in 1976. You cannot commit praetorian rape by halves. Conversely, transitions to democracy involve multiple actors—including mass publics, who must figure as actors, not victims. While such transitions may be relatively rapid, they typically span a series of liberalizing and democratizing steps. (We should, I think, make a firm distinction between pioneer democratizations—in Britain, for example—which cover decades, and redemocratizations, such as in South America, which can be compressed into a few years. Mexico, oddly, fits more within the first pattern). Yet even redemocratizations involve careful, cumulative steps; in particular, they involve placating and reassuring the outgoing authoritarian elites—above all, the military (Przeworski, 1991, ch. 2). (Incoming authoritarian regimes, of course, usually have no such scruples about the victims of their takeover; such victims may be removed altogether, by death, exile, or repression—an option incipient democracies do not possess.) At the same time, incipient democracies have to canalize mass publics in the direction not only of democratic politics (now the only game in town) but also of moderate democratic politics, thus appeasing residual authoritarians, placating the tutelary power of the military, and reassuring, perhaps, a skeptical middle class and foreign financial community. For, while the opposition to authoritarian regimes typically involves broadly mobilized mass publics—neighborhood associations, trade unions, "new social movements," church communities, human rights groups—the construction of a functioning democracy requires organized parties, preferably concentrated near the center of the political spectrum (Przeworski, 1991, 11).

This shift has important consequences for elite configuration, not simply because it introduces new elites and, if it is successful, new "consensual" ways of doing political business. It also affects the relationship of elites to mass publics and the relative autonomy of those elites. For the old protests against authoritarian government have often had a leaderless quality, or, we may say, leadership has been highly diffused, localized, and elusive (the better to avoid detection and repression). Who "led" the *madres de la Plaza de Mayo* in Argentina? Did they constitute an elite? If they did, their relationship to their "mass public" was very different from that which links Carlos Menen to the Peronist rank and file. In this sense, democratization nurtures and elevates its chosen elites, enhancing their relative autonomy. Stable democracy may, paradoxically, constrain the democratic impulses of its constituent parts. Thus, while a military takeover is inherently "critical," successful transitions to democracy precisely involve the avoidance of crisis, because crisis may involve runaway mass mobilization, confrontation, authoritarian reaction, even civil war—the classic sequence of the Spanish Republic after 1930.

The role of elites in authoritarian and democratic transitions is crucial, but different. Civilian elites sympathetic to and associated with the military played a role in the "bureaucratic authoritarian" coups of the 1960s and 1970s, as did some mass publics—for example, the middle class opponents of Salvador Allende. Such sympathetic elites—in business, the church, the media—also influenced the transition to democracy: first, because they felt that the military had done its job (crushing a threatening Left); second, because the arbitrary conduct of the military now posed a threat to their interests; third, because the international climate favored democracy (especially as the Cold War waned); and, fourth, because some elites retained a normative—as against a purely expedient—attachment to democracy. (All these considerations, by the way, influenced the military, too: few generals ever envisaged a permanent military regime, for which no legitimizing rationale existed; all military regimes—unlike civilian authoritarian regimes, such as Mexico's—were "regimes of exception," which knew they would have to end, sooner or later.) While the fourth factor—normative attachment to democracy—might be considered a relatively durable aspect of particular political cultures (hence, more evident in, say, Costa Rica than in El Salvador), the other three are distinctly conjunctural and, I would suspect, collectively more important in determining outcomes. Given a revived Left, a changing international climate, and a receding memory of military abuses (clearly more acute in some countries than others),[24] these conjunctural factors could lose their potency and, as a result, the current—conjunctural—democratic consensus could erode. This skepticism accords with Dogan and Higley's conclusion, suggesting that an analysis informed by historical comparison and (qualified) elite theory is less sanguine about the future of stable democracy than some others.

But elite theory does need to be qualified, since, as I have argued, regime transitions are not solely matters of elite deliberation. Elites do not act autonomously of either exogenous (international) factors or domestic mass publics (Mainwaring, 1992, 302–4). Currently, exogenous factors—U.S. policy, world opinion, globalization—tend to favor

Latin American democratization, in a way that they did not in the 1970s. The ending of the Cold War, by removing the monochromatic lens through which the United States viewed Latin America, has afforded democracy greater space; however, it is again unclear how durable—as against conjunctural—this situation may be. Before the Cold War (i.e., before 1945), the United States was often tolerant of friendly dictators. If the current conjuncture does not endure, the presumed equation of liberal politics and neoliberal economics may also collapse. The Southeast Asian model, not to mention Augusto Pinochet's Chile, shows that authoritarian politics can readily coexist with success in the global market economy. And, in a universe of democratic states, a major world recession would cull democratic victims—as it did in the 1930s—not authoritarian ones, as it did in the 1980s.

More important, the domestic autonomy of elites must be taken into account. At present, elites can generally rest assured that democratic politics contain no threat of militant leftism; in Samuel Valenzuela's terminology, there are ample "reserve domains" of military influence and power, which democratic leaders either cannot threaten or, more often, have pragmatically chosen to respect (Valenzuela, 1992, 64–65). (Mexico, in this regard, parallels most of Latin America, where Brazil's Workers Party represents the biggest leftist challenge, albeit one that remains squarely reformist and, thus far, unable to conquer national power.) This is true despite the role played by heterogeneous mass publics, including leftists, in the overthrow of authoritarian regimes. So long as the Left—despite the social ravages of neoliberal policies—remains weak, moderate, and democratic, the relative autonomy of elites offers a source of comfort, a guarantee against neopopulism and, in turn, against authoritarian reaction. Mexican politics—as they usually are under stable liberal democracies—amount to business as usual, in which parties respect the market (now more than ever), mass publics follow the cues of elite leaders and the mass media, and crisis is thereby kept off the political agenda.

But for how long? *Grosso modo*, the scenario reproduces that of the 1920s, in Europe and some of Latin America. We may assume that international financial agencies—the mutated Bretton Woods system—offer some guarantee against an economic debacle comparable to 1929–30. But the potential for both exogenous and endogenous crisis remains and will tend to increase as the memory of authoritarianism fades. If crisis ensues, if democracy fails, the result may not be a sudden and straightforward *cuartelazo* but, rather, "creeping" authoritarianism, engineered by overpowerful, discretionary executives and their elite allies. After all, if the Mexican case offers one clear lesson, it is that civilian (inclusionary) authoritariansm is vastly more flexible, responsive, and hence durable than outright (exclusionary) military rule. It would be ironic if the PRI, in its death agony, afforded a model for the recreation of authoritarianism, on civilian lines, elsewhere in Latin America.

Notes

1. For this reason, it may not be the best case on which to base generalizations and, in the concluding section, I hazard some broader comparisons.

2. This begs the questions of what are "essentials" and "nonessentials" and whether sufficient incremental change does not finally result in major transformation. Limits of space prevent a further discussion. The quote comes from Guiseppe Lampedusa's *The Leopard*.

3. Like many generalizations about Mexico, this was broadly valid until 1994. The Chiapas revolt—a major example of extraparliamentary protest—displayed the limitations of the PRI's hitherto successful strategy. It remains to be seen how the revolt will end; its transforming power, as of early 1997, seems to have waned.

4. After "winning" the presidential TV debate and watching his ratings soar, the PAN candidate, Diego Fernández de Cevallos, slipped out of the limelight during the final weeks before the election, giving rise to intense speculation: Was he bought off? ill? afraid of winning? Like many of the events of 1994, this will probably baffle future historians.

5. Even critics of the PRI acknowledge that the 1994 election was, in terms of electoral fraud, relatively clean, certainly cleaner than 1988, and capable of affording Zedillo a democratic mandate. Critical attention, therefore, switched to the bigger and more complex issue of the "level playing field," i.e., to what extent could an election be genuinely democratic when one party enjoyed such disproportionate access to resources, the media, and political decisionmaking? This, of course, is a particular version of a global argument. It raises the knotty question of where "procedural" criteria of democracy stop and more substantive matters of power and property begin.

6. An apt metaphor, given the popular designation of the PRI's old guard as "the dinosaurs."

7. Selection of the successor is accomplished by means of the famous *dedazo*—the pointing of the big finger. The 1987 attempt by de la Madrid to make this a more transparent process was not successful; Salinas reverted to executive fiat in 1993 (and 1994), provoking considerable resentment.

8. *Tesebonos* were dollar-denominated government bonds. They sucked in short-term foreign investment, propping up Mexico's deteriorating balance of payments. But in 1994–95, market confidence collapsed, and Mexico required massive financial support from the U.S. government to meet its obligations.

9. Of course, economic policy did not simply respond to political exigencies. The Salinas project embodied an ambitious economic reform, which was an end in itself (or, at least, which responded to goals that were not immedi-

ately political). However—with the caveat that Mexican policymaking is unusually opaque—I suspect that economic reform was seen as an important means of prolonging the PRI's control of Mexican politics. To put it more obviously: if economic reform had been seen as the PRI's death warrant, it would not have been pursued—however persuasive the economic arguments.

10. This may be true of many or most states. But the Mexican state is particularly adept at reaching decisions, particularly economic decisions, screened from public debate and input.

11. It is a moot point—perhaps *the* moot point—whether Mexican (and Latin American) insertion into a global free-trading market is unavoidable (ergo, an example of exogenous pressures over which Mexican and Latin American elites have little or no control). Of course, a latter-day Dr. Francia could try to cut his country off from the global economy; but that is not a plausible scenario today. More realistically, the question is whether qualified alternatives to outright neoliberalism exist, and not just for a giant economy like Brazil's.

12. The 1920s saw the early institutionalization of the revolutionary state; the 1880s witnessed the foundation of the Porfirian regime; the 1850s were years of liberal social and political innovation (the Reforma).

13. It should be stressed that "revolutionary" authoritarianism was very different from its Porfirian predecessor or many of its Latin American counterparts. Analysts have tended to see it as an "inclusionary" authoritarianism, weak on democratic procedure but strong on mass mobilization and "inclusionary" institution building.

14. It is tempting to draw a parallel with Tony Blair and "new Labour" in Britain and with Bill Clinton and "new Democrats" in the United States.

15. It should be remembered that the final years of presidential *sexenios* have frequently generated crises, often related to the succession. Any PRI recovery in 1999–2000 will have to buck that familiar trend. Like previous presidents, therefore, Ernesto Zedillo will probably have to recoup popularity and legitimacy during the first four or so years of his term (1995–98), before lame-duckery sets in. The notion of a six-year period of grace and opportunity is something of an illusion. At the midterm congressional and mayoral elections in 1997, for example, the PRI took a beating, losing control of both the Congress and the mayoralty of Mexico City. At national level, therefore, the PRI is far from staging a recovery, even if some regional bosses—such as Puebla's Manuel Bartlett—have managed to consolidate their power, often using traditional *(caciquista)* methods.

16. I am repeating a common opinion, but it raises the question how long it will take for the supposed "folk memory of revolution" to dissipate or, perhaps more relevant, how that memory is perpetuated, now that survivors of the revolutionary era scarcely exist.

17. This was the gist of, for example, Héctor Aguilar Camín's polemical critiques of Zapatismo: that it was a dangerous, atavistic throwback, out of place in "modern" Mexico.

18. On the emic/etic distinction, see chapter 2 in this volume.

19. Note the resurgence of former Communists in Russia and Eastern Europe.

20. My dating here is no more than a hunch; opinion polls are a relatively new phenomenon in Mexico, and, to my knowledge, none has asked this sort of question in the past. Even had they done so, I would not have placed great weight on the responses.

21. Perhaps "happily" is too strong, since some PANistas came to feel that the party was collaborating too closely with the PRI, and a (small) dissident minority even broke away in protest. This did not stop the process of detente.

22. I mention this because there is often an assumption that the demise of the PRI will usher in democracy—that the two events are virtually one and the same. This seems an overly sanguine view. Eastern Europe is different in many respects and may, therefore, be a poor guide; but it affords a salutary lesson. Recent events—notably the 1997 elections—have increased the possibility of an opposition victory in 2000; but they have not necessarily ensured that such a victory will signal a deep and definitive democratization.

23. This may constitute evidence of the superior stamina of institutionalized, civilian (though not necessarily democratic) regimes over military ones. After all, military regimes are a fairly peculiar, recent form of polity.

24. Thus, the double discrediting of the Argentine military (for what it did at home and for what it failed to do in the Falklands) offers a powerful guarantee against a revived militarism, at least for some time. The Brazilian military, in contrast, by governing with some success (according to its own lights) and withdrawing in good order, afforded no equivalent guarantee.

References

Basáñez, Miguel. 1990. *El pulso de los sexenios. Veinte años de crisis en Mexico.* Mexico: Siglo Veintiuno.

Camacho Solís, Manuel. 1978. *Las crisis en el sistema politico mexicano, 1928–77.* Mexico: Fondo de Cultura Economica.

Chalmers, Douglas A. 1977. "The Politicized State in Latin America." In *Authoritarianism and Corporatism in Latin America.* ed. James M. Malloy. Pittsburgh: University of Pittsburgh Press.

Diamond, Larry, Juan J. Linz, and Seymour Martin Lipset, eds. 1988–89. *Democracy in Developing Countries.* 3 vols. Baltimore: Johns Hopkins University Press.

Elizondo, Carlos. 1992. "Property Rights in Mexico: Government and Business after the 1982 Bank Nationalization." Ph.D. diss., Oxford University.

Foweraker, Joe. 1994. "Measuring Citizenship in Mexico." Paper presented at conference, Beyond Economic Reform: Mexico Under Zedillo. Institute of Latin American Studies, London, November.

Grindle, Merilee S. 1996. *Challenging the State. Crisis and Innovation in Latin America and Africa.* Cambridge: Cambridge University Press.

Knight, Alan. 1992. "Mexico's elite settlement: conjuncture and consequences." In *Elites and Democratic Consolidation in Latin America and Southern Europe,* ed. John Higley and Richard Gunther. Cambridge: Cambridge University Press.

———. 1996. "Mexico bronco, Mexico manso: Una reflexion sobre la cultura civica mexicana." *Politicy y gobierno* 3 (April).

Linz, Juan J., and Alfred Stepan, eds. 1978. *The Breakdown of Democratic Regimes.* Baltimore: Johns Hopkins University Press.

———. 1996. *Problems of Democratic Transition and Consolidation.* Baltimore: Johns Hopkins University Press.

Lipset, Seymour Martin. 1960. *Political Man.* New York: Doubleday.

Mainwaring, Scott, Guillermo O'Donnell, and Samuel J. Valenzuela, eds. 1992. *Issues in Democratic Consolidation.* South Bend: University of Notre Dame Press.

Mainwaring, Scott. 1992. "Transitions to Democracy and Democratic Consolidation: Theoretical and Comparative Issues." In *Issues in Democratic Consolidation,* ed. S. Mainwaring, G. O'Donnell and J. S. Valenzuela. South Bend: University of Notre Dame Press.

Molinar Horcasitas, Juan. 1991. *En tiempo de la legitimidad.* Mexico: Cal y Arena.

O'Donnell, Guillermo, Philippe C. Schmitter, and Lawrence Whitehead. eds. 1986. *Transitions from Authoritarian Rule.* 4 vols. Baltimore: Johns Hopkins University Press.

Pastor, Robert A. 1992. *Whirlpool: U.S. Foreign Policy toward Latin America and the Caribbean.* Princeton: Princeton University Press.

Przeworski, Adam. 1991. *Democracy and the Market.* Cambridge: Cambridge University Press.

Scott, James C. 1990. *Domination and the Arts of Resistance.* New Haven: Yale University Press.

Valenzuela, Samuel J. 1992. "Democratic Consolidation in Post-Transitional Settings: Notion, Process and Facilitating Conditions." In *Issues in Democratic Consolidation,* ed. S. Mainwaring, G. O'Donnell, and S. J. Valenzuela. South Bend: University of Notre Dame Press.

Part II

Case Studies

5

The Soviet Union:
Revolution and Transformation

Jack A. Goldstone

The events of 1989 in the former Soviet Union and Eastern Europe stunned observers with their suddenness and magnitude. Communist Party regimes that had deeply penetrated society and had been solidly institutionalized for decades (and in the Soviet Union for generations) simply came apart in a rapid-fire series of crises. Social scientists trying to explain these events confront a host of questions. Were these events revolutions, or something new in history? (For example, Timothy Garton Ash [1989] has called them a blend of reform and revolution, or "refolution," while Mattei Dogan and John Higley in chapter 1 of this book see the Soviet Union's demise as an "implosion.") Could they have been predicted? Do we have any knowledge in our theoretical arsenal to pin down the direction (or directions) in which such events will unfold? Is the democratic stabilization of post-Soviet Russia possible or even likely?

I believe that the events in the Soviet Union, in particular, constituted a true revolution. That being the case, we can—with some care and adjustments—build on current theories of revolution to obtain insights into the causes and aftermaths of those events. Moreover, close attention to debates among theorists of revolution can illuminate why observers were taken by surprise as well as help us avoid similar surprises.

What Happened in 1989, and Why Was It Such a Surprise?

A Revolution in the U.S.S.R.

Looking for historical parallels, some observers have identified 1989–91 as a repeat of 1848, when relatively short, mild revolutions—

aiming for constitutional liberties and nationalist political expression—challenged monarchies from France to Romania, leading variously to changes in regimes or regime policies (Devlin, 1995, 7). But the aftermaths of those events were generally conservative repressions, spearheaded by the armies of Prussia and Russia. In no case did a long-standing state simply dissolve and disappear; thus, 1848 provides little guidance for what will happen in the former U.S.S.R. and Eastern Europe. Some observers, including Dogan and Higley in chapter 1, have likened the events of 1989–91 to the dissolution of the Austro-Hungarian and Ottoman Empires after World War I, when old states did break up into an array of new nations. However, in those cases the dissolutions were clearly the outcome of war, and the dismemberment of the old regimes was overseen by military victors. In 1989–91, by contrast, one of the world's military superpowers collapsed without any military confrontation with its chief rivals. Finally, more optimistic observers have likened Mikhail Gorbachev's *perestroika* to cases of needed political and economic reforms, such as those instituted by Peter the Great centuries earlier (Hough, 1997). Needless to say, however, Peter's reforms represented adjustments in a growing and vigorous nation to international competition. The growing pains that produced the reforms never threatened to bring down the government, and they instead increased Russia's power on the world stage. Gorbachev's reforms appear more like those of the French monarchy in the 1780s, or those of the Chinese Empire in the early 1900s—desperate and ultimately unsuccessful efforts to head off impending collapse.

In sum, for the events of 1989–91, analogies with minor revolutions, the end of empires, and major economic reforms all fall short. What occurred was the collapse of the Communist Party and the end of party rule, the dissolution of all Soviet institutions of government and of the ideology that supported them, and economic and political chaos as new groups struggled to reconstitute new states. These changes would seem to qualify the events of 1989–91 in the U.S.S.R. as a major revolution.[1]

Claiming that the collapse and transformation of political, economic, and ideological institutions in the U.S.S.R. indicates a revolution as fundamental as that of 1789 in France or of 1917 in Russia, we are left with a question: How could such a major revolution have caught everyone unawares? It must be remembered that those two earlier revolutions also came as surprises to their nations. States can present strong facades, buoyed up only by history and habit, long after their real foundations have rotted. In 1916, no one thought that Lenin, a powerless exile, would in five years be the master of Russia; nor could anyone imagine in 1788 that a provincial lawyer from Arras named

Robespierre would, five years later, be presiding over a nation that had executed its king. Still, observers in the 1980s could have been better prepared, if they had known where to focus their attention.[2]

If one looked only at the Solidarity revolt in Poland during 1980–81, the Soviet events should not have been a surprise. Poles had begun actions of rebellion against their communist rulers many times—in 1956, in 1970, and again in 1980—with results ranging from repression to reform but usually resulting in a change in the policies, if not in the fundamental nature of the regime. Indeed, given that the death of Joseph Stalin in 1953, and the deposing of Nikita Khrushchev in 1964, were followed within a few years by uprisings against Soviet-sponsored regimes in Hungary and Czechoslovakia respectively, it should have been no surprise that following Leonid Brezhnev's death in 1982 Eastern Europeans would again test Moscow's commitment to dominating their nations.

The great surprise of 1989 was that in this case the rebellious actions of Poles, and shortly thereafter other Eastern Europeans, met with acceptance and even encouragement from Gorbachev's Soviet regime and that Gorbachev asked Eastern European governments—especially that of the Honecker regime in East Germany—to restrain their repression. Moreover, Gorbachev's regime itself soon began to shake, and at the end of 1991 Gorbachev was removed from the political scene and the U.S.S.R. ceased to exist as a sovereign state. Without denying the importance of economic hardships and government corruptions that fed popular resistance against the Soviet satellite regimes of Eastern Europe, the fundamental question behind the events of 1989 is why the U.S.S.R. was so weak. Why was it unwilling to exert itself to maintain its satellites, and moreover, why was it unable to contain its own centrifugal forces and avoid dissolution? In short, the essential surprise, the linchpin of events, was not that people in Eastern Europe rose up but that the Soviet regime thoroughly broke down.

Explaining Revolutions: Top-Down or Bottom-Up?

In identifying state breakdown as the fundamental issue of 1989–91, we confront a long-standing debate in the theory of revolutions. All theorists of revolutions have agreed that they involve at least two components—a populace motivated to rebel and a state too weak to resist popular action. But theorists (and mythmakers) have differed greatly among themselves over which component is primary. Today's generation of political leaders, commentators, and journalists received their schooling in a period when the dominant theories of revolution stressed popular action, or bottom-up efforts, as the key to revolution.

Theories of peasant revolution were used to account for the communist revolutions in Russia, China, and Vietnam.

This bottom-up view of revolutions was codified in a series of books during the 1960s and 1970s that marked a generation of bottom-up theorizing. Ted Robert Gurr's *Why Men Rebel* (1970) offers a persuasive account of popular frustration, caused by unmet aspirations for material and social progress, as the motive force of revolutions. Samuel P. Huntington's *Political Order in Changing Societies* (1968) similarly stresses popular frustration, although it focuses on the need for political participation as a source of popular demands for change. Chalmers Johnson's *Revolutionary Change* (1966) cites systemic dysfunction as the key to revolutions but argues that such dysfunction works by creating a search for new ideologies, leading to popular mobilization against the state. Neil Smelser's *Theory of Collective Behavior* (1962) similarly traces revolution to popular groups being increasingly drawn to value-oriented movements that oppose the state. And Charles Tilly's provocatively titled *From Mobilization to Revolution* (1978) argues that mobilizing and organizing popular groups is the prerequisite for revolutionary conflict.

Although all of these authors concede that popular frustration alone does not lead to successful revolution, because that requires the vulnerability of the state, all agree that the first stage of revolution is mounting popular unrest. Thus in looking for revolution on the horizon, popular unrest and mass mobilization by opposition leaders are regarded as the early warning signs. Leaders and commentators schooled in the bottom-up view of revolution were consequently amazed when revolutions broke out in East Germany, Czechoslovakia, Hungary, Romania, and finally the U.S.S.R. For in all these countries, there were few signs of popular unrest and no mass political mobilization prior to 1989. Visible opposition to the state consisted of a handful of brave dissidents, most of whose activities had been curtailed by time in prison or exile.

Yet, there is another tradition in the analysis of revolution, a top-down tradition that stresses changes in the strength of the ruling regime as the key to stability or change. This view grants that popular grievances are necessary, but instead of concentrating on popular actions, it stresses that international pressures or domestic economic changes may cause a state's power to decay. When this happens, state leaders and elites may come into conflict, and rulers may frantically try to reform the state to hold on to power. However, such internal conflict and frantic reform efforts only reveal the weakness of the state and invite restless elites to press for further changes. Competing elites may then seek to gain popular support for change—support that is more readily forthcoming as the old regime visibly crumbles. In this view, the dismantling of the old regime starts at the top, carried out by state leaders and social elites who perceive the old order as decaying. Popular mobilization and the expression of grievances then follow, indeed explode into the open when the decay of the old regime is fully apparent to all. Alexis de Tocqueville (1966, 188) may be credited with the first full expression of this view, in his work on the French Revolution, where he wrote:

> Louis XV did as much to weaken the monarchy and to speed up the Revolution by his innovations as by his personal defects, by his energy as by his indolence. . . . During his entire reign Louis XVI was always talking about reform; . . . in fact, he gave an impression of merely wanting to loosen [the regime's] foundations and leaving to others the task of laying it low. Some of the reforms he personally put through . . . prepared the ground for the Revolution not so much because they removed obstacles in its way but far more because they taught the nation how to set about it.

Machiavelli, too, warned rulers that late and frantic reforms are a sign of impending state breakdown, for when a crisis arises "you are too late for harsh measures; and mild ones will not help you, for they will be considered as forced from you, and no one will be under any obligations to you for them" (1961, 14).

More recently, Theda Skocpol (1979) and I (Goldstone, 1991, Goldstone, Gurr, and Moshiri, 1991) have elaborated theories of revolution in which state-centered, or top-down, problems initiate the process of revolution. Skocpol examines the French, Russian, and Chinese revolutions and argues that international pressures, particularly military competition or incursion, revealed weaknesses in the Old Regime states. Attempting to remedy those weaknesses, state leaders were led into conflict with political, economic, and social elites. Such conflicts further weakened or paralyzed the government, creating the opportunity for popular groups to mobilize and express their grievances. Unfortunately, Skocpol's structural analysis is too deeply rooted in the particular vulnerabilities of traditional peasant-based monarchical and imperial states, making it difficult to generalize to modern regimes. I therefore added the observation that long-term economic and demographic changes should be added to international pressures as sources of state weakness and elite conflicts and that one should look at the conjunction of (1) state fiscal weakness and debt, however it was caused; (2) competition and alienation among elites, both inside and outside the state; and (3) the growth of popular grievances among urban, not only rural, popular groups. When such long-term changes work *simultaneously* to weaken the state, intensify elite divisions, and raise popular grievances, the result has been massive state breakdown leading to revolutionary change. This pattern can be found in both early modern revolutions (Goldstone, 1991) and in revolutions of the twentieth century (Goldstone, Gurr, and Moshiri, 1991).

This top-down account is consistent with Dogan and Higley's view of elite dynamics, however constrained and shaped by the grievances and actions of the broader populace they may be, as the key to understanding regime transitions. However, as Alan Knight points out in chapter 2, elite dynamics do not fit any one simple pattern of crises and elite reactions to them. Instead, the roles of economic and military pressures, the responses of varied elite factions, and the impact of popular mobilizations on elites during crises must all be part of an analysis of crisis-induced regime changes. A bottom-up view of the collapse of the Soviet Union failed to provide adequate warning of impending events; but a state-centered view focusing on elite dynamics may provide a better explanation of how the revolutionary process began in the late 1980s. To test this proposition, however, and to move toward an understanding of the prospects for further revolutionary change or democratic stabilization, we must look more closely into the process of Soviet state decay during the decade prior to 1989.

A Model of State Breakdown and the Roots of the Soviet Collapse

Analysts of the Soviet collapse point to at least three "key" factors behind the Soviet state's breakdown: Gorbachev's political miscalculations, the growth of elite divisions, and economic failure. I have long argued that revolutions are *not* reducible to a single primary cause, so that a full-fledged state breakdown will occur only when there is a *conjunction* of several trends (Goldstone, 1991, Goldstone, Gurr, and Moshiri, 1991). Those trends are a decline in state effectiveness and fiscal strength, generally evidenced by inability to keep pace with international competitors and the growth of state debts or inflation; increased alienation and conflicts among the elites, generally evidenced by clogged routes of social mobility producing heightened competition or frustration among aspirants to elite status and sharp elite disagreements over how to respond to the state's declining effectiveness and fiscal problems; and an increase in mass mobilization potential, created in the first instance by declining living standards but multiplied by increased urbanization and increases in the size of youth cohorts in the population.

With the exception of increasing youth cohorts, every one of these trends was in evidence in the Soviet Union from 1970 to 1989. Therefore, I suggest we focus our attention on three questions: (1) Was the Soviet state losing effectiveness in a manner visible to state leaders and Soviet elites? (2) Were the elites of the Soviet state and society experiencing increasing alienation and divisions due to failures in social mobility, and thus becoming sharply divided in their responses to such problems? (3) Were declines in living standards and shifts in urbanization evident to an extent that they could provide a basis for growing mass mobilization potential among the populace? If the answers to all three questions are yes, then I would argue that the collapse of the Soviet regime, though novel in form, is not only comprehensible but, in fact, conforms to the general causal pattern of revolutions. Moreover, to the extent that events in the former U.S.S.R. conform to that pattern, we can derive from past revolutionary history better guesses regarding the aftermaths of the breakdown.

The Decay of State Effectiveness

Michael Mann (1986) has suggested that there are four types of power: economic (the power of resources and production), ideological (the power of inspiring ideas), military (the power of coercion), and political (the power of legitimate authorities, particularly when supported by control of complex organizations, to command obedience). Until roughly 1970, the relative success and stability of the Soviet regime rested on all four power forms. But thereafter, the four bases of Soviet power decayed steadily, with the decay accelerating greatly after 1985.

Some observers' postmortems on the U.S.S.R. have declared its entire history since World War II to be "forty years of failure" (Brown, 1991, 2). In this view, the 1989–91 revolution was simply the inevitable breakdown of a creaking, failed system. Other scholars believe Soviet material failures to be moderate. "What had gone wrong economically? . . . The simple answer is that nothing had. . . . In Moscow something like 90 percent of the people have their own apartments. . . . They are neither hungry nor cold. They're quite well dressed. Public transport is excellent. Things are bad only by comparison to the West" (Gellner, 1992, 112). In this view, the revolution was produced by the bravery of dissidents and the impatience of the Soviet (and Eastern European) peoples, who revolted not out of poverty but out of disgust with a bland, relatively choice-poor, and morally impoverished unfreedom, which lost all appeal when compared with the free and exciting Western consumer-oriented democracies.

The truth lies between these extreme views. After establishing much legitimacy through its costly victory in World War II, the Soviet regime scored numerous economic and political victories during the next twenty-five years. Economically, steady industrial growth rates of more than 6 percent per annum established modern industrial conditions throughout Soviet territory (Rostow, 1991, 62). The U.S.S.R. rose to world leadership in the output of oil, steel, and other basic industrial goods. In space and nuclear technology, it became one of two superpowers.

Militarily, the U.S.S.R. and its allies kept NATO and the United States on the defensive throughout the world. The Berlin Wall, and the Cuban missile crisis in the 1960s, though seen as Western victories, were only defensive victories that did no more than slightly limit Soviet gains from its increased control of East Germany and Cuba. In Vietnam, the United States suffered a costly defeat at the hands of Soviet-supported opponents. Soviet automatic rifles (the Kalashnikov), tanks, and jet fighters challenged U.S. arms manufacturers for dominance on the battlefield and in world arms markets.

Ideologically, America's civil rights battles, student movements, antipoverty campaigns, and interventions in the Dominican Republic and Vietnam during the 1960s gave the world the impression of a capitalist society that was racist, oppressive, imperialistic, and rife with poverty. In contrast, the socialist ideology of the Soviet Union, which appeared free of unemployment and discrimination and had led Russia's rise in a few short decades to challenge American power, had great international appeal. In 1975, when the United States withdrew in defeat from Vietnam, America's capitalist ideology seemed weak. In Angola and Mozambique, Egypt and Syria, Cuba, and even among significant communist parties in Western Europe, communist ideology seemed to be gaining influence.

Politically, the CPSU (Communist Party of the Soviet Union) under Khrushchev and Brezhnev gradually institutionalized its control of Soviet society. The police state and mass gulags under Stalin were replaced by extensive, but less heavy-handed, political authority, which operated as much by favoritism and incentives for successful managers, scientists, artists, and athletes as by coercion and terror. Political opposition was reduced to a few thousand dissidents, while political allegiance was gained from silent millions who benefited from the extension of industrial amenities and services. From 1958 to 1971, Soviet infant mortality was halved, from 40.6 to 22.9 deaths per thousand (Davis and Feshbach, 1980, 3).

The strength and stability of the Soviet regime from 1945 to 1970 was therefore evident. But after about 1970, conditions in all these domains began to deteriorate. Economically, Soviet productivity faltered. An economy geared to producing heavy industrial commodities could not make the adjustment either to the next industrial generation of micro-computer technology or to the provision of diversified consumer goods and services (Chirot, 1991). From 1945 to 1970, the Soviet Union increased its economic output by producing increasing numbers of tractors, tons of concrete, and sheets of steel. But by about 1970, the society's ability to absorb basic industrial commodities came into ques-tion. Giving a farm two tractors where there had been none greatly increased output. Giving a farm four tractors where there had been two (especially since there were insufficient spare parts to keep even two running full time) did not add to output and thus did not cover the cost of producing the additional tractors. Producing more tractors, concrete, and sheet steel simply meant more goods piled up on rail-road sidings or severely underutilized in fields and plants; what was needed were cars and light trucks, plastics, and more sophisticated alloys and castings.

Thus, during the 1970s the Soviet economy poured enormous re-sources into basic investments while achieving less and less growth in outputs. Manufacturing and agriculture stagnated, and the U.S.S.R. became more dependent on production and trade of raw materials. Annual industrial growth fell from 6.4—6.5 percent in 1961–70 to 5.5 percent in 1971–75 and then sank to 2.7 percent in 1976–80 and 1.9 percent in 1981–85 (Rostow, 1991, 62). In 1955, 28 percent of the U.S.S.R.'s exports to Western Europe had been manufactured goods. By 1983, as a result of shortages in the U.S.S.R. and the inferiority of Soviet manufacturers, that figure had fallen to 6 percent (Aslund, 1991, 19). Shortages of consumer goods, even of basic items such as housing, increased sharply. No more houses were built in the U.S.S.R. in 1984 than had been built in 1960, despite a substantially increased popula-tion; thus, the stock of housing relative to the population "actually decreased by 30 percent" over these years (Aganbegyan 1989, 228).

In 1985–86, Gorbachev followed Yuri Andropov's lead in trying to improve the economy mainly by enforcing work discipline and "accel-erating" work efforts. But these efforts failed (Goldman, 1994). Follow-ing these failures, early efforts at more severe restructuring under the banner of *perestroika* simply disrupted production and led to severe shortages of goods (Filtzer, 1994, 72–73). Finally, attempting to buy rather than force reform, Gorbachev literally bankrupted the Soviet state. Printing rubles to underwrite unrealistic promises of raises and investments in key sectors of the economy, the currency multiplied dramatically. The state budget deficit, stable at 15–18 billion rubles per year in 1980–85, suddenly rose to 90 billion rubles per year in 1988–89 (Aslund, 1991, 190, 192). The sizable inflation that followed further undermined the legitimacy of Gorbachev's government.

Militarily, after 1975 the tide of Soviet influence and effectiveness began to recede. Vietnam and Cuba became burdens rather than areas of further expansion in Asia and Latin America. Egypt threw off its Soviet alliance, leaving only a badly defeated Syria as the U.S.S.R.'s main Middle East ally. Most critically, the communist regime in Afghanistan faced an internal rebellion in 1979 and looked to Soviet troops to defend it. But following ten subsequent years of unsuccessful warfare, Soviet troops withdrew from Afghanistan, leaving the Afghan rebels in control of the countryside and, three years later, Kabul. In a striking parallel to America's experience in Vietnam, Soviet withdrawal in 1989 marked the most dramatic military failure in Soviet history.

Ideologically, the failure of socialism became most marked in the environmental arena, especially in the wake of the Chernobyl disaster. Capitalism had been castigated as an economic system that exploited and ravaged its workers for the sake of profits for the few. The U.S.S.R. claimed to be a workers' state whose economy operated with the welfare of its workers as its chief aim. Yet the explosion of the nuclear power plant at Chernobyl, and more especially the inept reaction of the authorities, comprehensively undermined the Soviet claims. Because of the Chernobyl disaster's watershed political consequences, it deserves closer examination.

On April 26, 1986, one of the four reactors at Chernobyl nuclear power station overheated, leading to steam explosions and fires that spread highly radioactive materials over the countryside and into the atmosphere. Yet Soviet authorities did not even admit to an accident until three days later, when Swedish authorities who had suddenly detected a major increase in radioactive fallout in their country began to press through private and public channels for an explanation of what had occurred. Although more precise figures are becoming available only as this paper is being written, even early estimates place the total radiation release as *eighty times* that of the Hiroshima or Nagaski explosions (Haynes and Bojcun, 1990, 44).

Nonetheless, Soviet authorities made no announcement to people in the regions affected by fallout, advocated no precautions. Party leaders ordered schools, shops, and workplaces to remain open, while sending their own families away. May Day parades went on in Kiev (whose 2.4 million residents lived only seventy-five miles from the reactor site) while radiation plumes were still spreading overhead. As the extent of the disaster slowly became clear, Western reports on Radio Free Europe increasingly conflicted with the reassurances of the Soviet authorities. As the truth gradually became known in the U.S.S.R., it became clear to Russians, Ukrainians, Belorussians, and Latvians that the Soviet regime had been encouraging them to feed their children with contaminated foods and left them uncertain about the safety of their homes. The myth that they lived in a society chiefly concerned with workers' welfare vanished, replaced by a cynical reevaluation of the "authorities."

Moreover, the Chernobyl explosion was just the tip of the iceberg of environmental disasters that began to come to light. It raised, for example, concerns about pollution of the Dnieper River, the main source of drinking and irrigation water for the Ukraine. However, a search for possible alternatives revealed that none existed; industrial pollution had already rendered every other major river in the central and southern Ukraine unfit for human consumption (Haynes and Bojcun, 1990, 118). In the port of Ventspils in Latvia, schools periodically had to issue gas masks to children due to the venting of the petrochemical and tanning works in the city. Radioactive wastes, chemical effluents, fertilizer and pesticide misuse, and poorly designed and managed irrigation schemes had left much of the U.S.S.R. and Eastern Europe an ecological nightmare, encompassing some of the most dangerously polluted lands on earth and wreaking destruction of habitats and resources (such as the shrinkage of the Aral Sea and the disappearance of the Volga sturgeon fishery) on an unprecedented scale.

Growing indications of ecological disaster were accompanied by declines in health care and mortality. From its low point in 1960–61 to 1975–76, the Soviet death rate increased 30 percent, from 7.2 to 9.4 deaths per thousand per year. Infant mortality, which had steadily fallen to 22.9 per thousand in 1971, swiftly rose (according to Soviet official statistics) by almost half, to 31.1 per thousand by 1976 (Davis and Feshbach, 1980, pp. 2–3). Things then deteriorated even further. By 1980–81, adult life expectancy had fallen four full years from 1964–65, from 66.1 to 62.3 years (Treml, 1991, 126). In the city of Ventspils in Latvia (noted above for heavy chemical pollution), the percentage of deformed newborns quintupled from .8 percent of all births in 1977 to 4.3 percent in 1984. At the later date, 14 percent of newborns had illnesses requiring hospitalization. Indeed in Ventspils only 27 percent of all pregnancies went to term and produced normal births as opposed to ending in miscarriages or problem births. For Latvia as a whole the figure was 50 percent; in the United States the comparable figure is 90 percent (Cullen, 1991, 118). By 1987, the Soviet health minister admitted that infant mortality in the U.S.S.R. ranked no better than fiftieth in the world, after Barbados and the United Arab Emirates (Field, 1991, 79).

Shortages of medical supplies contributed to the decline of public health. As Mark Field notes, "The health service, as constituted at the end of the 1980s, [was] indeed in such poor shape that it help[ed] to undermine the legitimacy of the Gorbachev regime" (1991, 79). Increasing numbers of industrial accidents, as workers suffered with worn-out machinery and deteriorating mines and factories, probably also contributed to greater mortality. Under such conditions, in which public health and mortality sharply deteriorated while party officials evaded responsibility and shielded themselves, any ideological claims about the superiority of socialism and its greater regard for the working man and woman, provoked anger rather than assent.

Coming together with great force in the late 1980s, these trends and conditions eroded the CPSU's political authority. Managers complained that central economic directives were unproductive and out of touch with local needs. Military officials, bruised in Afghanistan, questioned national policy priorities. Local party officials sought to defend their regions against pollution excesses. Previously passive miners began to strike for safer conditions. Writers and artists increasingly gave expression to the mounting problems. Under this drumbeat of problems, the formerly cohesive party structure weakened amid a host of evasions of responsibility for the apparent deterioration in every main area of Soviet life.

The Growth of Elite Alienation and Conflict over Access to Elite Positions

A top-down view of revolution suggests that unrest and alienation among elites can carry a state far down the path to collapse well before popular mobilizations occur. In the French Revolution, it was the Finance Ministry's admitted bankrupting of the Crown, as well as the rejection of the Crown's proposed reforms by the Assembly of Notables, that precipitated the calling of the Estates General. It was only after the Estates General met that Parisian crowds surged to the Bastille. Similarly, in the U.S.S.R., it was elites inside the party structure that issued calls for reform, and later for the dissolution of the regime.

Elite alienation grew rapidly as the trends discussed above became evident; indeed, the trends were most evident to party leaders and to middle-level and provincial elites. As J. F. Brown (1991, 3–4) has noted, "the communist ruling elite . . . began to lose confidence in its ability to rule, and more to the point, to lose the willingness to use the means to retain its rule." Among middle-level and provincial elites, the change in attitudes was exemplified by the disgust of Leonid Teliatnikov, who had been chief of the Chernobyl Nuclear Plant Fire Station at the time of the accident. Learning that local political leaders neither informed nor prepared to evacuate the affected population, he told the journal *Smena*, "I felt sick in my soul and ashamed that I should belong to the same Party as these people. . . . I stopped respecting many city leaders" (cited in Haynes and Bojcun, 1990, 51).

Teliatnikov's reaction was indicative of the attitudes of increasing numbers of technical school graduates. From the 1960s to the 1980s, the Soviet Union experienced an explosion of graduates in engineering and other technical subjects. Yet as the structure of the Soviet economy did not become more information- and skill-intensive but stayed mired in its heavy industry structure, there were few suitable outlets for the career ambitions of these graduates. Instead of rising in income and influence, these "technical specialists," as they were called, remained subordinate to party officials and a small cadre of enterprise managers, who thwarted their efforts to rise in the system. Much of the support for reform came precisely from these specialists, who joined the more exalted academicians and the upper intelligentsia of writers, television and radio workers, artists, and professionals in thoroughly rejecting the Communist Party (Hough, 1997).

Table 5.1 shows trends in the occupational structure of the Soviet Union's labor force from the 1950s to the 1980s. What is most striking in this table, and in marked contrast to trends among North American and European labor forces during the same period, is the utter stagnation in the proportion of the labor force engaged in professional and administrative positions from the 1960s to the 1980s. We see here the

TABLE 5.1
Social Mobility and Competition in the U.S.S.R., 1930–1989.
(Percentage of Population)

	1930s	*1940s*	*1950s*	*1960s*	*1970s*	*1980s*
Manual	33	37	42	48	51	41
Clerical	6	6	7	10	12	16
Educational and Services	7	8	9	14	14	19[a]
Professional and Elites	2	3	4	5	5	—

Note: Columns do not add up to 100 due to the exclusion of agricultural and miscellaneous workers.

[a]Educational/Services and Professional/Elite categories merged.

Sources: Gordon, L., and A. Nazimova (1986, 48–50); Aslund (1991, 21); Garcelon (1995, 249).

U.S.S.R.'s clear failure to shift from an industrial to an information-based economy.

This occupational stagnation occurred despite a huge increase in the proportion of the population with higher degrees. Thomas Remington (1990, 166) estimates that the number of those whose jobs qualified them as "specialists" due to advanced technical or college training rose from roughly one million in 1940 to perhaps ten million by 1970. In 1959, only 2 percent of the population had postsecondary degrees; by 1989, the proportion had risen to 9 percent (Dunlop, 1993, 68). During the 1970s and 1980s, the proportion of persons with higher degrees appeared to outstrip the number of specialized and professional jobs available for them. As Remington notes, "The decline in the number of auxiliary and unskilled jobs is painfully slow, and the increase in the number of jobs requiring a specialist's training lags far behind the output of specialists" (171).

The overproduction of specialists produced both economic problems and political frustrations. In 1988, Alexei Kochetov argued that many specialists "are employed at a level lower than that of the qualifications they received," with low salaries and few or no prospects for promotion (quoted in Garcelon, 1995, 297). Many engineering graduates "came to be regarded as a pool of skilled manual labor" (Remington, 1990, 172). In recognition of the widespread alienation among the workforce, one of Gorbachev's first reforms was to raise the wage differential between specialist and manual laborers. But as with so many of his efforts, the practical effect was to make things worse: the benefits went mainly to enterprise directors and superintendents, further disappointing and alienating large numbers of technical specialists (Filtzer, 1994, 61–62).

These aggrieved specialists, numbering in the millions and concentrated in the major cities and industrial centers, represented a pool of energetic, educated, mostly younger people who were frustrated aspirants to elite status and who targeted the Communist Party hierarchy, and the latter's control of the economic system, as the reason for their plight. They provided the core of support for the election of Boris Yeltsin and the Democratic Russia Party in the Russian and all-U.S.S.R. elections. In the 1989 balloting for the Congress of People's Deputies in Moscow, 73.5 percent of the winning candidates were faculty, researchers, artists, engineers and technical specialists, managers, public administrators, and professionals (Colton, 1990). Marc Garcelon's (1995, 247) survey of the Moscow branch of the Democratic Russia movement, the key popular support group for Yeltsin, similarly found more than 75 percent drawn from the ranks of specialists.

Although the main social divide among the elites ran between the younger, better educated, and more urban artists, writers, academicians, professionals, and technical specialists on the one hand, who supported first Gorbachev and then Yeltsin, and the older, more provincial party careerists and officials who supported the status quo, the split ran through all the ranks of the elite. Even Gorbachev's advisers, the party elite, and the Supreme Soviet were divided over whether the remedy for the U.S.S.R.'s problems lay in strengthening current institutions or in fundamental reform (Lane, 1996). "The divisions at the top were mirrored at all levels" (Gill, 1994). Even within the Army and the KGB, there were severe splits rather than consensus or overriding loyalty to the regime (Castoriadis, 1989, 64).

During the attempted coup against Gorbachev and Yeltsin in August 1991, the chief of police in Leningrad immediately went over to the side of the liberal mayor against the coup plotters. General Evgenii Shaposhnikov, commander of the Soviet air force, and General Pavel Grachev, head of Soviet paratroops, supported Yeltsin and sent paratroopers to help defend the Russian Parliament (Dunlop, 1993, 234–37, 248–49). In sum, the entire elite structure was divided over the best course for Russia and the U.S.S.R.

Nonetheless, what happened in the Soviet Union from 1989 to 1991 was not a mere coup or elite rebellion. The degree of fracture in the party would not have developed, nor its consequences been so great, without considerable mass mobilization for the cause of reform.

Mass Mobilization and the Collapse of the USSR

After what has been said about the deterioration of health, life, environment, and economy in the Soviet Union, the intensification of popular grievances after 1975 requires no further comment. What is remarkable is the extent to which Western observers refused to believe that this deterioration existed or that it affected popular attitudes in the Soviet Union and Eastern Europe.

The marked deterioration in infant mortality was evident to Western demographers, who suggested that the data on its steep rise in the 1970s indicated fundamental problems in the Soviet system (Davis and Feshbach, 1980). But imported consumer goods on display in Moscow (often purchased with borrowed funds) gave foreign observers a sense that the regime was meeting consumer needs. The drabness and disrepair of East Berlin was often contrasted with the liveliness of West Berlin. But some observers downplayed the import of this distinction, assuming that modern factories lay behind the pockmarked walls and that contented workers lived in the crumbling tenements. Speaking of East Germany, but using words applicable to the entire Soviet bloc,

Amos Elon (1992, 36) notes that when "Eduard Reuter, head of Daimler Benz, returned from his first thorough tour of East German industrial installations he is reported to have said that the problems there could only be resolved by bulldozers." Elon further observes, "Many now wonder at the apparent willingness of so many governments and 'experts' in the West over the years to swallow as a fact the myth of East Germany as the 'eleventh' industrial world power. The one successful public relations coup of the East German regime—a regime otherwise so disreputable—was to make so many people believe in the myth." One might also add westerners' willingness to believe, as a converse to the bravery of Soviet dissidents, in the myth of the "stoic" Russian people and their immunity to suffering.

Mikhail Gorbachev had come up through the party hierarchy as a talented, ambitious manager. But it was under Yuri Andropov, when he had led an intensive review of the country's situation, that he became a committed reformer (Aslund, 1991, 27). Gorbachev thought the way to overcome entrenched conservative interests was to encourage the population to make apparent the shortcomings of Soviet society and hold guilty authorities responsible. Thus, his policy of *glasnost* was developed as the essential precursor to restructuring, or *perestroika*.

Glasnost, however, led as certainly to state breakdown in the Soviet Union as the policy of the French Crown two centuries earlier when it invited peasants, bourgeoisie, and nobles throughout France to meet in local assemblies to discuss the problems of the nation and elect representatives to the Estates General. Once a far-reaching debate on the problems of the U.S.S.R. was encouraged by the authorities, they could neither set the terms of that debate nor resist the demands for solution of pressing problems that followed. Given an opening, the intelligentsia, who had earlier faced a hard choice between conforming to or opposing the regime, leapt at the chance to highlight myriad problems that had previously been concealed. The vast range of problems that came to light, and conflicts between conservative and reformist elites over their solution, led to policy paralysis. Confronted with inaction and waffling from the central authorities, local and regional grievances quickly blossomed into demands for greater autonomy and later into nationalist separatist movements.

Gorbachev first encouraged the formation of independent social clubs, where citizens could share opinions. Apparently thinking that these would remain amenable to party control, Gorbachev was surprised when these clubs quickly formed cross connections, coalescing into popular fronts in support of reform. When Gorbachev decreed that popular elections would now be required for selecting local leaderships and representatives to the All-Soviet Congress, communist politicians had to orient themselves to winning popular support; the popular fronts quickly became independent political organizations (Brovkin, 1990).

What form would these take? While Gorbachev apparently envisaged popular action by Soviet citizens, he failed to realize that local organizations would follow the preexisting lines of local organizations created by the U.S.S.R., which emphasized the national identity of the constituent republics. Led by the Marxist-Leninist belief that only class, and not nationality, would be a lasting source of political divisions, the Communist Party made permanent, and even magnified, nationalist identities in the Soviet Union. The nationalities not only received distinctive passports, and support for traditional cultures and languages; the regime went so far as to provide extended apparatuses of sovereignty, including duplicate republican ministries, scientific and cultural academies, and communist parties (Milanovich, 1994; Brubaker, 1994). The officially recognized form of political organization alternative to the central Soviet authorities was *territorial and nationalist.* As Branko Milanovich notes, when the center had overwhelming authority, this did not matter. But "when the whole system became shaky, these 'shells' could be easily filled with substance; the proto-states became real states" (Milanovich, 1994, 63).

The electoral campaigns forced upon local party officials by Gorbachev quickly ceased to become confrontations of corrupt officials by loyal Soviet citizens. Instead, they became true contests based on popular appeal. And given the sense of betrayal and frustration felt by so many with the Communist Party, nationalist alternatives were frequently compelling. The election of nationalist governments seeking autonomy in the Baltic and the Caucasus began the process of making the "republics" real competing centers of power with the Communist Party in Moscow.

The challenge to the authority of the Communist Party from non-Russian nationalist republics was abetted by popular demonstrations in the major cities of Russia. In the years from 1959 to 1989, Russia had transformed itself from being a mainly rural to a mainly urban nation; its urban population almost doubled, from 100 million to 188 million, in those three decades (Devlin, 1995, 11). These urban centers became the focus for popular mobilization in support of Boris Yeltsin and against the communist regime. On February 4, 1990, more than 250,000 people demonstrated in Moscow demanding the end of the Communist Party's constitutionally guaranteed monopoly of power; almost a year later, on January 20, 1991, 200,000 demonstrated in Moscow against the efforts of the Soviet regime to militarily intimidate the Baltic republics (Devlin, 1995, 149; Garcelon, 1995, 473; Urban, Igrunov, and Mifrokhin, 1997, 191). In March 1991, "Yeltsin's supporters held vast demonstrations in support of Russian sovereignty throughout the republic," with hundreds of thousands turning out in Moscow and tens of thousands in Leningrad, Yaroslavl, Volgograd, and other cities (Dunlop, 1993, 32–34). And during the crucial days of August 19–21 in Moscow, during the attempted coup, perhaps 500,000 turned out at some time in support of Yeltsin against the coup, including perhaps 50,000 or more who took part in the defense of the White House during the crucial night of resistance on August 20 (Garcelon, 1995, 562; Dunlop, 1993, 223).

The efforts of the non-Russian republics to secure autonomy and the efforts of the Russian reformers to throw off communist domination reinforced and fed on each other. As the republics drew away, violence over borders and refugees broke out, particularly in Armenia, Azerbaijan, and Moldova. Interethnic conflict in 1988–91 killed more than a thousand people and created hundreds of thousands of refugees and tens of billions of rubles of damage; and "the inability of the U.S.S.R. government to control nationalist violence . . . was one of the major factors leading to the collapse of the Soviet state, reinforcing perceptions of the frailty of Soviet power, . . . impelling some groups toward secession, and provoking a sense of desperation" among conservative elites (Beissinger, n.d., 12–13).

The third element of popular mobilization that contributed to the fall of the Communist Party was strikes, particularly among the coal miners, who provided the essential energy for Soviet industry and heat for Soviet homes. Massive strikes in 1989 and 1991 rocked Gorbachev's authority and provided a base for Yeltsin, who was able to rally the miners' support. The 1989 strike involved more than four hundred thousand workers who organized themselves in new grass-roots unions (Filtzer, 1994, 94–95). The 1991 strike helped persuade Gorbachev to support Yeltsin, a turn that provoked the August coup. And the costs of settling the strikes contributed to the financial unraveling of the regime.

Glasnost had put Gorbachev in an untenable position. Having decided, after Chernobyl, that the policy of covering up errors would lead to further decay, it was clearly necessary to expose faulty state policies. Seeking to undermine party conservatives, it was essential to demand responsibility, support the intelligentsia, and encourage popular representation. But when such actions unleashed increased opposition, Gorbachev could not suppress that opposition without handing power to conservatives and silencing future complaints against the system's faults. In Eastern Europe and the Baltics, in particular, massive armed intervention to suppress autonomy would dash Gorbachev's hopes for increased autonomy and support for his reforms from Soviet society. When mild interventions in the Baltics drew harsh international and domestic criticism, Gorbachev had to decide whether to act like Stalin to preserve the dominance of the party or to leap ahead with still greater reforms. Having begun his career attempting to change all that was associated with Stalin, Gorbachev had little hope but to attempt, like a surfer, to keep ahead of the wave of popular discontent he had aroused, hoping to ride it to greater power and further reform.

Waves ultimately break, overturning the surfer. Gorbachev lost his balance as his own allies in reform in the military and in his ministries saw that his policies were leading to greater disorder and the destruction, not the salvation, of party authority. In their attempted 1991 coup, they admitted the bankruptcy of Gorbachev's party-led reform policy. However, their failure left no authority at all to the party, or to Gorbachev.

Of course, one could argue that much could not have been foreseen. As Timur Kuran (1991) has demonstrated, and Vaclav Havel (1990) has eloquently described, it was to the advantage of ordinary people to falsify their observed preferences as long as the communist regimes remained in power. Depths of discontent could be hidden behind positive, if unenthusiastic, affirmations of support for the regime. Moreover, official economic statistics, even to 1980, could be interpreted as showing sustained growth. No doubt Gorbachev believed he had the people on his side in his efforts to renew the party.

Nonetheless, by the end of the 1980s, the deterioration in the economy, environment, and credibility of the Soviet Union and its government were manifest. Perhaps only a Marxist like Gorbachev, rather than a follower of Tocqueville, could believe that under such conditions encouraging popular identification of problems and hamstringing repressive capacities could lead to anything other than state collapse. If, as Marx and Lenin taught, a committed leader can mold the understanding of the people and overthrow a corrupt state, then Gorbachev might have succeeded. But if, in fact, revolutions follow upon state decay rather than upon popular mobilization, Gorbachev was bound to fill the role, as many ambitious reformers before him, of hastening the forces that would overwhelm him and his regime. The structural conditions for the Soviet state to unravel from the top down, unleashing elite and popular discontent, were too far advanced to be reversed. Gorbachev's attempt to undermine party conservatives could only remove the remaining props of the regime, not overcome its manifold deficiencies.

Elite Configurations and the Outcome of
Revolution in the U.S.S.R.

The Soviet Union in the 1980s showed all the major trends typical of a society headed for revolution: a weakening state hamstrung by economic and political failures; an elite sharply divided over how to respond to the state's problems and with a vast number of educated and talented but frustrated aspirants to elite and subelite positions who had come to reject the legitimacy of the leadership and the system that sustained it; and a population suffering marked declines in living standards and readily mobilized to support elites seeking radical change. As in prior revolutions, each of these trends, by unfolding simultaneously, led to mutually reinforcing challenges to the regime's survival. The state's efforts at reform provoked resistance from conservative elites, excited ambitions for change among reform-minded elites and their supporters among the frustrated aspirants to elite and subelite positions, and triggered waves of popular mobilization. The reform-minded elites encouraged popular mobilization to pressure conservative elites. The elites polarized, dividing between conservatives seeking to maintain the status quo and reformist elites seeking to overcome their adversaries by pressing for ever more radical changes. Finally, a military confrontation (the August coup of 1991) pitted reformist elites against conservatives; a combination of splits in the military and popular support for the reformers led to their victory, sweeping away the Soviet regime and beginning a struggle to consolidate the successor Russian regime in the face of various recalcitrant regional and conservative groups.

It is thus not a serious distortion to say that, while of course manifesting its own distinct elements (as does every revolution), the demise of the Soviet regime in the U.S.S.R. basically followed the script of past major revolutions such as the English Revolution of 1640 and the French Revolution of 1789. As in the past, a key part of the revolutionary dynamic was a split among elites amid a developing crisis or crises—initially economic stagnation, which spurred Gorbachev's efforts at reform, then popular rejection of communist authority under glasnost and perestroika, which polarized elites and left Gorbachev squeezed between Yeltsin and his anticommunist reformers and staunch communist conservatives in the army, the bureaucracy, and the KGB.

While the future of the former Soviet republics will of course be shaped by the conditions that existed in Russia and the Commonwealth of Independent States (CIS) before and during 1989–91, are there nonetheless lessons from the past that we might use for guidance in assessing this future? And more specifically, can we gain any insights from the discussion by Dogan and Higley in chapter 1 of elite configurations and regime change?

Democratic institutions can be brought forth with the stroke of a pen, but to give them power and stability is another matter. Michael Burton and John Higley in chapter 3 (see also Higley and Gunther, 1992) argue that an essential component of democratic transitions is an elite settlement, which creates a consensus among elites about core political values and practices. Where elites remain disunited, divided by ethnic or other oppositions, and unwilling to compromise their disputes, democracies cannot be consolidated. The classic example is Germany's Weimar Republic, and Alan Knight in chapter 4 provides many additional Latin American examples.

In France in the 1790s, as in most revolutions, divisions among the leaders and aspiring leaders of the postrevolutionary regime led to turmoil, coups, and eventually Napoleon's populist and expansionist authoritarian rule. It required another century of political turbulence before something approximating stable democracy came into being in France. From 1789 until at least the inception of the Third Republic in 1875, French elites remained deeply divided into monarchist, republican, and Bonapartist camps, each of which enjoyed a brief ascendancy during the century that followed the revolution but whose conflicts and unrestrained competitions kept France in periodic turmoil and revolutionary upheavals.

In its divisions, the postrevolutionary elite configuration of Russia today appears similar to that of postrevolutionary France. In the terms that Dogan and Higley employ in chapter 1, an "ideocratically united elite" during the heyday of communist power has been replaced by a "disunited elite." The elite structure of present-day Russia (and probably of all the former Soviet republics) is crippled by divisions among economic reformers, various stripes of conservatives and ultranationalists, and the managers of enterprises not yet privatized. These divisions prevent the elite consensus necessary for stable democracy from taking root.

The economic reformers believe that establishing a market economy is the best way to rebuild and advance the Russian economy and restore the power of the Russian state. Yet the Soviet economy was constructed in such a way as to make marketization extraordinarily difficult. Market organization of production depends on competing firms making similar products and on small firms providing the basis for the market to work its magic, with successful small firms growing and unsuccessful ones failing without, however, disrupting the entire economy. However, the Soviet economy operated with a disdain for competition and small enterprises. By share of total industrial employment, in the United States only a quarter of industrial enterprises have one thousand or more employees; the comparable proportion in the last years of the Soviet Union was nearly three-quarters of all enterprises. In terms of Soviet ideology, "if a Soviet factory or dam . . . was not the biggest, there was some explaining to do." Moreover, of 7,664 products in metallurgy, chemicals, and construction, 77 percent were produced by monopoly enterprises providing the entire country's supply. (All data and the quote are from Goldman, 1994, 13.) Under these conditions, enterprise managers had tremendous monopoly and labor-control power. It was in part the growing independence of enterprise managers, and their ability to evade and manipulate the central planning authorities, that led to the massive inefficiencies of the Soviet economy.

Since the collapse of the Soviet regime, the power of enterprise managers has actually grown (Burawoy and Krotov, 1992, 1993). They control tremendous amounts of resources and labor and hold industry hostage through their ability to create bottlenecks by withholding essential products. In lieu of either central government regulation or market constraints, the result has been increased anarchy in production and more bartering among enterprises. These independent fiefdoms are resistant to the imposition of markets and have so far frustrated every attempt of market reformers to impose market discipline (McFaul, 1995).

At the same time, the new political elite in Moscow has failed to build a nationalist ideology capable of uniting the nation. This new elite—David Lane and Cameron Ross (1996, 4) calculate that of 479 high officials in Russian government as of January 1995, 306 had no prior posts in the Soviet regime, and 76 had five years or less of such experience—has failed to take either nationalism or ideology seriously, except as pathologies. Mainly technocratic in background, its members have instead focused on technical economic solutions and titularly democratic political competitions. Nationalists of varying strikes have tried to fill the resulting ideological vacuum. Within both Russia and the other former Soviet republics, nationalists and populists have presented themselves as alternatives to the colorless, increasingly unsuccessful democratic technocrats who hold power. It is ominous that following previous revolutions, whenever a similar competition has emerged, the nationalists and populists (Napoleon, Mao, Lenin, Hitler) have ultimately emerged victorious.

Observers initially were surprised and disturbed at the emergence of strong nationalist tendencies in Eastern Europe and the former Soviet Union. Nationalist feelings fueled the independence of the Baltic states, the Ukraine, Belarus, and the Caucasian and Central Asian republics (Beissinger, n.d.). Further nationalist mobilization threatens to create additional independence movements in the new Russian republic and add to internal and cross-border conflicts in Moldava, Georgia, Armenia, and Azerbaijan. The war in Chechnya has been the most dramatic manifestation of these tendencies. Yet, this growth of nationalist mobilization should have been expected in a revolutionary situation.

In analyzing past revolutions (Goldstone, 1991, 424–28), I have noted that new governments taking power in the wake of revolutionary collapses of old regimes must struggle to gain the allegiance of their populations. Respect for the legitimacy of a new regime, and even more, the kinds of commitments necessary to overcome severe social problems, is far from automatic. Revolutionary governments typically proceed through a series of steps in trying to gain such legitimacy and commitment.

The first step is usually rectification of the old regime's abuses, followed by efforts to redistribute assets and give rewards to those who were previously excluded or abused. Yet rectifications and redistributions are rarely sufficient to build legitimacy; as I have elsewhere observed, they are "inherently a short-lived basis for building a revolutionary coalition. . . . Redistribution has its limits; the wealth of the privileged elite, when diluted and redistributed, is generally far from sufficient to relieve the wants of the general populace." Moreover, while retribution for abuses and redistribution can create short-term satisfaction among the populace, "if the revolutionary leadership is to retain the support of skilled elites and middle groups, redistribution must stop short" (Goldstone, 1991, 427).

The viability of revolutionary governments, therefore, depends on finding an alternative basis of commitment to the new regime. "The ideal, and most common, alternative popular principle is nationalism. By identifying the revolutionary leadership as the new carrier of authentic national aspirations and identity, revolutionaries can hope to maintain the loyalty of a broad, cross-class coalition" (ibid.). Fanning nationalist feelings has great risks: competing territorial claims can lead to war, as has already occurred in Azerbaijan, Armenia, and the former Yugoslavia. Fanning nationalist feelings also can lead to persecution of ethnic minorities, who become suspect in newly emerging nations (Gurr, 1994).

Faced with this paradox, should governments embrace or try to suppress growing nationalist claims? Given that people need a sense of identity, and a sense of strong and legitimate authority to turn to in times of pressing crises, suppression or denial of nationalist claims is likely to lead only to more intense nationalism and the emergence of more extreme groups. Greater conflict and violence are the likely result.

If the past pattern of revolutionary governments is that support and unity are built on nationalism, what does this imply about current struggles between Yeltsin and his opponents? Although Yeltsin has been a brilliant political tactician, he probably committed a grave strategic error in failing to build a nationalist party through which he could portray his commitment to democracy and economic reform as a way to recover Russia's international power and prestige. Leaving the field open to nationalisms of the left and the right, Yeltsin has invited major challenges to his rule and to the Russian democratic regime.

Although Yeltsin won reelection in the second round of the June 1996 presidential election, the first-round votes were still telling. Nationalist votes went to the communist-cum-nationalist Gennady Zyuganov, to the military nationalist Alexander Lebed, and to the far-right nationalist Vladimir Zhirinovsky. Taken together, those votes far exceeded Yeltsin's support. Indeed, it is remarkable that in the first round, despite energetic campaigning, open-ended campaign coffers, total control of the media, and support of the best Western election strategists, Yeltsin gained barely 2 percent more votes than Zyuganov.

It was thus a brilliant stroke by Yeltsin and his advisers to co-opt the nationalist Lebed as special assistant for defense and security. Adding Lebed's nationalist popularity to his own reform message allowed "the collective Yeltsin" to trounce Zuganov in the second round. However, Yeltsin's opponents remain in control of the Duma, and they remain popular among voters.

Moreover, Yeltsin won his presidency only with the overwhelming support of the enterprise managers, who contributed enormous amounts of money and media resources to Yeltsin's campaign. To these enterprise managers, Yeltsin's reform government was not entirely welcome, but it was far less threatening than the communists, who would have restored central control over these now liberated economic fiefdoms (Hough, 1997). The alignment of the reformers and the enterprise managers to defeat the conservatives (nationalists and communists) was effective, but it represented a shifting alignment of elite factions, and not the emergence of elite unity.

In sum, the democratic and technocratic elites that have captured the Kremlin, for all the support they garnered for their fight against autocratic communist rule, have failed to build either a firm economic base (that remains with the enterprise managers) or a firm ideological base (that remains with various nationalist politicians). Russia's political future, therefore, depends to a considerable extent on whether elite groups will come together to forge an elite settlement that would be the basis of a stable democratic regime.

The two most apt historical parallels are Turkey after the Kemalist revolution and dissolution of the Ottoman Empire, and Germany, after the ineffective Weimar Republic that followed the overthrow of the imperial regime. In both cases, a reforming center tried to make its way between strong economic power centers outside of government (landlords in Turkey and industrialists in Germany) while trying to restore ideological vigor to a defeated and dissolved empire.

In Turkey, the Kemalist government was able to appropriate a nationalist ideology, although this resulted in terrible conflicts with Armenians and Greeks. However, the regime was not able to gain command of the economic resources of the nation, which remained for the most part in the hands of landlords, who came to control local and regional governments. A weak central government thus persisted for decades, mainly on the strength of its upholding the ideal of a secular, modern Turkish national state. But real power was in the countryside (Trimberger, 1978). Only recently, with the advent of substantial industrialization, has this begun to change. But at the same time, the central government has lost much of its ideological luster, and resurgent Islamic parties are mounting a strong challenge for the mantle of nationalist leadership.

In Germany, the Weimar government completely failed to command nationalist enthusiasms, which were captured instead by Hitler's National Socialist Party. Indeed, Hitler succeeded to such a degree that industrialists and other politicians were willing to accede to his plans in the pursuit of restored national power (Goldhagen, 1996). The coalition of populist nationalist leadership and outside economic interests swept the Weimar Republic away and created a newly imperialistic Reich.

Modern Russia could go either way. If Yeltsin retains control of the Russian state and gradually builds a nationalist party that remains committed to pro-Western economic and democratic reforms, he may yet don the mantle of a reformist *and* nationalist leader. In this eventuality, there would be something resembling a Kemalist state in Russia. But with real economic power in the hands of local enterprise managers and real political power in the hands of local and regional elites, it would be a much weaker version of the Kemalist model. On the other hand, if a nationalist leader should come to power who does not continue Yeltsin's commitment to democracy and integration with the broader world but instead makes common cause with enterprise leaders and provides a measure of protectionism to receive their economic support, we could have, in broad outline, the Hitlerian outcome (without, it is hoped, the same degree of venom)—a more confrontational, aggressively nationalist and expansionist regime.

Conclusion

Much can be learned about both the causes and aftermaths of the Soviet Union's demise by recognizing it as resulting from a true revolutionary crisis. This recognition tempers optimism about Russia's future political course. Although new elites have replaced the old, ideocratically unified communist elite, the new elites are disunited. Unless a more consensually united elite emerges, the prospects are either a weak state and economic autarky or an aggressively nationalist regime, with elite factions waging relatively unchecked power struggles in either scenario.

On the other hand, the recognition that a fundamental shift in elites has occurred also points to the fundamental nature of the regime transformation that has occurred and, therefore, to the possibility that a democratic regime may emerge. It would be premature to conclude pessimistically—though there will surely be short-term setbacks—that in the longer run the most likely result will be a recycling of authoritarian rule under some new name.

Notes

1. Some commentators (e.g., Shevtsova, 1995) have pointed to continuity of many government personnel from the Gorbachev era to the Yeltsin regime as evidence that not much really changed in 1991 and after. Yet such perceptions of continuity are typical of revolutions, and they date back to Tocqueville's observations of the French Revolution. Napoleon soon restored the ranks of nobility and awarded places to leading nobles of the *ancien régime*, and he was followed by restoration of the Bourbon monarchy. Similarly, the Stuarts returned to the throne after the English Revolution, and even the Bolsheviks used large numbers of former tsarist personnel to staff their civil service. The fact is that revolutions do not destroy the need for skilled, experienced personnel, and thus all revolutionary regimes rely, to a greater or lesser extent, on carryover personnel from the prerevolutionary regime. What truly changes is the taken-for-granted monopoly of political power held by the old institutional and ideological frameworks. Even the "reborn" Communist Party under Zyuganov is more nationalist than Marxist-Leninist in outlook (Remnick, 1996).

More recently, a number of authors have come to agree that the events of 1989–91 in the Soviet Union constituted a major revolution, a "Second Russian Revolution." See, for example, Hough (1997) and Urban, Igrunov, and Mitrokhin (1997).

2. A major exception is Cornelius Castoriadis (1989), who before 1989 accurately perceived the degree of social change in the Soviet Union and the weakness of the state and who thus forecast the occurrence of a major revolution.

References

Aganbegyan, Abel. 1989. *Inside Perestroika: The Future of the Soviet Economy*. New York: Perennial/Harper and Row.

Ash, Timothy Garton. 1989. "Revolution: The Springtime of Two Nations." *New York Review of Books*. June 15, 3–10.

Aslund, Anders. 1991. *Gorbachev's Struggle for Economic Reform*. Rev. ed. Ithaca: Cornell University Press.

Beissinger, Mark R. n.d. "Violence as Nationalist Contention." Unpublished ms., University of Wisconsin.

Brovkin, Vladimir. 1990. "Revolution from Below: Informal Political Associations in Russia 1988–89." *Soviet Studies* 42 (June): 233–58.

Brown, J. F. 1996. *Surge to Freedom: The End of Communist Rule in Eastern Europe*. Durham: Duke University Press, 1991.

Brubaker, Rogers. 1994. "Nationhood and the National Question in the Soviet Union and Post-Soviet Eurasia: An Institutionalist Account." *Theory and Society* 23 (April): 47–78.

Burawoy, Michael and Pavel Krotov. 1992. "The Soviet Transition from Socialism to Capitalism: Worker Control and Economic Bargaining in the Wood Industry." *American Sociological Review* 57 (February): 16–39.

———. 1993. "The Economic Basis of Russia's Political Crisis." *New Left Review*, no. 198: 49–70.

Castoriadis, Cornelius. 1989. "The Gorbachev Interlude." In *Gorbachev: The Debate*, ed. Ferenc Feher and Andrew Arato. Atlantic Highlands N.J.: Humanities Press, 61–84.

Chirot, Daniel. 1991. "What Happened in Eastern Europe in 1989?" In *The Crisis of Leninism and the Decline of the Left: The Revolutions of 1989*, ed. D. Chirot, Seattle: University of Washington Press, 3–32.

Colton, Timothy. 1990. "The Politics of Democratization: The Moscow Election of 1990." *Soviet Economy* 6 (October): 285–344.

Cullen, Robert. 1991. *The Twilight of Empire: Inside the Crumbling Soviet Bloc*. New York: Atlantic Monthly Press.

Davis, Christopher and Murray Feshbach. 1980. *Rising Infant Mortality in the USSR in the 1970s*. Washington, D.C.: U.S. Department of Commerce.

Devlin, Judith. 1995. *The Rise of the Russian Democrats: The Causes and Consequences of the Elite Revolution*. Aldershot, U.K.: Edward Elgar.

Dunlop, John B. 1993. *The Rise of Russia and the Fall of the Soviet Empire*. Princeton: Princeton University Press.

Elon, Amos. 1992. "In a Former Country." *New York Review of Books* 39: 34–39.

Field, Mark G. 1996. "Soviet Health Problems and the Convergence Hypothesis." In _Soviet Social Problems_, ed. Anthony Jones, Walter Connor and David E. Powell, Boulder, Colo.: Westview, 78–94.

Filtzer, Donald. 1994. _Soviet Workers and the Collapse of Perestroika_. Cambridge: Cambridge University Press.

Garcelon, Marc. 1995. _Democrats and Apparatchniks: The Democratic Russia Movement and the Specialist Rebellion in Moscow 1989–1991_. Ph.D. diss., University of California, Berkeley.

Gellner, Ernest. 1992. "A year in the Soviet Union." _Contention_ 1 (June): 107–20.

Gill, Graeme. 1994. _The Collapse of a Single Party System: The Disintegration of the CPSU_. Cambridge: Cambridge University Press.

Goldhagen, Daniel Jonah. 1996. _Hitler's Willing Executioners_. New York: Alfred Knopf.

Goldman, Marshall. 1994. _Lost Opportunity: Why Economic Reforms in Russia Have Not Worked_. New York: Norton.

Goldstone, Jack A. 1991. _Revolution and Rebellion in the Early Modern World_. Berkeley: University of California Press.

Goldstone, Jack A., Ted Robert Gurr, and F. Moshiri. 1991. _Revolutions of the Late Twentieth Century_. Boulder, Colo.: Westview.

Gordon, L. and A. Nazimova. 1986. "The Socio-occupational Structure of Contemporary Soviet Society: Typology and Statistics." In _Social Structure of the U.S.S.R._, ed. M. Yanowitch. Armonk, N.Y.: M.E. Sharpe.

Gurr, Ted Robert. 1970. _Why Men Rebel_. Princeton: Princeton University Press.

———. 1994. "Minorities in Revolution." In _Revolutions: Theoretical, Comparative, and Historical Studies_, 2nd ed., ed. Jack A. Goldstone, 308–14. Fort Worth, Texas: Harcourt Brace.

Havel, Vaclav. 1990. "The Power of the Powerless." In _Without Force or Lies: Voices from the Revolution of Central Europe in 1989–90_, ed. W. M. Brinton and A. Rinzler, 27–104. San Francisco: Mercury House.

Haynes, Viktor and Marko Bojcun. 1990. _The Chernobyl Disaster_. London: Hogarth Press.

Higley, John and Richard Gunther, eds. 1992. _Elites and Democratic Consolidation in Latin America and Europe_. Cambridge: Cambridge University Press.

Hough, Jerry. 1987. "Gorbachev Consolidating Power." _Problems of Communism_. (July–August): 21–43.

Hough, Jerry. 1997. _Democratization and Revolution in the USSR 1985–1991_. Washington, D.C.: Brookings Institution.

Huntington, Samuel P. 1968. _Political Order in Changing Societies_. New Haven: Yale University Press.

Johnson, Chalmers. 1966. _Revolutionary Change_. Boston: Little-Brown.

Kuran, Timur. 1991. "Now Out of Never: The Element of Surprise in the East European Revolution of 1989." _World Politics_ 44 (April): 7–48.

Lane, David. 1966. "The Gorbachev Revolution: The Role of the Political Elite in Regime Disintegration." _Political Studies_ 44 (April): 4–23.

Lane, David, and Cameron Ross. 1996. "From Soviet Government to Presidential Rule. In _Russia in Transition_, ed. D. Lane, 3–20. London: Longman.

McFaul, Michael. 1995. "State Power, Institutional Change, and the Politics of Privatization in Russia." _World Politics_ 47 (January): 210–44.

Machiavelli, Niccoló. 1961. *The Prince*. Harmondsworth, Eng.: Penguin.

Mann, Michael. 1986. *The Sources of Social Power*, Vol. 1. Cambridge: Cambridge University Press.

Milanovic, Branko. 1994. "Why Have Communist Federations Collapsed?" *Challenge* 37: 61–64.

Remington, Thomas. 1990. "Regime Transitions in Communist Systems: The Soviet Case."*Soviet Economy* 6 (June): 160–90.

Remnick, David. 1996. "Hammer, Sickle, and Book." *New York Review of Books* 43 (May 23): 45–51.

Rostow, W. W. 1991. "Eastern Europe and the Soviet Union: A Technological Time Warp." In *The Crisis of Leninism and the Decline of the Left: The Revolutions of 1989*, ed. D. Chirot, 60–73. Seattle: University of Washington Press.

Shevtsova, Lilia. 1995. "Russia's Post-Communist Politics: Revolution or Continuity?" In *The New Russia: Troubled Transformation*, ed. Gail Lapidus, 5–36. Boulder, Colo.: Westview.

Skocpol, Theda. 1979. *States and Social Revolution*. Cambridge: Cambridge University Press.

Smelser, Neil J. 1962. *Theory of Collective Behavior*. New York: Free Press.

Tilly, Charles. 1978. *From Mobilization to Revolution*. New York: Random House.

Tocqueville, Alexis de. 1966. *Democracy in America*. Edited by J. P. Mayer. Translated by G. Lawrence. New York: Harper and Row.

———. 1955. *The Old Regime and the French Revolution*. Translated by Stuart Gilbert. New York: Doubleday/Anchor Books.

Treml, Vladimir G. 1991. "Drinking and Alcohol Abuse in the U.S.S.R. in the 1980s." In *Soviet Social Problems*, ed. Anthony Jones, Walter Connor, and David E. Powell, 94–118. Boulder, Colo.: Westview.

Trimberger, Ellen Kay. 1978. *Revolution from Above*. New Brunswick, N.J.: Transaction Books.

Urban, Michael, Vyacheslav Igrunov, and Sergei Mitrokhin. 1997. *The Rebirth of Politics in Russia*. Cambridge: Cambridge University Press.

6

Russia: Elite Continuity and Change

Stephen White and Olga Kryshtanovskaya

Revolutions, for Vilfredo Pareto (1935), were above all a matter of elite change. And for many there was a revolution in this sense in Eastern Europe at the end of the 1980s, with changes in government and a shift toward pluralist and democratic politics throughout the region. Several years later, the change looked less decisive. Former communist parties had returned to power in Hungary and Albania; they had won parliamentary and presidential elections in Lithuania and Poland and parliamentary elections in Bulgaria. In Romania, there was a change of leadership but less clearly—until the 1996 elections—a change of regime; while in Moldova, a former member of the CPSU Politburo won the presidential election that was held at the end of that year. Former communists maintained their position in Serbia and, with a change of nomenclature, in most of former Soviet Central Asia. In Mongolia, former communists won and lost a parliamentary majority but then won the presidential election of 1997. In Russia itself, the Communist Party left office, but it revived in early 1993, polled strongly in the elections in December of that year, and was by far the largest party, with a third of the seats in the new Duma after the election that took place in December 1995. The Russian public, for their part, remained committed to the concept of a U.S.S.R., they rated their political system less highly than the one they had experienced in the Soviet years, and in any case they thought the communists were still in power (*Argumenty i fakty* 35 [1994]: 2, and 23 [1994]: 2).

There were differing views about the extent to which communists or former communists were, in fact, still in power throughout the Central and Eastern European countries. There was relatively little direct continuity in the Czech Republic, where the Communist Party quickly be-

125

came a marginal force (Mansfeldova, 1994), and only a limited degree of continuity of leading personnel in Poland (Pogorecki, 1994; Szelenyi, 1995a; but see also Wasilewski, chapter 7, this volume). In Russia, some argued similarly, there was "relatively little overlap between the Gorbachev and Yeltsin political elites" (Lane and Ross, 1995, 68), although the same authors reported elsewhere that more than a third of the postcommunist political elite had held full-time executive positions within the CPSU—a very narrow definition of elite status in the Soviet period—and that, at the regional level, more than half of those in post in January 1995 had done so (Lane and Ross, 1997, 171–72). Others agreed that there were particularly high levels of continuity at the local or regional level (*Rossiiskaya gazeta,* March 4, 1992, 2) and went on to emphasize the continuities in postcommunist governments more generally (see, for instance, Baylis, 1994). If an observer had gone to sleep in Russia at the start of 1990 and had woken up later to be shown a list of the current Russian government, as a commentator in *Nezavisimaya gazeta* put it, he or she would be bound to conclude that the reformist wing of the Communist Party headed by Boris Yeltsin had finally come to power (December 3, 1992, 5).

The more considerable the changes at leadership level, clearly, the more readily we can consider the Russian and Eastern European transition a revolution. But we need to differentiate at the same time between changes in central government and changes in the regions; between changes in different sections of the central government; and between rates of change in different subperiods. We need to know if the elite has been changing in terms of age and gender, in its social and geographical origin, in its national composition, and in its levels of education. We need to know to what extent the postcommunist elite has recruited its members from the nomenklatura of the Soviet period—by which we mean the list of positions of authority to which appointments could only be made with the approval of the relevant level of the CPSU apparatus. And, for the purposes of this volume, we need to relate elite change to regime crisis: in particular, to a crisis that deepened throughout the 1980s and then led to a change of regime at the end of 1991 as the state itself was dissolved and communist rule was brought to an end.

Continuity and change are never simple notions, least of all through political crises. The Russian crisis, for instance, had been developing over a long period, and it persisted after the end of communist rule—arguably, even after a bloody confrontation between Boris Yeltsin and the Russian parliament had led, in December 1993, to the adoption of a new and strongly presidential constitution. Equally, questions of continuity span two political regimes and a change of social system.

The Soviet elite was more than proportionately Russian, but it was also representative of a society in which Russians accounted for barely more than half the total population and in which the various republics had an automatic share of elite positions. Most of them, clearly, were likely to pursue their interests in one of the newly independent states after 1991, not in postcommunist Russia. And while the political elite, in the 1980s, could be identified with the central nomenklatura of the CPSU, by the postcommunist 1990s the "holders of strategic positions in powerful organizations and movements" included the leaders of a variety of parties and of a variety of organized interests, including private business. The passage of time, moreover, would in itself have brought about a substantial degree of change in the composition of the elite, given the age of the central party nomenklatura in the later stages of Soviet rule (the average age of the Central Committee in 1986 was fifty-eight, close to the male retirement age of sixty). In the discussion that follows we consider, first, some of the operating principles of the former nomenklatura, and second, some of the evidence that has been collected about the extent to which it persisted into the postcommunist period. We conclude with a sociological portrait of the postcommunist Russian elite after a change of regime that, for its proponents, was nothing less in its significance than the great French Revolution (Gaidar, 1996, 8) but which, for Russians themselves, was just the latest stage in a power struggle within the elite that left them with even less influence on the process of government than they had enjoyed under communist rule (Rose, 1994, 28, and more generally Miller, White, and Heywood, 1998).

The Soviet Nomenklatura

Following other chapters in this volume, we define the Soviet and Russian elite in positional terms: in other words, on the basis of their occupancy of posts that involve or had in the past involved the making of decisions of national importance. In the Soviet regime, such elite posts were exclusively located in the highest echelons of the nomenklatura.[1] "Almost certainly," as one of its members in the late Gorbachev period has written, "there was never a system constructed with such attention to detail and so well protected from dangerous innovations as the party nomenklatura" (Shakhnazarov, 1993, 229). Lists of leading positions were maintained in the Central Committee apparatus, and appointment to these leading positions was impossible without the agreement of the party hierarchy. The highest-placed members of the nomenklatura—that is, the holders of positions to which appointments required the approval of the Politburo or Secretariat of the CPSU Central Committee—were in effect the national elite. Equally, in spite of the varied character of the positions that were included in the upper nomenklatura, the Soviet elite was unitary in nature, extending across all spheres of party, state, and social life. Its unitary character was assured by the fact that all (or virtually all) its members were communists and by the manner in which all leading appointments had to be made, or at least approved, by higher-level party bodies. Elite members, clearly, might differ in emphasis on matters of policy, and they might well press the claims of the institutions or regions with which they were associated, but they were all obliged to espouse Marxism-Leninism and, in the last resort, to observe the other conventions of the system to which they owed their position.

The Soviet nomenklatura elite, moreover, was strictly hierarchical. All nomenklatura positions as early as the Stalin era were divided into fourteen ranks (for the development of this system, see Voslensky, 1984; Rigby, 1990, ch. 4; and Korzhikhina and Figatner, 1993). At the highest level was the general secretary of the CPSU Central Committee, followed by members of the Politburo, candidate Politburo members, and the Central Committee secretaries. The next rank in the hierarchy consisted of the nomenklatura of the Politburo—that is, the list of positions to which appointments were made or approved at Politburo level. This list included the first and (sometimes) second secretaries of republican party organizations, the first secretaries of regional party committees and of the largest towns, all-union ministers, the military hierarchy, ambassadors to all the socialist countries and to the largest capitalist countries, directors of the largest military-industrial enterprises, the leading officials of the creative unions, and the editors of central newpapers and journals. The level below this was the nomenklatura of the Central Committee Secretariat, including a more junior list of positions: deputy ministers, the second secretaries of regional party committees, the heads of regional soviet executives, and so forth. Then came positions that required the approval of the relevant Central Committee department, and after it positions that required the approval of regional, urban and district party committees and even (at the lowest level) of local party branches (a complete inventory of centrally regulated positions, as of summer 1991, is available in the party archives: see "Tsentr," 1991). The hierarchical principle required a steady progression through these stages, from level to level: it was similar in many ways to an army hierarchy, and, as in the armed forces, exceptions were rare.

The nomenklatura system had a number of mechanisms that limited the tendency to self-recruitment, or *semeistvennosti*. According to an informal convention, for instance, the children of higher-level officials never inherited positions with the same level of seniority as their fathers. Rather, "elite children" had a series of special professional niches, often connected with work abroad. This was supported by a special system of nomenklatura education at elite institutions, particularly those that trained economists, diplomats, and journalists specializing in international affairs. As a result of the restriction upon internal recruitment, the nomenklatura was replenished to a large extent by new members from other sections of society, including the intelligentsia, the working class, and the collective-farm peasantry. The biographies of Central Committee members for the whole period of Soviet rule demonstrate how few, for instance, had a Moscow or big city background, and there were almost no members who had themselves been brought up in a nomenklatura household. (This principle began to be violated only in 1986, when Brezhnev's son and son-in-law joined the Central Committee; however, both had lost their jobs and been expelled by the following party congress, in 1990.)

The nomenklatura, in addition, required of its members and particularly of those who were likely to obtain advancement that they serve in different parts of the country. The traditional nomenklatura career trajectory began with study in Moscow and then went on to the soviet, Komsomol (Young Communist League), economic, or party apparatus at district level, followed by recall to Moscow for a one- or two-year stint in the Central Committee headquarters and then a return to the provinces to a higher-level post (often a regional party first secretaryship). Apart from geographical mobility, another characteristic was a change in career specialization. Over the Brezhnev period, a number of typical nomenklatura career patterns developed, all of them under Central Committee auspices: party-economic, Komsomol-party, soviet-party, and party-diplomatic. The most typical was a career that moved upward from Komsomol to party work, or from party to soviet work and back, or from economic to party work and back. There were also "pure" career progressions, most often on the part of economic administrators. In cases of this kind, the people involved moved upward at the same factory to the level of director, then into the relevant ministry, and eventually to the rank of minister. The party-diplomatic career type, by contrast, was a feature of the decline of the nomenklatura, with ambassadorial posts in less important countries being filled by disgraced politicians as a form of honorary retirement.

The nomenklatura was served by a comprehensive and finely differentiated system of privileges. In Michael Voslensky's words (1984, 213 ff), its members lived in "Nomenklaturia, . . . another, entirely different, and special country" from which ordinary citizens were "carefully isolated." The existence of a system of this kind was related to the chronic deficits that existed throughout the Soviet period. Members of the nomenklatura were not rich in the conventional sense, but they were removed by virtue of their position from the hardships of daily life and allowed to enjoy a better quality of life. Their money incomes were generally high, but their living standards were sustained more directly by a whole system of indirect payments or benefits. Prices in official restaurants, for instance, were significantly below their real cost; places in recreation homes were heavily subsidized. Nomenklatura members were also accorded flats and dachas in the most fashionable areas, for rentals that were symbolic (see, for instance, Matthews, 1978; Zemtsov, 1986).

Apart from this, there was a well-developed distribution system that supported the special needs of nomenklatura members. At food processing plants, for instance, there was always a workshop producing higher-quality foodstuffs for the elite. Special construction companies looked after their housing requirements at a level far above that offered to ordinary citizens. There were special ateliers, special shops, special polyclinics, and even (a labor veteran complained) special graveyards (*Moskovskie novosti* 17 [1988], 9). Privileges were strictly according to rank, and each rank in the nomenklatura ladder had its own list of benefits. In addition, there was a system of special nomenklatura education. It included the Higher Komsomol and Party Schools, the Academy of Social Sciences attached to the CPSU Central Committee, and the Academy of the National Economy. The Higher Schools were generally concerned with the training of local and regional-level nomenklaturists and sometimes provided a local official with the educational qualifications that were felt to be appropriate. The Moscow Party School, the Academy of Social Sciences, and Academy of the National Economy were, by contrast, institutions for raising the qualifications of nomenklatura members. A placement at any of these institutions meant, in practice, that the official concerned was being prepared for advancement to a still higher position.

Regime Change, Elite Change

As the Soviet system began to change under the impact of the Gorbachev reforms, so, too, did the patterns of elite advantage that had become established over decades of Soviet rule. And as political position became a less secure guarantee of those advantages, the emphasis shifted to private property—as Trotsky (1937), many years earlier, had predicted. Several recent studies have considered the extent to which the former elite was able to maintain its position in this and other ways, using a variety of methodologies: some have adopted a positional approach, based for the most part on the data available in biographical handbooks, while others have favored a reputational approach based on interviews with elite members (see, for instance, Lane, 1994). Others still have employed interview methods, not to obtain subjective judgments but to collect biographical data for members of the elite that are not included in printed sources (see, for instance, the studies included in Szelenyi, 1995b, which draw on four thousand personal interviews conducted in six postcommunist countries). All of these methods have their strengths and weaknesses: interviews give access to the values and beliefs of elite members but are a problematic source of biographical information—even communist party membership may be "forgotten" once a change of regime has made it a liability (see White, 1996); printed biographical sources, on the other hand, can give no impression of opinions and judgments, but they allow much larger data sets to be collected and are, in principle, less open to retrospective adjustment. What do these studies suggest about elite continuity and change?

The most substantial interview-based study, with respect to the Soviet and Russian elite, was conducted in 1993–94 by B. V. Golovachev, L. B. Kosova, and L. A. Khakhulina (1995, 1996) as part of a more general study of elite change in postcommunist Europe (on the larger project see Szelenyi, 1995b). Golovachev and colleagues based their research on interviews with more than eighteen hundred individuals who had occupied positions in the political elite in 1988 and with the same or different individuals who occupied elite positions in 1993. The "old" elite included the CPSU leadership, members and candidate members of the Central Committee, ministers and deputy ministers, the heads of mass organizations like the Komsomol and trade unions, directors of the largest factories, those holding leading positions in the media and in scholarly life, and diplomats and other members of the foreign service. The common characteristic of such positions was that any appointments to them required party approval: they were, in other words, nomenklatura positions. The "new" elite were, as far as possible, comparable in the social positions they occupied: they included members of the presidential administration and government, trade union officials and party leaders, parliamentary deputies, the directors of the largest state enterprises, managers and owners in the private sector, newspaper editors, and members of the Academy of Sciences. No attempt in this case was made to interview members of the diplomatic service, most of whom were working abroad; but inquiries were conducted in nineteen Russian regions. Use was also made of reference

works, such as the (formerly secret) list of Central Committee nomenklatura appointments, of biographical guides of other kinds, and of
commercial information. What were their conclusions?

The Soviet ruling group and the new Russian elite were, it appeared,
"in many respects very similar" (Golovachev, Kosova, and Khakhulina, 1995, 20). Both were predominantly male (95 percent of the Soviet
nomenklatura, 93 percent of the Russian elite). Nearly all (97 percent)
of the Soviet elite, and 78 percent of the new elite, had been CPSU
members; 71 and 47 percent respectively had maintained a much closer
association with the former regime as holders of elective positions
within the party apparatus. The new elite were rather younger, with
an average year of birth of 1944 as compared with 1934 for the Soviet
nomenklatura. Almost 90 percent of both elites identified themselves
as Russian, and both were highly educated: 97 percent of the Soviet
nomenklatura had a university or college education, as did 94 percent
of their successors in the Russian Federation. Both groups, equally, had
material advantages or privileges, such as a motor car (62 percent of
the Soviet elite compared with 70 percent of their postcommunist successors). At the level of individuals, there had been a turnover comparable with the circulation that had taken place at the start of the 1930s;
but this renewal had largely been a result of the advance of those in
"prenomenklatura" positions, such as a divisional head in a ministry
or party office, and only 16 percent of the new Russian elite had never
held such positions. It was, in other words, a "revolution of deputies."
And there was greater continuity in governing and managing than in
other positions: 57 percent of the "old" nomenklatura retained elite
positions in government or the economy, and altogether "three-
quarters of former nomenklatura staff either remained in high state
and management posts, or occupied positions that were close to them"
(Golovachev, Kosova, and Khakhulina, 1996, 37).

In another study that derived from the same project, Eric Hanley,
Natasha Yershova, and Richard Anderson (1995) found that substantial
advantages were associated with former CPSU membership, particularly "political capital in the form of enduring networks." More than
half (51 percent) of the 1993 elite had their occupational origins in the
nomenklatura of 1988, and another 33.4 percent had been managers in
the economy or elsewhere; conversely, 64.2 percent of the 1988 nomenklatura continued to occupy positions within the Russian postcommunist elite of 1993, often moving across institutional boundaries. The
formation of the postcommunist elite, moreover, closely paralleled the
nomenklatura selection process. The typical form of advancement was
vertical, from an immediately subordinate position; the most obvious
effect of postcommunist change was that it accelerated the rise of indi-

viduals who were well on their way to the top before the old system collapsed. The changes that had taken place under Gorbachev's auspices had opened up new routes to elite status, including the electoral process and private business; but at the same time, the vast majority of the members of the 1988 nomenklatura retained elite and quasi-elite positions in 1993, with little downward mobility occurring. Overall, 61 percent of the party nomenklatura of 1988 had found elite positions by 1993, most of them in the state apparatus; when compared with former party elites in Hungary and Poland, Russia was clearly exceptional in the extent to which the former party nomenklatura had been able to reproduce its elite status after the collapse of the party itself.

There were similarities in other respects as well. In particular, the social backgrounds of the old nomenklatura and the new elite were practically identical, with both groups reporting very high social origins. Well over 50 percent in both groups had fathers who had worked as administrators or professionals; about a third in both groups had fathers who had a higher education; and 51.7 percent of the 1988 nomenklatura and 51 percent of the Russian elite had fathers who had been members of the CPSU, a rate of membership much greater than that among the general population and one that demonstrated the privileged origins of both Communist- and postcommunist-era elites. These were levels that, once again, comfortably exceeded the corresponding levels in Hungary and Poland; and they made clear that even if some of the personnel had changed, the social group occupying command posts in postcommunist Russia society had not changed. Despite institutional innovations, members of the Russian elite continued to be recruited from the social group that had dominated the Soviet Union for decades.

In a related study, Mawdsley and White (forthcoming) have examined the continuity of political elites, and more particularly of the CPSU Central Committee, using inclusion in a national "Who's Who" as an indicator of elite status. The first substantial directory that can be used for such purposes appeared in 1993, covering Russia as well as the other former Soviet republics (Kto, 1993); it has been used to define elite status, for instance, in *Mir Rossii*, (1995, no. 3–4, 5). Of the largely Brezhnevite Central Committee of 1986, 64 members (14 percent) were listed; of the Gorbachevian Central Committee of 1990, however, nearly a quarter—99 of the total 412 members—were included. About the same proportion of the 1986 Central Committee were listed in a "Who's Who in Russia" that appeared in 1996 (61 of the 307 full members), and a slightly higher proportion of the Central Committee that had been elected in 1990 (86 of the 412). Many of the old Central Committee, indeed, were prominent in government in postcommunist Russia. President Yeltsin had served on the Central Committee since 1981, as had his prime minister, Viktor Chernomyrdin, and his foreign minister, Yevgenii Primakov, since 1986. In the Council of the Federation, the upper house of the new parliament, there were ten members of the 1990 Central Committee; among them were a series of regional first secretaries, including the secretaries of North Ossetia, Ul'yanovsk, Belgorod, Buryatia, Kaluga, and the Tatar first secretary, Mintimer Shaimiev (who, after June 1991, was president of the Council). Another was the former Orel first secretary and later Politburo and Secretariat member, Yegor Stroev, who became speaker of the upper house in January 1996.

Continuity was considerably greater in the lower house, the State Duma, particularly after the December 1995 election had brought success to the Communist list of candidates and to Communist-sponsored candidates in the single-member constituencies. In all, twenty-two members of the 1986 or 1990 Central Committee were elected to the Duma in 1993 or 1995, and nine were elected in both years. Not all the former Central Committee members, admittedly, were elected to the new parliament as communists. Alevtina Fedulova, deputy head of the Soviet Women's Committee and a Central Committee member from 1990, stood for the Duma on the list put forward by Women of Russia and won election in 1993. Vladimir Gusev, a former vice premier who had been first secretary of the CPSU in Saratov, stood as a member of Vladimir Zhirinovsky's Liberal Democrats in 1993 and 1995 and won election on both occasions. More commonly, members of the Central Committee in the late Soviet period stood as Communists or independents and won election as individual members as well as members of the list of candidates sponsored by the Communist Party. In December 1995 successful candidates on the party's list included the former Vologda and Russian first secretary Valerii Kuptsov; Viktor Zorokalítsev and Aleksei Pomorov, both former first secretaries in Tomsk; the Udmurt first secretary Nikolai Sapozhnikov; and the Krasnodar second secretary Boris Kibirev.

Some former members of the Central Committee stood as individual candidates, and they often enjoyed remarkable success. The former North Ossetian first secretary Alexander Dzasokhov, for instance, took more than half the vote of his constituency in 1995, as did former prime minister Nikolai Ryzhkov, standing under the auspices of his own "Power to the People" movement. Perhaps the most remarkable success was that of Sergei Manyakin, who had been elected first secretary in Omsk as far back as 1961; a Central Committee member from that year up to 1990, Manyakin was also chairman of the Committee of People's Control, which was supposed to ensure the prudent use of public funds. In this capacity, he spoke at the Central Committee plenum that met in October 1987, taking the floor immediately after Boris Yeltsin had delivered a remarkable and unexpected broadside against the existing leadership. Manyakin denounced the future president for failing in his job in Moscow—there were unacceptable shortages of fruit and vegetables and numerous examples of waste and inefficiency—and for "political immaturity" in offering his resignation, and Manyakin went on to detail Yeltsin's "character faults" (Izvestiya TsK KPSS 2, 1989, 243–4). Aged seventy-two and a pensioner in 1995, he nevertheless took more than half of the vote in a constituency in his native region on behalf of Ryzhkov's "Power to the People." Another member of the late Soviet Central Committee, newspaper editor Gennadii Seleznev, was elected speaker of the Duma when it convened after the election in January 1996.

The Postcommunist Elite

In this final section, we offer an analysis of the characteristics of three generations of the Soviet and Russian elite—under Brezhnev, Gorbachev, and Yeltsin—in order to sustain some of the generalizations advanced in earlier sections and to provide our own evidence about the extent to which the nomenklatura of the Soviet period maintained its position into the postcommunist 1990s. Tables 6.1 through 6.6 present demographic data on the three elite generations.

One of the clearest conclusions (see table 6.1) is that the elite has become significantly younger over the past ten years; overall, by about eight years. Under Brezhnev, the oldest groups within the elite were the Politburo and Soviet government groups, that is, the most powerful functionaries of all, while the youngest was the group of deputies to the U.S.S.R. Supreme Soviet. There was, in fact, a direct relation between age and political influence: the greater the age, the greater the authority. The same tends to be true of professional groups in all societies, but it is less clearly the case elsewhere that youth is an indicator of lowly status. In the Brezhnev elite, the relation was almost linear: the youth of parliamentarians was a direct reflection of their relatively low position in the nomenklatura hierarchy. Under Gorbachev, the ages of the various sections of the elite became more similar: the traditional party-state elite became more youthful, while the relatively freely elected parliament became three years older. And then under Yeltsin, there were further changes: the government and regional leadership became almost ten years younger, while the parliament aged on average by a further four and a half years as it lost the youthful workers and Komsomol members that had formerly been imposed upon it. As the December 1993 elections made clear, Russian voters, given a choice, generally preferred candidates who were in their late forties, married, and male, with some experience in other spheres of public activity.

The social composition of the elite in the Brezhnev period was also subject to a quota. About a third of the seats in the U.S.S.R. Supreme Soviet were reserved for women, for instance, and this was the reason for their relatively substantial representation in parliament compared with other sections of the elite (see table 6.2). At levels of the nomenklatura where power was actually and not simply formally exercised, however, women were much less conspicuous and sometimes nonexistent. Under Gorbachev, there was some increase in the number of women in positions of real authority (they almost doubled their share of the CPSU Central Committee in 1990), but this was matched by a fall in female representation in parliamentary institutions, and the political significance of the Central Committee was declining as their presence within it was increasing. The old nomenklatura had been predominantly rural, as well as male: more than half of the Moscow-based party and government leaders had a rural background, and in the regions the proportion was even higher. Under Gorbachev, there was very little change in this respect in the regions, although in the central institutions of party and state there was a considerable increase in the proportion of leaders who were of urban origin. But the real change took place in the years that followed. Yeltsin was able to attract a new group of young and well-educated professionals into his administration, and those of rural origin dropped to a small proportion, not only in the top leadership but also in the regions, where a rural origin might have been expected to survive rather longer. Overall, the proportion of elite members who had been born in rural areas fell to less than half of its level in the years before Gorbachev's accession, and elite social origins involved a very different set of experiences, although its members were still far from representative of a society that had largely urbanized.

It is more difficult to consider changes in the nationalities composition of the elite from the Brezhnev to Yeltsin eras, given the collapse of the U.S.S.R. and the formation in its place of fifteen independent states. A direct comparison of the Brezhnev and Gorbachev elites with the elite of the Yeltsin years would in these respects be very misleading. It is clear, however, that Gorbachev was making some effort under the pressure of events to increase the representation of non-Russians: in the top party leadership, their share more than doubled (this reflected a change in the composition of the Politburo, which in 1990 became a

TABLE 6.1
Average Age of Soviet and Russian Elite (years)

	Top Leadership (Politburo)	Party Elite (Central Committee)	Parliamentary Elite (Supreme Soviet)	Government Bureaucracy	Regional Elite	Business Elite	Average by Cohort
Brezhnev cohort	61.8	59.1	41.9	61.0	59.0	—	56.6
Gorbachev cohort	54.0	54.9	44.0	56.2	52.0	—	52.2
Yeltsin cohort	53.1	—	46.5	52.0	49.0	42.1	48.5

TABLE 6.2
Women in the Elite (percentage of elite group)

	Top Leadership (Politburo)	Party Elite (Central Committee)	Parliamentary Elite (Supreme Soviet)	Government Bureaucracy	Regional Elite	Business Elite	Average by Cohort
Brezhnev cohort	3.9	4.3	32.8	0	0	—	8.2
Gorbachev cohort	5.7	8.4	8.4	2.9	0	—	5.6
Yeltsin cohort	2.3	8.6	11.2	2.9	0	0	4.2

body made up of the heads of republican party organizations); and in the Central Committee it increased in proportion. Only at the regional level was there a relative fall in the proportion of non-Russians. Under Yeltsin, by contrast, the clearest tendency has been for the nationalities' composition of each section of the elite to become more similar: under Gorbachev there had been a fourfold difference in the share of non-Russians in the central leadership as compared with the regions, while under Yeltsin the share of non-Russians within each section of the elite has varied much less, around an average of just over 20 percent—which is itself just above their share of the total population.

The elite has always been one of the most educated groups in the society (see table 6.3). Even in the Brezhnev years, when the leadership was made up predominantly of those of lower socioeconomic status, a higher education of some kind was all but universal. A significant proportion of the nomenklatura of those years, admittedly, had a party or Komsomol higher education, of whose quality there could be some doubt. During the 1980s it was, in fact, the parliamentarians who distinguished themselves, by virtue of the fact that all groups of the society—including the highly educated—had their allocated share of seats in representative bodies. Under Gorbachev, the relative advantage of parliamentarians declined, while regional party first secretaries moved to the fore. The educational level of parliament nonetheless increased considerably in the Gorbachev years, following the relatively open elections of 1989 and 1990; and there were still more considerable changes in all elite groups during the Yeltsin years, with tertiary-level degrees becoming all but universal and with a shift from a technological education to training in law or economics.

What, finally, about recruitment and renewal? Under Brezhnev, as we have noted, it had been all but impossible to enter the elite without passing through the nomenklatura hierarchy and each of the normal stages of advancement. There were some non-nomenklaturists within the CPSU Central Committee and the U.S.S.R. Supreme Soviet, but these (as in other areas) were "planned" exceptions. There were some changes in the perestroika years, and even the party leadership became accessible to relative outsiders. The most important means of recruitment to the leadership by other than the nomenklatura route was, however, the elections of 1989 and 1990. During the postcommunist years, a still greater proportion of persons who were not previously members of the nomenklatura have been recruited to the elite (see table 6.4): nearly half of all party leaders, and two-fifths of the business elite, have been "new people" and so, too, have two of every five parliamentary deputies. More striking, however, has been the degree of continuity at leading levels of government: three-quarters of the presidential

TABLE 6.3
Higher Education among Elite Members (percentage of elite group)

	Top Leadership (Politburo)	Party Elite (Central Committee)	Parliamentary Elite (Supreme Soviet)	Government Bureaucracy	Regional Elite	Business Elite	Average by Cohort
Brezhnev cohort	100	92.6	51.3	100	100	—	88.8
Gorbachev cohort	88.6	74.4	67.9	100	100	—	84.1
Yeltsin cohort	100	100	94.0	100	97.1	93.0	97.4

TABLE 6.4
Elite Members from Outside the Nomenklatura (percentage of elite group)

	Top Leadership (Politburo)	Party Elite (Central Committee)	Parliamentary Elite (Supreme Soviet)	Government Bureaucracy	Regional Elite	Business Elite	Average by Cohort
Brezhnev cohort	0	6.0	51.3	0	0	—	11.4
Gorbachev cohort	8.5	28.8	40.6	—	0	—	19.5
Yeltsin cohort	25.0	42.8	39.8	25.7	17.7	39.0	35.0

administration and nearly three-quarters of the Russian government were former nomenklaturists, and among the regional leadership more than 80 percent had that background.

Most of the Yeltsin leadership spent a considerable length of time in leading positions in the former regime (see table 6.5). Within the Yeltsin elite as a whole, more than a third had begun their progress through the nomenklatura in the Brezhnev years, and more than a third under Gorbachev; only one in ten were new to power circles in the sense of having begun their professional careers in the post-Soviet period. More than half of the current regional leadership began their nomenklatura careers under Brezhnev, and all had inherited, rather than acquired, their current elite status. Among those in the Yeltsin leadership who were former nomenklaturists, the average length of service was 11.4 years, ranging from an average of 10 years among members of the Yeltsin government to 14.5 years among his regional administrators.

Just as there were typical career paths in all three periods, there were typical paths from one period to another (see table 6.6). Regional first secretaries, for instance, became chairmen of local soviets and then heads of local administrations. The presidential administration and the regional elite tended to emerge from former structures of government; the business elite was more likely to have a background in the Komsomol. The Russian government, for its part, became more professional, with its origins increasingly in economic management, diplomacy, and the former security services.

Russia, Political Elites, and Regime Crisis

This discussion has largely shared the conclusions of those who have argued that in the composition of postcommunist elites, "plus ça change. . . ." It would, of course, be surprising if the political managers of a post-Soviet system were very different from those who had been responsible for its operation for many years; and this was particularly true in Russia, where communist rule had lasted for more than two generations and where many of its assumptions—surveys suggested—retained a great deal of public support (for a review, see Wyman, 1997). So it was appropriate that the postcommunist Russian state should be headed by a president who had been a member of the CPSU Politburo and Secretariat, by a prime minister who had been a member of the Council of Ministers and of the party's Central Committee, and by a foreign minister who had also been a member of the ruling Politburo; indeed, seven of the twelve presidents in the Commonwealth of Inde-

TABLE 6.5

The Yeltsin Elite Cohort According to When its Members Entered the Nomenklatura (percentages, by column)

Entered Nomenklatura	Government	Top Leadership	Regional Elite	Average
Under Brezhnev	31.3	22.7	57.4	37.1
Under Gorbachev	42.9	36.4	39.7	39.7
Under Yeltsin	20.0	11.4	0	10.5

TABLE 6.6

Recruitment of the Yeltsin Cohort, by sector (percentage of elite group)

	Top Leadership	Party Elite	Government	Regional Elite	Business Elite	Average
Recruited from the nomenklatura as a whole	75.0	57.1	74.3	82.3	61.0	69.9
Recruited from sectoral subelites:						
party	21.2	65.0	0	17.8	13.1	23.4
Komsomol	0	5.0	0	1.8	37.7	8.9
soviets	63.6	25.0	26.9	78.6	3.3	39.5
economy	9.1	5.0	42.3	0	37.7	18.8
other	6.1	0	30.8	0	8.2	11.0

pendent States were the former first secretaries of their Soviet republics' communist parties, with three more only a level or two below (Rigby, 1997). The more "indigenous" the regime, it would appear, and the greater its longevity, the greater the extent to which its post-communist leadership is likely to have its origins in the nomenklatura of the Soviet period.

A broader elite continuity coexisted, in the Russian case, with a process of elite circulation as a younger and less compromised cohort rose to leading positions. This was what a former Gorbachev adviser calls the "revolution of the second secretaries" (Grachev, 1994, 9) or what Golovachev, Kosova, and Khakhulina term a "revolution of deputies" (1996, 37); it was similar, in some ways, to the military coups in Africa that were typically headed by junior officers, not complete outsiders. For the Hungarians, a change of this kind was best described as a "power metamorphosis"*(metamorphozisa)*; it was not a transition from one system to another but the resolution of an intrasystem crisis and the recuperation of a system of authoritarian power. Trotsky long ago argued that the elite would find their privileged position unsatisfactory, as (under Soviet conditions) it depended on their control of office. Far better, from their point of view, to protect their advantage from the vagaries of the political process and make it heritable across generations in the same way as ruling groups in other societies: by the private ownership of property and wealth (Kotz, 1997, argues that this was the conscious strategy of the Yeltsin reformers from the late Soviet period). It was access to the market, in the first instance, that allowed the nomenklatura to begin to protect their position as the future of the regime became uncertain; afterward, for many, it was the market, and particularly banking, that allowed them to retain their position of advantage.

The Russian case, accordingly, can make a number of contributions to a more general theory of elite change and political crisis. The post-communist regime certainly originated in a crisis; but a complex and continuing one. There was no obvious *Wendepunkt*, like the breaching of the Berlin wall or the overthrow of the Ceausecus in Romania. A referendum in March 1991 had confirmed the popularity of a "renewed federation," the U.S.S.R. was still in existence and President Gorbachev was still in office after the attempted coup of August 1991 had been suppressed, and there was little popular involvement in the resistance to the coup or, even less so, in the hasty decision to terminate the U.S.S.R. the following December—an elite pact of a rather peculiar kind, conducted by a Russian president who allegedly was inebriated at the time. The crisis was a more systemic one, reflected in steadily falling rates of economic growth, and it persisted after December 1991, particularly in the continuing confrontation between President Yeltsin and a largely communist parliament. Arguably, it persisted even longer, with the economy continuing to contract, a population that had little confidence in its postcommunist institutions, and a constitution that was still contested because of the manner in which it had been imposed in December 1993 after the parliament had been bombed into submission.

The ambiguous nature of regime change in Russia was paralleled by the partial nature of the elite change that accompanied it. Initially, President Yeltsin was determined to appoint ministers who had no career association with the Gorbachev administration, and his early governments were dominated by politically inexperienced academics like Yegor Gaidar. But there was much less change in the administration as a whole, including the government bureaucracy, and much less in the regions, where local first secretaries were able to maintain their position and in most cases secure legitimation through the ballot box as voters looked for experienced leaders who knew how things were done, whatever their ideology or their former career. Indeed, given the CPSU's monopoly of positions of political influence up to the end of the 1980s and the absence (as Mattei Dogan and John Higley note in chapter 1) of church, trade union, business, or other counterelites, there was no other source from which a postcommunist leadership could be derived. After the crisis of late 1993 and the shock of the election result that followed it, Yeltsin began to recruit again in a more balanced way, and he ended the "anti-Gorbachev cadre 'blockade' " (Kostikov, 1997, 271) that had marked his first years of office. But the outcome was not a consensually united elite, as rival clans associated with a variety of competing banks and sectoral monopolies competed for influence over an ailing president. It was rather, and to borrow Dogan and Higley's formulations in chapter 1, a "congeries of cliques and factions," and it seemed likely, as elsewhere, to "continue the disunited configuration which had sparked or contributed to the crisis in the first place."

Note

1. Our analysis is based on a series of investigations conducted between 1989 and 1994 by the Section for Elite Studies of the Institute of Sociology of the Russian Academy of Sciences (for a fuller discussion, see Kryshtanovskaya and White, 1996). The main methods of study included informal in-depth interviews with elite members; formal interviews; surveys of expert opinion; observation; the study of official biographies; press analysis; and the study of official documents and statistics. The core of the study was based on an examination of official biographical directories, as well as a series of interviews with elite members themselves conducted by the Section for Elite Studies in associa-

tion with the University of Glasgow. Altogether, 3,610 biographies were analyzed, consisting of members of the Leonid Brezhnev elite (57 members of the government, 1,500 deputies of the U.S.S.R. Supreme Soviet, 282 members of the CPSU Central Committee, 26 Politburo and Secretariat members, and 131 regional party first secretaries); the Mikhail Gorbachev elite, from 1985 to August 1991 (consisting of 251 Russian Supreme Soviet deputies, 371 members of the CPSU Central Committee that was elected in 1990, 35 members of the Politburo and Secretariat, and 132 regional party first secretaries); and the Yeltsin elite, from September 1991 (consisting of 35 members of the Russian government, 44 members of the higher ranks of the Presidential Administration, 68 heads of regional administrations, 35 party leaders, 100 members of the business elite, and 543 members of the Federal Assembly).

Our elite groups consist of six main sections:

1. the government executive (before 1985, during the Gorbachev years, and in 1993),
2. parliament (for the Brezhnev period, the Eleventh Supreme Soviet of the U.S.S.R. that was elected in 1984; for the Gorbachev period, the Supreme Soviet of the RSFSR (Russian Soviet Federative Socialist Republic) that was elected in 1990; and for the Yeltsin period, the Federal Assembly of the Russian Federation that was elected in December 1993),
3. the party elite (for the Brezhnev period, the CPSU Central Committee that was elected at the Twenty-seventh Party Congress in 1986; for the Gorbachev period, the Central Committee that was elected at the Twenty-eighth Party Congress in 1990; and for the Yeltsin period, the leaders of the major Russian parties as they stood in 1993—despite the change from a single to a multiparty system, this was the section that manifested the greatest degree of direct continuity),
4. the top leadership (for the Brezhnev period, the members and candidate members of the Politburo and the Secretaries of the Central Committee as of January 1985; for the Gorbachev period, the members and candidate members of the Politburo and the Secretaries of the Central Committee as of January 1991; and for the Yeltsin period, the president's immediate associates, the leading members of his administration, his advisers, and members of the Presidential Council),
5. the regional elite (for the Brezhnev period, the regional party first secretaries who were in office at the start of 1985; for the Gorbachev period, the regional party first secretaries who were in office in 1990; and for the Yeltsin period, the heads of regional administrations as of 1993); and finally,
6. the business elite (for the Yeltsin period alone, consisting of the heads of the largest banks, exchanges, and industrial-financial groups).

References

Baylis, Thomas A. 1994. "Plus ça Change? Transformation and Continuity amongst East European Elites." *Communist and Post-Communist Studies*, 27 (Sept): 315–28.

Gaidar, Egor. 1996. *Dni porazhenii i pobed*. Moscow: Vagrius.

Golovachev, B. V., L. B. Kosova, and L. A. Khakhulina. 1995. "Formirovanie pravyashchei elity v Rossii." part 1. *Ekonomicheskie i sotsialínye peremeny: monitoring obshchestvennogo mneniya*, no. 6: 18–24,

———. 1996. "Formirovanie pravyashchei elity v Rossii." part 2. *Ekonomicheskie i sotsialínye peremeny: monitoring obshchestvennogo mneniya*, no. 1: 32–38.

Grachev, Andrei. 1994. *Dalíshe bez menya. Ukhod Prezidenta*. Moscow: Progress-Kul'tura.

Hanley, Eric, Natasha Yershova, and Richard Anderson. 1995. "Russia: Old Wine in a New Bottle? The Circulation and Reproduction of Russian Elites, 1983–1993." *Theory and Society* 24 (October): 639–68.

Korzhikhina, T. P. and Yuri Figatner. 1993. "Sovetskaya nomenklatura: stanovlenie, mekhanizmy deistviya." *Voprosy istorii*, no. 7: 25–38.

Kostikov, Vyacheslav. 1997. *Roman s Prezidentom*. Moscow: Vagrius.

Kotz, David with Fred Weir. 1997. *Revolution from Above: The Demise of the Soviet System*. London: Routledge.

Kryshtanovskaya, Olga, and Stephen White. 1996. "From Soviet Nomenklatura to Russian Elite." *Europe-Asia Studies* 48 (July): 711–33.

Kto estí kto v Rossii. 1996. ed. Yuri S. Andreev. Moscow: Russkaya kadrovaya assotsiatsiya/RAU korporatsiya.

Kto estí kto v Rossii i v blizhnem zarubezhíe: spravochnik. 1993. Moscow: Novoe vremya/vse dlya vas.

Lane, David. 1994. "Gorbachev's Political Elite in the Terminal Stage of the U.S.S.R.: A Reputational Analysis." *Journal of Communist Studies and Transition Politics*, 10 (March): 104–16.

Lane, David and Cameron Ross. 1995. "The Changing Composition and Structure of the Political Elites." In *Russia in Transition*, ed. D. Lane, 52–75. London: Longman.

———. 1997. "Russian Political Elites, 1991–1995: Recruitment and Renewal." *International Politics* 34 (June): 169–92.

Mansfeldova, Zdenka. 1994. "The Emerging New Czech Political Elites." Paper presented at the European Consortium for Political Research Joint Sessions, at Madrid, Spain (April).

Matthews, Mervyn. 1978. *Privilege in the Soviet Union*. London: Allen and Unwin.

Mawdsley, Evan and Stephen White. Forthcoming. *The Soviet Elite*.

Miller, William L., Stephen White, and Paul Heywood. 1998. *Values and Political Change in Postcommunist Europe*. London: Macmillan.

Pareto, Vilfredo. 1935. *Treatise on General Sociology*. New York: Harcourt, Brace, Jovanovich.

Pogorecki, Adam. 1994. "The communist and postcommunist nomenklatura." *Polish Sociological Review*, 106, no. 2: 111–23.

Rigby, T. H. 1990. *Political Elites in the USSR*. Aldershot, Eng.: Edward Elgar.

———. 1997. "New Elites for Old in Russian Politics." Mimeo, Research School of Social Sciences, Australian National University.

Rose, Richard. 1994. *New Russia Barometer III: The Results*. Glasgow: Centre for the Study of Public Policy, University of Strathclyde, Studies in Public Policy no. 228.

Shakhnazarov, Georgii. 1993. *Tsena svobody: Reformatsiya Gorbacheva glazami ego pomoshchnika*. Moscow: Rossika/Zevs.

Szelenyi, Ivan, ed. 1995a. *Elity w Polsce,w Rosji i na Wegrzech*. Warsaw: Instytut Studiow Politicznych.

————, ed. 1995b. "Circulation vs. Reproduction of Elites during the Postcommunist Transformation of Eastern Europe." Special issue of *Theory and Society* 24 (October).

Trotsky, Leon. 1937. *The Revolution Betrayed*. London: Faber.

"Tsentr po khraneniyu sovremennoi dokumentatsii." 1991. *Fond 89, perecheni* 20, document 77, August 7.

Voslensky, Michael. 1984. *Nomenklatura: Anatomy of the Soviet Ruling Class*. London: Bodley Head.

White, Stephen. 1996. "Interviewing the Soviet Elite." *Russian Review* 55 (April): 309–16.

Wyman, Matthew. 1997. *Public Opinion in Postcommunist Russia*. London: Macmillan.

Zemtsov, Ilya. 1986. *Chastnaya zhizni sovetskoi elity*. London: Overseas Publications Interchange.

7

Hungary, Poland, and Russia: The Fate of Nomenklatura Elites

Jacek Wasilewski

What happened to the elites based in the *nomenklaturas* of the Hungarian, Polish, and Soviet communist regimes during the crises that engulfed them between 1988 and 1991? The answer is important to several audiences. For sociologists, the fates of the nomenklatura elites are of great interest because they reveal much about the impacts of deep political crises on elites, regimes, and social hierarchies. The postcommunist locations and powers of the old elites are significant indicators of the depth of change between communist and postcommunist social structures. For political scientists who study transitions from authoritarian to democratic regimes, the nomenklatura elites' fates are also of much importance. For some of these scholars theorize that peaceful democratic transitions necessarily involve significant amounts of elite continuity and, furthermore, that such elite continuity may even contribute to democratic consolidation.

Beyond the concerns of scholars, the locations and powers of the old nomenklatura elites are at the heart of current political struggles in all three countries. Staunch democratic and marketizing reformers want to made a clean break with the previous communist regimes by removing all holdover elites; others argue that a significant degree of continuity in elites and leaders is essential if further economic, political, and social disarray is to be avoided. For Hungarian, Polish, and Russian mass publics, meanwhile, the postcommunist status of the old nomenklatura elites is closely tied to communism's bankruptcy and disappearance. People hold strong emotional views about this question, and they tend to draw far-reaching conclusions on the basis of individual cases of elite continuity or replacement. Whether these views are right or wrong, it is an important political fact that societal attitudes toward the new postcommunist regimes and their policies are powerfully shaped by peoples' perceptions of the nomenklatura elites' place and role in today's regimes.

Three Regime-Destroying Crises

The crises that ultimately destroyed the Hungarian, Polish, and Soviet communist regimes had their immediate genesis in the abrupt Solidarity challenge to the Polish regime in 1980–81. This was a paradigmatic case of a political crisis of the revolutionary kind. Organized masses of workers, led by a cohesive counterelite of trade union officials and opposition intellectuals, demanded political and economic reforms that struck at the heart of the state socialist regime. One should not be misled by the "self-limited" character of the Solidarity revolution. With the Brezhnev Doctrine still in effect and with the doctrine's author still residing in the Kremlin, the revolution could not have been "unlimited." Nevertheless, paying only lip service to socialist slogans, Solidarity targeted the twin pillars of state socialism: the Communist Party's (formally, the Polish United Workers' Party) hegemony and state control of the command economy. The crisis of 1980–81 involved several paroxysms and it triggered a significant reshuffle at the top and middle levels of the power hierarchy, though it did not eventuate in wholesale elite replacement. Nor did the declaration of martial law on December 13, 1981, resolve the crisis. Military rule merely froze the crisis and gave the ruling elite time to look for measures that might defuse it. But when none of these measures succeeded, the crisis reached the boiling point again in 1988.

At first glance, the predicaments of the Polish communist regime in 1988 do not seem to fit the definition of political crisis provided by Mattei Dogan and John Higley in chapter 1. Taken alone, that year's political and social turbulence, including serious strikes during May and August, could not be deemed "an abrupt and brutal challenge to the survival of a political regime." In the larger Polish context of 1988, however, the events of 1988 constituted precisely the conditions of crisis that Dogan and Higley have in mind.

During and after the Solidarity revolt in 1980–81, the Polish ruling elite tried all possible means to shore up its power position, regain political and economic stability, and reverse its profound loss of legitimacy. It sought, alternately, to co-opt a moderate wing of the opposition into the regime, to outmaneuver Solidarity by including it as a legitimate player in the political game, to crush Solidarity by naked force, to disarm Solidarity by lifting martial law and speeding economic liberalization, and to mollify Solidarity by adopting several institutions typical of a democratic polity (e.g., an ombudsman, a supreme administrative court) and by broadening civil freedoms and economic reforms. All this was in vain; each effort was rejected by the regime's opponents. Simply put, what would have been willingly accepted before December 13, 1981, was completely unacceptable after that date. The ruling elite lost whatever credibility it had left, and the response to each of its ploys and proposals was a flat "no." Its last-gasp effort—a national referendum in November 1987 to ratify liberalizing political and economic reforms—was boycotted by most voters. Thus, by 1988 the ruling elite had reached a dead end, and with Mikhail Gorbachev's proclamation of the so-called Sinatra Doctrine (according to which the Soviet Union's satellite regimes in East Central Europe were left to "do it their way"), the Polish elite's arsenal of weapons was empty.

In this situation, the strikes during May and August 1988 posed a mortal threat to the regime. Led by young and radical labor leaders of the post-Solidarity generation, the strikers had just one demand: relegalize Solidarity. The new leaders were fed up with both the "self-limited" efforts of the established Solidarity leadership and the regime's power-preserving tricks. They were bent on using Solidarity's popularity and organizational assets to achieve far-reaching, if poorly defined, goals that were mostly articulated in strong anticommunist terms. With the utmost difficulty, Lech Walesa, the chairman of Solidarity, and Tadeusz Mazowiecki, a moderate leader of the democratic opposition, gained control over the young Solidarity radicals. But all this left the communist establishment with just one option: to negotiate a power-sharing arrangement with its opponents that signified a regime change.

The situation of Hungarian elites in the 1980s was an outgrowth of political practices that were followed in the wake of the bloody and failed 1956 revolution, which practices Janos Kadar, the general secretary of the Socialist Workers' Party, encapsulated as "he who is not against us is with us." In line with this slogan, and accompanied by a bevy of economic reforms, the communist elite successfully co-opted most of the discontented intelligentsia into the regime. This left the Hungarian ruling establishment better prepared than its Polish and other Eastern European counterparts to cope with the accelerating demise of communist power throughout the region toward the end of the 1980s. Hungarian reforms "from within" constituted a unique pattern within the Soviet bloc—a mixture of communist authoritarianism, private market practices, and significant political liberalism.

A basic transformation of this pattern was initiated jointly by party reformers and democratic opponents beginning in 1988 (Bruszt, 1992; Tokes, 1996). The party accepted de facto multiparty competitions in political matters and substantially unrestricted capitalism in the economic realm. To a large extent, the Hungarian "refolution" (Timothy Ash's term for the interplay of reform and revolution) had an intraelite character in which oppositional leaders communicated and cooperated intensively with reform-minded communist leaders. Even before tripartite Roundtable negotiations commenced in June 1989, the Hungarian regime had been transformed profoundly "from above." Although a large part of the Socialist Workers' Party elite was at the forefront of this regime transformation, the party (repackaged as the Socialist Party in the autumn of 1989) had to pay a price for its previous hegemony. In the first fully democratic elections, during the spring of 1990, it won fewer than ten percent of the seats in parliament, and it was driven from power.

The political crisis that felled the Soviet regime was exceptionally dramatic. As in Poland and Hungary, long economic decline, or at best economic stagnation, steadily undermined whatever legitimacy the regime had once enjoyed. With Gorbachev's loosening of ideological uniformities and requirements, which proved to be the heterogeneous Soviet elites' only unifying force, elite groups divided into distinct factions that began to fight each each ferociously. The Soviet Union was torn apart by this elite fighting and by the inability of Gorbachev and the topmost political elite to deal with it in any way other than coercion and violence. The crisis climaxed during the second half of 1991 with the attempted state coup of August 19–21, the banning of the Communist Party three months later, and the final disintegration of the Soviet state in December.

Elite Change: Appearance or Reality?

Academics, politicians, and ordinary citizens are strongly divided over the political status of former communist elites and the composition of new elites in the postcommunist environments of the 1990s. Some see the nomenklatura elites as major winners in the transitions from communist to postcommunist regimes; others see them as major losers. Those who hold the former view argue that the nomenklatura elites, where they did not simply retain their previous political and administrative posts, successfully converted their political and bureaucratic capital into market assets. Those who perceive the nomenklatura elites as losers point out that many elite persons not only lost their ruling positions within the former partocratic apparatuses, but they have also been prevented from obtaining the higher-level positions in the new economic, political and social orders for which their educational credentials and occupational skills qualify them. Taking these controversies as the point of departure, let me summarize three hypotheses about the postcommunist destinations of the nomenklatura elites.

The first, a "power-conversion" hypothesis, was formulated during the last years of communist rule by two prominent sociologists, Elemer Hankiss (1990, 1991) in Hungary, and Jadwiga Staniszkis (1991a, 1991b) in Poland. It holds that, threatened by accelerating changes and failures in the Soviet system of state socialism, the nomenklatura elites sought to secure their authority and social status through adept moves to convert their political and bureaucratic power into market assets and capital. In a word, they saw the handwriting on the wall and acted accordingly. Observing developments in Hungary at the end of the 1980s, Hankiss argued that the power conversions by incumbent elites amounted to the formation of a new ruling class:

> There can hardly be any doubt today that a new ruling class, a kind of grand bourgeoisie, is emerging in this country. It is, or in all likelihood will be, the alliance of four social groups: first, the most dynamic members of the younger generation of the Kadarist oligarchy; second, the same type of people coming from the upper and upper-middle layers of the state bureaucracy; third, the managerial class, i.e., the managers of great state companies, and agricultural cooperatives (called the red and green barons); fourth, the most successful members and families of the emerging entrepreneurial class. (Hankiss, 1990, 240).

In Poland, Staniszkis focused her attention on the spontaneous and mostly pathological forms that privatization of the state sector was taking during the second half of the 1980s. This was, she observes, already "making owners of the nomenklatura." The process, which she calls "political capitalism," consisted of taking advantage of one's managerial or political position to establish private or semiprivate firms working within a state enterprise or in close cooperation with it. On the one hand, these "private profit-oriented cooperatives," as Staniszkis calls them, made the operation of state enterprises more efficient. On the other hand, they acted against interests of the enterprises with which they were affiliated, freely using their machinery, energy, and producer-distributor networks, while transferring all profits to private hands (Staniszkis, 1991a, 38–72).

The course and pace of this power conversion, as well as the social attitudes toward it, varied in Hungary, Poland, and Russia. In Hungary, as I have already noted, Kadar's policy of placating growing discontents by allowing a "second economy" safety valve created a large semientrepreneurial class as early as the 1970s. Thus, the "embourgeoisment of the nomenklatura" had some ideological justification in Hungary well before the collapse of communism. In Poland, although there existed a large and private agricultural sector and "peasantry," there was no official approval of a Hungarian-type second economy, so that the practices of political capitalism outlined by Staniszkis evoked much criticism and strong condemnations. In Russia, the processes that unfolded in Hungary and Poland got under way only somewhat later, and then in quite limited forms. But in all three countries the outcome was the same: nomenklatura elites managed to enter the postcommunist orders as a privileged category in purely economic terms. Thanks to "spontaneous privatization," the leading groups of the old regime had market assets at their disposal even before postcommunist privatization programs began. The new free market environment merely enabled them to increase these assets. In this fashion, an elite "reproduction through conversion" took place, in which one resource (political or managerial power) was exchanged for a different resource (property ownership and economic wealth), so that many individuals and groups simply perpetuated their status as elites.

The power-conversion hypothesis will receive empirical support if the nomenklatura elites are found to have been running their own firms (no matter whether they were also employed elsewhere) before the regime changes in 1989–91 or to have held managerial positions in significant private firms after those changes. It is necessary to consider both ownership and managerial positions, because the separation of ownership and control has not advanced very far in postcommunist economies. Owners and co-owners frequently perform managerial functions, while nominally salaried managers frequently have some ownership stake in the firms they manage.

A second hypothesis might simply be labeled "no change." It is not as well grounded theoretically as the power-conversion hypothesis, but it is widely held among radical democratic and marketizing opponents of incremental political and economic reforms in the three countries. According to this hypothesis, changes among elites have been limited to the very top of the communist power pyramid, that is, to the figurative handful of Politburo members, party secretaries, state presidents, premiers, and secret police heads. Below this highest echelon, however, most nomenklatura elites have managed to hold on to their command positions in the state-controlled economic sectors and state administrative apparatuses. Although the positions and actions of these holdover elites are not the stuff of front-page headlines, they are sufficiently influential to affect national and especially regional political outcomes quite profoundly. A corollary is that those who lost their offices as a result of "plebiscitary" elections during 1989–91 succeeded in regaining their positions or equivalent ones after the second round of democratic elections between 1993 and 1995. Therefore, nothing has really changed: the old rulers still dominate in both the economy and politics. The only difference is that now they operate in a new environment, which forces them to use somewhat different methods to achieve their goals. They try to keep lower public profiles, but this does not mean that they have less power than before. In short, the nomenklatura elites have simply reproduced themselves, often managing to hold the same offices as before and retaining their holds on the major institutions.

The no-change hypothesis stresses the retention of leadership posts in all domains of public life. It will receive empirical support if the old nomenklatura elites are found to hold elite positions in the same political domain (legislature, government, administration), the same state-run sector of the economy (economic domain), or the same media and cultural institutions (cultural domain) during the 1990s. In this connection it is necessary to note that the data I analyze below were collected before the electoral comebacks of the formerly communist (and in Russia the still communist) parties between late 1993 and 1995. Those comebacks began with the Democratic Left Alliance's victory in Poland's September 1993 elections, continued with the Socialists' victory in Hungary's May 1994 elections, and could also be seen in the strong showings made by the Communists in Russia's State Duma elections at the ends of both 1993 and 1995. Because they do not measure the positional restorations that these political comebacks involved, my findings actually underestimate the recent and current proportions of nomenklatura elites, especially the "political nomenklatura," in all three countries.

The third hypothesis—let us call it "revolutionary victimization"—is usually formulated by the nomenklatura elites themselves. It stands in clear opposition to the preceding two hypotheses because it portrays those who previously led the countries, or even all members of those countries' communist parties, as more or less innocent victims of the 1989–91 upheavals. Accordingly, no matter what their qualifications and level of involvement in the ancien régime, the nomenklatura elites have not only been forced to step down from their bureaucratic posts, but they have also been deprived of the right to compete equally for posts in the new postcommunist orders. In other words, elites who now rule have applied the principle of "collective responsibility" to their predecessors, in the process victimizing all those who had no more than formal and perfunctory connections to the communist regimes. In short, the nomenklatura elites have experienced severe and undeserved downward mobility, or, if one prefers, they have been unfairly displaced in a "circulation of elites."

To make the victimization hypothesis operational in an accurate way, the ages of respondents have to be taken into account, because it is hard to consider retirement as downward mobility or elite circulation when the persons in question had already reached a pensionable age (sixty years for women and sixty-five for men). I therefore arbitrarily assume that if someone had achieved pensionable age by 1993, his or her retirement was a natural event that does not signify coerced political or structural change in elite composition. The victimization hypothesis will thus receive empirical support if members of the nomenklatura elites who had not yet reached retirement age are found to have been unemployed or employed in manual or routine nonmanual occupational positions in 1993.

The Main Patterns

An international research project on social stratification in Eastern Europe after 1989, in which I participated, produced a considerable body of data relevant to the hypotheses I have stated. The project focused on Hungary, Poland, and Russia, and it had two main components: (1) survey interviews conducted in the autumn of 1993 with random samples of people holding elite positions in each country in 1988 ("the nomenklatura elites") and in 1993 ("the new elites"); and (2) simultaneous survey interviews with representative samples of the adult populations of all three countries.

To assess the extent of elite continuity between communist and postcommunist regimes, the nomenklatura elites were defined as persons holding command positions that were controlled by the Central Committees of the Hungarian, Polish, and Russian communist parties in 1988. They consisted of position holders in the party apparatuses at national and regional levels, legislators and top state administrators at both levels, and leaders of mass organizations (all of these persons constituting "the political nomenklatura"), together with directors of the largest state enterprises ("the economic nomenklatura") and decision makers in the spheres of science, education, media, and the arts ("the cultural nomenklatura").

It is important to stress at once that because systemic transformations occurred in Hungary, Poland, and Russia, social positions and roles that were outwardly the same in 1993 as in 1988 may have changed greatly in their real powers and functional importance. In tracing the nomenklatura elites' fates, I make no attempt to measure the extent to which their real powers changed between 1988 and 1993. Neither do I speculate about the wider economic and political consequences of such power shifts. These issues are beyond the scope of this chapter, because they call for data about the overall powers of elites in the new postcommunist settings; to obtain such data, a comprehensive analysis of the current power structures of Hungary, Poland, and Russia would be necessary.

There were sizable differences in the sectoral compositions of Russian, Hungarian, and Polish nomenklatura elites in 1988 (table 7.1). Reflecting the politically unifying function of the nomenklatura system itself, the political nomenklatura (i.e., party, state, and mass organization leaders) constituted a majority of the elite sample in each country. In the Russian and Hungarian cases, however, the second largest elite sector consisted of leaders in the ideological (cultural) spheres (media, science, education, science, and the arts), whereas in Poland it consisted of economic leaders. This cross-national difference reflected local variations in the personnel policies of the three communist parties: the Russian and Hungarian parties seemed to pay more attention to ideological mobilization, while the Polish party apparently focused more closely on the economy. But I cannot exclude the possibility that differences in the nomenklatura elites' sectoral makeups result at least in part from deficiencies in sampling procedures and interviewing. In all three countries, our researchers had serious problems compiling complete lists of the incumbents of nomenklatura posts, and in Poland and Russia our interviews with elites were conducted amid serious political tensions that might have influenced response rates significantly. In Poland, interviews were conducted in the summer and early

TABLE 7.1
Composition of the 1988 Nomenklatura Samples in Russia, Hungary, and Poland (percentage)

1988 Nomenklatura	Russia	Hungary	Poland
N	848	812	888
Political nomenklatura	67.6	64.4	56.5
Party	18.3	19.2	18.6
State	42.2	33.0	31.5
Mass organizations	7.1	12.2	6.4
Economic nomenklatura	7.2	12.6	29.6
Cultural nomenklatura	25.2	23.0	13.9

fall of 1993, shortly after the collapse of the government led by Hanna Suchocka and President Lech Walesa's dissolution of parliament. In Russia, the interviews were conducted during the growing conflict between President Boris Yeltsin and what was still called the Supreme Soviet, a conflict that culminated in the shelling of the House of Soviets (the White House) in early October 1993.

In addressing the three hypotheses discussed in the preceding section, let me first note that they are neither comprehensive nor mutually exclusive. Specifically, the locations of some nomenklatura elites in 1993 may not have accorded clearly with any of the hypothesized patterns (e.g., persons who worked as teachers), or they may have accorded with more than one pattern (e.g., retirees running their own businesses). I have constructed a typology of the elites' postcommunist destinations that tries to take such ambiguities into account (table 7.2). In particular, I classified those who had more than one job or position in 1993 according to their "higher" status and usually better remunerated job. For instance, an engineer working for a state-owned firm while also running a part-time business has been classified as an entrepreneur; a retired teacher who was nevertheless elected to parliament or some other office has been classified as a politician. The resulting typology consists of nine categories, and it serves as a major tool for testing the three hypotheses.

In table 7.2 the "business" category includes all self-employed persons (irrespective of their firm's size and monetary turnover), as well as all those who held managerial posts (corporate managers and general managers[1]) in the private sector. Party leaders, members of parliament and government cabinets, and higher officials of national and regional

TABLE 7.2
The 1993 Destination of Nomenklatura Elites (percentage)

1993 Destination	Russia	Hungary	Poland
N	848	812	888
Business	15.1	26.2	24.4
Politics	24.6	5.2	6.1
Business and politics	2.5	1.2	.6
Directors in state sector	25.6	12.1	17.1
Managers and professionals	19.7	23.5	19.1
Nonmanual	2.0	1.6	5.1
"Lower" classes	.2	2.8	2.8
Early retirees	5.3	16.7	18.1
Emeriti	5.0	10.6	6.6

administrations have been included in the "politics" category. The "business and politics" category groups together all those who were both entrepreneurs and politicians or senior state officials. This category was introduced in order to test claims by the advocates of radical democratizing and marketizing reforms that many nomenklatura elite members were simultaneously and actively involved in private business and politics. If by "active political involvement" we mean holding high-ranking offices in the political and state administrative organs, these claims are poorly grounded—as seen in table 7.2. This does not necessarily invalidate such claims, however, because the data do not allow assessment of other ways in which nomenklatura elites may have had continuing political involvements and influence in 1993.

The next category in table 7.2—"directors in state sector"—refers mainly to the economic and cultural sectors of the nomenklatura elites (i.e., directors of large state enterprises and decision makers in the media, scientific, educational, and arts spheres). The "managers and professionals" category includes middle-level managers in the public sector and salaried professionals. The "nonmanual" category includes the remaining white-collar workers. The "lower classes" category combines manual or blue-collar workers with those who were unemployed in 1993 (the very small number of unemployed persons in our samples warrant combining them with blue-collar workers). Persons who retired from their jobs before achieving pension ages make up the "early retirees" category. The last category, "emeriti," consists of persons who had left the labor market due to their ages and were not involved in any occupational, economic, or political activities.

The typology shows that nomenklatura elites followed four major routes from their positions in 1988 to their postcommunist destinations in 1993. The first route led to business, the second to command positions in politics, administration, and the state sector of the economy, the third to nonmanual (mostly professional and managerial) jobs, and the fourth route led out of the labor market altogether. The data in table 7.2 show that the hypothesis about a conversion of political power into market assets gains empirical support in Hungary and Poland. In both countries roughly a quarter of all nomenklatura elites moved to command positions in private business. The Russian elites, by contrast, were less successful in converting political capital into market assets. Nevertheless, one cannot say that the conversion hypothesis is invalid in Russia. Considering that market-oriented reforms and privatization programs were initiated later there, the 15.1 percent of nomenklatura elites who by 1993 were successful in business suggests that the power-conversion process was well under way in Russia, too.

Naturally, it is not clear just how many members of the nomenklatura elites would have to become entrepreneurs in order for the power-
conversion hypothesis to be fully confirmed. Is one-quarter in Hungary
and Poland or 15 percent in Russia a lot or a little? Some light can
be shed on this through comparative analysis. Table 7.3 presents data
pertaining to the makeup of the three countries' employed workforce
in 1988 and 1993. To make these workforce data comparable to the
nomenklatura categories, I selected those workers who in 1988 were
economically active and older than twenty-one years of age (because
all nomenklatura members were economically active in 1988 and the
youngest among them were twenty-two at that time). Table 7.3 shows
the proportions of the socio-occupational categories in the 1988 workforces who had become entrepreneurs by 1993, defining entrepreneurs
in the same way as I did for the nomenklatura elites, i.e., all who
owned a business or held a managerial job in the private sector. I excluded self-employed farmers from the entrepreneur category.

The patterns of movement toward entrepreneurship between 1988
and 1993 were very similar in all three workforces. The only major
variation occurred among farmers, and this doubtless reflected the
quite different organization of the agricultural sector in the three countries under communist rule. Self-employed farmers hardly existed in
Russia and Hungary (there were just four of them in the Russian sample and twenty-six in the Hungarian sample). One should not, therefore, make too much of the differences between the 1993 destinations
of Russian, Hungarian, and Polish farmers. In all three countries, in
any event, the category of persons who most frequently became entrepreneurs by 1993 consisted of those who were already self-employed
in 1988. This is, of course, a relatively trivial observation, and it does

TABLE 7.3
Outflow from the 1988 Socio-occupational Categories into 1993
Entrepreneurial Positions (percentage)

1988 Category	Russia	Hungary	Poland
N	3,586	2,770	2,340
Managers	11.1	28.3	25.0
Professionals	3.5	13.9	10.5
Self-employed (nonfarmer)	83.3	67.7	75.5
Nonmanual	3.0	8.2	6.7
Skilled manual	3.2	6.4	9.6
Unskilled manual	0.8	2.8	4.1
Self-employed farmers	—	15.4	3.6

little to help us understand the shift to entrepreneurship among the nomenklatura elites.[2] The second most successful category in this respect were managers. The proportions of 1988 managers who became entrepreneurs by 1993 were almost exactly the same as the corresponding proportions among the nomenklatura elites. This implies that holding a managerial job under communist rule, even one that was not an elite job, was quite crucial to moving to the private sector during the period under discussion. Compared with the other elite and workforce categories, large proportions of both the nomenklatura elites and communist subelite or middle-level managers moved to entrepreneurial roles immediately before or after the transitions to postcommunist regimes. These proportions are several times greater than the proportions of nonmanual and skilled and unskilled manual workers who became entrepreneurs, and they are at least twice as high as the proportions of professionals who made such moves. Clearly, the set of factors linked with managerial jobs and status were critical to attaining entrepreneurial positions in the postcommunist orders, and this was true at both elite and nonelite levels.

Regarding the no-change hypothesis, it receives weak support in Poland and even less support in Hungary. If we look again at table 7.2, we see that in neither country was overt political power in 1988 transferred with any frequency into comparable political power in 1993. In the latter year, a few nomenklatura elites still held top government positions in each country, and an even more marginal number combined such positions with private business activities. On the other hand, a considerable proportion of the nomenklatura elites in Poland (17.1 percent) and Hungary (12.1 percent) still held top command posts in state-owned firms. All in all, in 1993 about one-fifth of Hungarian nomenklatura elites and about one-fourth of their Polish counterparts continued to hold top decision-making positions in various domains of public life (although their 1988 and 1993 positions were not necessarily the same). The no-change hypothesis is, therefore, far from being without foundation in both countries. Nonetheless, the evidence hardly justifies the often-heard claim that "everything is as it was before." In Russia, however, the no-change hypothesis receives much stronger support: in 1993, one-half of the 1988 nomenklatura elites still held top command positions in politics and the state-owned sector of the economy. But even in the Russian case the no-change hypothesis is seriously misleading, for it ignores the half of the elites who are not holdovers from communist rule.

The third hypothesis, which claims that nomenklatura elites have been victims of acute social degradation, is not strongly supported by the evidence. Where, as in Russia, more than 60 percent of leading entrepreneurs, enterprise directors, and other national and regional decision makers are former nomenklatura elites and where, as in Hungary and Poland, the comparable proportions are more than forty percent, one can hardly refer to the nomenklatura elites as "victims." Some nomenklatura elite persons clearly did experience downward mobility, but the mere fact that someone has lost his or her political office during a period of crisis-induced changes cannot be interpreted as a sign of vengeful discrimination and victimization. Downward mobility for some elites routinely accompanies any change of government, not to mention transitions from one kind of regime to another.

The subjective element is an important aspect of the nomenklatura-as-victim hypothesis: to what extent do members of the nomenklatura elites feel that they have been degraded socially and politically? Lacking data on subjective perceptions, we must restrict ourselves to the available "objective" data. Those nomenklatura elites who were unemployed or who held manual jobs in 1993 had clearly experienced a drastic occupational degradation. Those who were employed as routine white-collar workers could also be seen in this light. But only 2 percent of the Russian nomenklatura elite, 4 percent of the Hungarian elite, and 8 percent of the Polish elite held such occupational positions in 1993. It is more difficult to draw conclusions about the extent to which early retirees reflect a process of degradation or victimization. We do not know whether their retirements were unwelcomed necessities or merely voluntary actions reflecting ill health and other personal circumstances. In any event, drastic occupational and accompanying social degradation appears to have been the fate of only tiny proportions of the three nomenklatura elites. According to standard social mobility measures such as occupational prestige scales and socioeconomic indices of occupations, nearly all members of the nomenklatura elites, to be sure, experienced some amount of downward mobility. Measured by these devices, their 1993 occupational positions were usually lower than their 1988 ones. In 1988, however, nearly all of them were at the very top of the social hierarchy, so that virtually any change in position involved downward mobility. But the generally limited extent of these downward movements by no means warrants the "victim" label.

The typology of elite destinations in table 7.2 reveals that significant proportions held professional and middle- or lower-management positions in 1993. Presumably, the majority of these persons had returned to the professions and managerial functions they held before they entered nomenklatura elite positions. Many of them were recruited into top nomenklatura positions during the 1980s, when in all three countries substantial changes in the makeup of elites were taking place (cf. Hanley, Yershova, and Anderson, 1995; Wasilewski and Wnuk-Lipinski, 1995; Szelenyi, Szelenyi, and Kovach, 1995). Here are a few typical cases of individuals in the Polish elite sample who had landed in the "managers and professional" category by 1993: a university chancellor who reverted to the rank of professor, a department director who became an adviser in the same ministry, a regional party secretary who returned to his previous job as teacher in a technical school, a director of a firm who became head of the design section of another firm, a magazine editor in chief who in 1993 was a journalist for the same magazine. Persons like these (as well as some early retirees and emeriti) declared during interviews that their departures from former elite positions did them no harm; on the contrary, they claimed to have achieved a much-desired release from the stresses their involvement in communist politics had caused.

Additional light on elite social mobility is provided by the data presented in tables 7.4, 7.5, and 7.6, which compare the 1988 and 1993 positions held by each country's nomenklatura elite. Let me briefly examine the most interesting patterns. First, the route from nomenklatura to business was followed by persons in all elite sectors. Thus, it was not a channel open only to those who were directly involved in economic management ("enterprise directors") under communist rule. Whether this pattern stemmed from the workings of what Staniszkis called "political capitalism" under communism—the increasing conversion of political capital into market assets—is uncertain, however. Tracing the origins of postcommunist economic elites to that earlier process is difficult, because former communist government officials and high-ranking party apparatchiks are not numerous enough among postcommunist business leaders to demonstrate that "political capitalism" before 1989 in Hungary and Poland and before 1991 in Russia was a key determinant of the nomenklatura elites' destinations. The fact, nevertheless, that persons in all nomenklatura sectors had moved in more or less equal proportions to command positions in private business by 1993 does strongly suggest that general political capital under communism, and not just first-hand access to enterprise resources and decision making, was important for elite continuity.

Second, in Hungary and Poland three nomenklatura elite groups were virtually eliminated from top political positions during and after the regime transitions: persons in the Communist Party apparatuses and those in the economic and cultural nomenklaturas. In Russia, members of the economic and cultural nomenklatura groups were also poorly represented in postcommunist political elite positions (although there were more of them in such positions than in Hungary

TABLE 7.4

Outflow from the 1988 Nomenklatura Categories into the 1993 Destination, Russia (percentage of elites) ($N = 848$)

1988 Nomenklatura Category	N	Business[a]	Politics	Directors in State Sector	Managers and Professionals	Nonmanual and "Lower Classes"[b]	Early Retirees	Emeriti
Party	155	14.2	31.6	19.4	19.4	.6	5.8	9.0
State	358	18.4	34.1	20.1	13.7	3.1	5.6	5.0
Mass organizations	60	25.0	40.0	10.0	13.3	1.7	6.7	3.3
Economy	61	32.8	6.6	45.9	11.5	—	1.6	1.6
Media, culture	214	12.1	4.7	37.9	34.1	2.8	5.1	3.3
		17.6	24.6	25.6	19.7	2.2	5.3	5.0

Note: Chi-square = 160.8; $p < .001$.
[a]Due to small frequencies, "business and politics" category was combined with "business."
[b]Due to small frequencies, "nonmanual" and "lower classes" categories were combined.

TABLE 7.5
Outflow from the 1988 Nonmenklatura Categories into the 1993 Destination, Hungary (percentage of elites) ($N = 812$)

1988 Nomenklatura Category	N	Business[a]	Politics	Directors in State Sector	Managers and Professionals	Nonmanual	"Lower" Classes	Early Retirees	Emeriti
					Destination				
Party	156	26.3	5.1	5.8	23.6	1.9	1.3	25.6	5.1
State	268	26.9	7.5	10.4	23.1	2.2	6.0	16.0	7.8
Mass organizations	99	31.3	12.1	2.0	16.2	3.0	5.1	17.2	13.1
Economy	102	44.1	1.0	15.7	5.9	—	—	23.5	9.8
Media, culture	187	18.2	.5	23.0	33.2	.5	—	6.4	18.2
Average		27.5	5.2	12.1	23.5	1.6	2.8	16.7	10.6

Note: Chi-square = 163.5; $p < .001$.
[a]Due to small frequencies, "business and politics" category was combined with "business."

TABLE 7.6
Outflow from the 1988 Nomenklatura Categories into the 1993 Destination, Poland (percentage of elites ($N = 888$))

1988 Nomenklatura Category	N	Business[a]	Politics	Directors in State Sector	1993 Destination Managers and Professionals	Nonmanual	"Lower" Classes	Early Retirees	Emeriti
Party	165	25.5	1.8	6.1	24.8	13.9	9.1	17.0	1.8
State	280	20.0	12.5	5.0	23.2	5.4	2.5	21.1	10.4
Mass organizations	57	35.1	26.3	5.3	8.8	3.5	1.8	10.5	8.8
Economy	263	30.8	.4	34.2	10.6	1.9	.4	17.5	4.2
Media, culture	123	18.7	—	28.5	25.2	—	.8	17.9	8.9
Average		25.0	6.1	17.1	19.1	5.1	2.8	18.1	6.6

Note: Chi-square = 296.6 p < .001
[a]Due to small frequencies, "business and politics" category was combined with "business."

and Poland). However, one-third of the Soviet Union's Communist Party elite still held command positions in political institutions in 1993.

Third, in all three countries significant numbers of communist governmental bureaucrats could be found in the new state administrations. In Russia, as many as 30 percent of these bureaucrats retained their governmental posts. In Poland and Hungary the proportions were smaller, but not negligible.

Fourth, in Hungary and Poland downward mobility was more severe among party officials and communist state administrators than among the other nomenklatura groups. Such differing fates were not apparent in Russia, however.

Fifth, outflow patterns among both economic nomenklatura and the cultural nomenklatura differed between Poland and Hungary. For example, a substantial proportion of Polish state-enterprise directors remained in their positions despite the regime change, whereas in Hungary a larger proportion of state-enterprise directors left their positions, either moving to private business or retiring.

Who Won and Who Lost?

The political crises and regime changes that occurred in Poland, Hungary, and Russia clearly involved important changes in elite composition and structure. Yet, none of the three hypotheses I have examined tells the whole truth about these changes. Each does, however, tap into a significant aspect of them.

My data show that the conversion of political capital into economic assets, which was hypothesized by Hankiss (1990, 1991) and Staniszkis (1991a, 1991b), did occur, particularly in Hungary and Poland. The proportions of former Communist Party rulers who became capitalist entrepreneurs were exceeded only by the proportions of managers of state-owned enterprises who made this jump. The data do not reveal the specific mechanism by which party leaders converted their political capital into market assets, but the result of the conversion process was, by 1993, exactly as Elemer Hankiss predicted: the state, party, and economic nomenklatura elites (and, I may add, the communist managerial stratum in general), together with the communist-era petite bourgeoisie, constituted the core of the emerging postcommunist capitalist class. Reproduction through conversion was, thus, an important aspect of the elite transformation in the countries I have studied.

In a strict sense, the no-change hypothesis is patently false when applied to the three countries. However, it draws attention to the limited nature of the elite changes that occurred, especially in Russia, where about one-third of the former political elite and nearly one-half of the old economic elite retained their elite status during and after the regime change. In fact, this simple continuity of elites is arguably the Russian case's dominant feature. In Poland and Hungary, simple elite continuity was less pronounced, though still clearly evident; thus, one-third of Polish state-enterprise directors retained their positions during and after the regime change in Warsaw.

Assessing the fates of the nomenklatura elites in terms of winners and losers is a subjective matter. In my interpretation, the winners should be considered those nomenklatura members who in 1993 were located in my "business," "politics," and "directors in state sector" elite categories. Those who constituted the "emeriti" category in each country should be excluded from a winners-losers analysis, since they presumably would have left the labor market regardless of political events. The apparent losers are those in my "lower classes" and "non-manual" categories. All early retirees should probably be considered losers. All in all, then, 50 percent of the nomenklatura elites were winners in Hungary, 51 percent were winners in Poland, and 71 percent were winners in Russia. When the "emeriti" are excluded, the ratio of winners to losers was 90:10 in Russia, 21:10 in Hungary, and 19:10 in Poland. Clearly, nomenklatura elites largely survived the dramatic political crises and regime changes that occurred in these three countries. Only minorities of elites suffered serious social or political demotion. In Poland and Hungary, these minorities were fairly sizable, whereas in Russia the seriously demoted made up an almost negligible minority. The three cases show that even during and after profound political upheavals, elites strongly tend to persist.

Notes

1. These are terms used in standard occupational classifications. Under the International Standard Classification of Occupations (1990), supervising occupations that are concerned with the control of the quality of work done are not included in managerial categories. Consequently, respondents who performed supervisory functions in private firms in 1993 were not included in the economic elite.

2. A nontrivial question in this context is why a quarter of Polish, one-third of Hungarian, and 15 percent of Russian communist-era business leaders ceased to run their own businesses after the change from a centrally planned to a market economy.

References

Bruszt, Laslo. 1992. "The Negotiated Revolution of Hungary." In *Post-Communist Transition: Emerging Pluralism in Hungary*, ed. A. Bozoki. London: Pinter.

Hankiss, Elemer. 1990. *East European Alternatives.* Oxford: Clarendon Press.

———. 1991. "Reforms and the Conversion of Power." In *Upheaval Against the Plan,* ed. P. R. Weilemenn, G. Brunner, and R. L. Tokes. Oxford: Berg.

Hanley, Eric, Natasha Yershova, and Richard Anderson. 1995. "Russia—Old Wine in a New Bottle? The Circulation and Reproduction of Russian Elites, 1983–1993." *Theory and Society* 24 (October): 639–68.

Staniszkis, Jadwiga. 1991a. *The Dynamics of the Breakthrough in Eastern Europe.* Berkeley: University of California Press.

———. 1991b. "Patterns of Change in Eastern Europe." In *Upheaval Against the Plan,* ed. P. R. Weilemenn, G. Brunner, and R. L. Tokes. Oxford: Berg.

Szelenyi, Szonja, Ivan Szelenyi, and Imre Kovach. 1995. "The Making of the Hungarian Postcommunist Elite: Circulation in Politics, Reproduction in Economy." *Theory and Society* 24 (October): 697–722.

Tokes, Rudolf L. 1996. *Hungary's Negotiated Revolution.* New York: Cambridge University Press.

Wasilewski, Jacek, and Edmund Wnuk-Lipinski. 1995. "Poland: The Winding Road from Communist to Post-Solidarity Elite." *Theory and Society* 24 (October): 669–96.

8

Germany: Twentieth-Century Turning Points

Ursula Hoffmann-Lange

Momentous crises in 1918–19, 1933, 1945, and 1989 have constituted the major turning points in Germany's twentieth-century political history. These crises triggered five changes of political regimes, and they illuminate the connections between elites, crises, and the origins of regimes. Comparatively extensive research on the composition and configuration of German elites before, during, and after the crises has yielded rich data that facilitate an analysis of these connections.[1]

The 1918–19 crisis was triggered by military defeat in World War I, and it resulted in the introduction of the Weimar parliamentary regime. In 1933, a deep economic crisis intersected with the Weimar regime's endemic instability to produce the totalitarian Nazi regime. A third crisis in 1945 began with the Nazi regime's defeat in World War II, and it resulted in the division of Germany into two fundamentally different regimes. The liberal democratic Federal Republic of Germany (FRG) was established in the west, and the state-socialist German Democratic Republic (GDR) was created in the east, where it remained in power for the next forty-five years. In October and November 1989, after the Soviet Union renounced its supremacy in East Central Europe, the GDR state-socialist regime collapsed in the course of a few weeks. In that crisis, new political leaders turned immediately to the FRG for economic and political support, thereby enabling the government in Bonn to determine the conditions under which German reunification took place in October 1990. All these crises are well known, and there is little to be gained from rehearsing them here. I want, instead, to examine the extent to which they were accompanied by fundamental changes in elites that help to account for the origin and

169

character of Germany's successive political regimes during the twentieth century.

The Crisis of 1918–1919 and the Formation of the Weimar Republic: Military Defeat, Regime Change, and Elite Continuity

To understand the crisis of 1918–19 and the subsequent failure of the first German democratic regime, the Weimar Republic (1919–33), one has to go back to the formation of the German Empire in 1871 and the political regime it produced. Historians and social scientists have often claimed that Germany at that time was following a *Sonderweg,* or unique track, because its socioeconomic modernization and democratization did not coincide (e.g., Dahrendorf, 1967; Blackbourn and Eley, 1985). Defying democratizing trends in other Western European countries, the kaiser retained constitutional power to appoint governments that were exclusively answerable to him, instead of depending upon majority support in the popularly elected parliament, the Reichstag. The Reichstag's power was limited to vetoing legislation initiated by the executive. This dual political structure strongly affected the development of political parties. Lacking responsibility for governing, the parties used the Reichstag primarily as an arena for articulating far-reaching and unrealistic political goals while at the same time engaging in pragmatic wheeling and dealing with the executive to promote the interests of their respective clienteles. This clientelistic politics contributed to a widespread perception of parties as representatives of narrow interests, in contrast with the prestigious, mainly Prussian civil service, which was perceived as the only defender of the public interest. In the typology of regimes that Mattei Dogan and John Higley adopt in chapter 1, the German Empire is best classified as a traditional (monarchical) regime.

The empire brought a multitude of kingdoms and principalities under one German state, and it realized the long-standing desire for German unity. Only a few dissident elite groups felt that the monarchical regime did not correspond to the demands of the time. Thus, the regime enjoyed widespread legitimacy, especially because it oversaw rapid economic growth. However, the regime was not capable of accommodating the emerging labor movement, whose support among the working class grew steadily. By 1912, the Social Democratic Party (SPD) was the largest party in the Reichstag, though its representatives were generally treated as political and social outsiders. At the outbreak of World War I, nonetheless, most Germans enthusiastically greeted

Germany's entry into the war, and even the Social Democrats voted in favor of the government's war loans. But as the war dragged on, public support eroded and economic and political discontents increased, especially during the winter famine of 1917–18, the *Steckrübenwinter*. Labor movement elites, whose clienteles were most seriously affected by shortages in food and other goods, split over the question of renewing vital war loans, and a left-wing Independent Social Democratic Party (USPD) opposed to the war effort was formed in 1917. In November 1918, after the General Staff admitted that the war was lost and a parliamentary-backed government had been created, mass discontents erupted in several revolutionary insurgencies. These made it clear that merely installing a government with parliamentary support would not placate discontents, and on November 9, 1918, the last government of the German Empire resigned and handed power to Friedrich Ebert, the SPD's leader. On the same day, the kaiser abdicated, and Germany was declared a republic.

The high degree of elite and organizational continuity that characterized this crisis-driven regime change has been documented extensively by Wolfgang Zapf (1965, 140) and highlighted by Ralf Dahrendorf (1967, 215). No large-scale displacement of existing elites analogous to that which occurred in Russia following the Bolshevik seizure of power in late 1917 took place in Germany. Instead, revolutionary insurgencies remained localized, and they were short-lived. To be sure, the introduction of a parliamentary democracy shifted governmental power from the executive to the legislature. But this was only grudgingly accepted by right-wing parties and by elites in other sectors, especially the business, judicial, and military elites. Crucially, most members of the civil service elite, who were accustomed to playing a central role in policy making, resented the decrease in their power that parliamentary dominance involved. Not a few members of all these entrenched elite groups awaited an opportunity to revise or even reverse the constitutional change of regime.

The numerical strength of center-left parties in the Reichstag made them the obvious candidates to form and lead a new government. Handing power to center-left forces also seemed the only way to prevent insurgencies from becoming more widespread. The previously marginalized but electorally powerful SPD thus moved to the center of the Weimar stage. But SPD leaders faced many difficulties. Apart from labor union leaders, they had few elite allies. Most existing elites refused to accept the former SPD outcasts as the core of an altered political elite. In particular, conflict-of-interest rules under the old regime had prevented civil servants from becoming members of the SPD and had thus contributed to a homogeneously conservative political outlook among leaders of the bureaucracy. Social Democrat Party ministers nevertheless had to rely on these bureaucratic leaders, who quite frequently used their expertise to subvert the programs of their new political masters. Reflecting their generally humble social backgrounds, moreover, SPD leaders lacked assertiveness and were overly cautious and deferential in dealing with the civil service and other elites.

The obstacles to cooperation between SPD leaders and other party elites were exacerbated by the fact that political leaders were, in general, ill-prepared to operate a parliamentary democracy. They had little understanding of their new responsibilities in democratic governance, they shared no code of democratic political behavior, and they lacked any serious consensus about democratic institutions and procedures. Their conflicting ideological goals had not been tempered, and their clientelistic practices remained unchanged. A deep socioeconomic cleavage continued to separate the Social Democrats from their bourgeois opponents. In short, the crisis and resulting regime transition of 1918–19 were unaccompanied by a significant change in the mode of elite behavior. Accommodation and cooperation were conspicuously absent, and as a consequence all coalition governments in the Weimar regime were highly unstable. When another crisis in the form of drastic economic decline began in the late 1920s, even short-lived coalitions with majority support in the Reichstag became untenable.

Weimar Breakdown and the Nazi Ascendancy

While there is agreement that constitutional and economic factors exacerbated the Weimar Republic's political problems,[2] the refusal of most elite groups to cooperate within a democratic institutional framework and to bridge traditional cleavage lines was clearly the primary cause of its breakdown. Unchecked mass mobilizations by competing and disunited elites fueled widespread public dissatisfaction and eventually brought Germany to the brink of civil war. Political pragmatism was denounced for the "foul compromises" it involved, and extremists on the left and the right regularly blamed the "party system" for the country's economic and political woes. The party system was, in fact, a classic example of polarized pluralism (Sartori, 1976), involving a centrifugal "politics of outbidding" and a consequent erosion of electoral support for moderate parties. This was shown clearly by the rapidly increasing support for extremist parties during the last electoral period in which a government backed by a parliamentary majority could be formed. Between 1928 and 1930, the Communist Party (KPD) share of the vote rose from 10.6 percent to 13.1 percent, and the National Socialist Party (NSDAP) vote increased from 2.6 percent to 18.3 percent. In the July 1932 election, the combined share of these two anti-system parties rose to 51.6 percent (NSDAP: 37.3 percent; KPD: 14.3 percent; cf. Bracher, Funke, and Jacobsen, 1988, 630–31).

A special feature of the Weimar constitution nevertheless provided a way to avoid total government paralysis. This was the (in)famous Clause 48, which gave the directly elected president the right to issue emergency decrees. Its purpose was to ensure that governmental institutions would function even in the absence of a government supported by a Reichstag majority. While the first president, Friedrich Ebert, only rarely made use of this instrument, his successor, Wilhelm von Hindenburg, increasingly invoked it to avoid ungovernability in the midst of an ever more drastic economic crisis, which by 1932 saw six million persons, more than 40 percent of the labor force, unemployed (Lepsius, 1978, 61; Bracher, Funke, and Jacobsen, 1988, 636–37). In the summer of 1930, the last majority-backed government resigned, and Hindenburg appointed Heinrich Brüning, of the Center Party, to head a government that relied entirely on the president's emergency decree power. This in effect restored the dual structure of government that had existed during the German Empire, changing the Weimar regime's fundamental character even before its final collapse in 1933.

Elite recruitment patterns reflected these developments. At the beginning of the Weimar Republic, members of the executive were drawn predominantly from parliament in conformance with the customary pattern of parliamentary democratic regimes. By the end of the 1920s, however, the predemocratic pattern of recruiting government members from the administration and from among nonpolitical experts (the so-called *Fachleute*) had reemerged (Best, 1989). Moreover, entirely new political elites had emerged at the head of movements situated at both extremes of the political spectrum, the communists on the left and the Nazis on the right. The social composition of these new elites differed greatly from that of the established civil service, military, and business elites, as well as from the elites of the democratic parties. Consequently, elite change was more pronounced during the second half of the 1920s than during the 1918–19 regime transition. However, this change did not derive from elite circulation within established institutions and organizations; rather, it resulted from basic changes in the structure of the political party system.

The rise of the Nazis would not have been possible without the support of sizable portions of the established elites, who perceived them as a vehicle for restoring their own dominance. The Nazi regime's initial measures during and after 1933 appeared to confirm this perception.

They were mainly directed against the left-wing elites and their supporters, allowing right-wing and centrist elites to continue their usual
activities. But the Nazi elite was in no way inclined to share power
with traditional conservative groups, and it gradually assumed control
over ever wider areas of Germany's political and social life. After Hitler was appointed chancellor in January 1933, the Nazis first abolished
what remained of the Weimar parliamentary system. By the so-called
Enabling Act of March 1933, the Nazi government granted itself legislative powers and curbed its responsibility to the Reichstag. The Enabling Act was passed by the Reichstag with the approval of the center-
right parties. Within a year, the Nazi government subjected all important interest groups (labor unions, churches, professional associations,
and even business associations) to government control by installing
Nazi loyalists in strategic leadership positions. Recognizing the particular importance of the mass media, the Nazi government also took full
control of the state-owned radio system as early as the spring of 1933
(Diller, 1980).

This "streamlining" *(Gleichschaltung)* of German society was accomplished without dismantling established organizational structures.
Most elites were allowed to remain in their positions, provided they
accept the Nazi policy guidelines for their organizations. Acquiescence
by the majority of German elites in the gradual usurpation of power
was remarkable. Rainer Baum (1981) attributes it to the prior absence
of elite consensus about standards of political conduct, which he traces
back to the cultural heterogeneity and value dissensus of the wider
German society. Baum argues that this heterogeneity and dissensus
fostered a "moral indifference" among German elites that enabled
them to collaborate in even the worst atrocities perpetrated by the Nazi
regime.

Initial continuity in organizational structure and elite position holding were part of the Nazis' legalistic strategy that was intended to reassure established elites and the populace. However, from the mid-1930s
on, once the Nazis had entrenched themselves, the established elites
became expendable, and they were increasingly replaced by Nazi Party
functionaries. The business elite was the only one that was left largely
untouched. Cooperation between political and business elites resembled that which occurred during the years of the German Empire. The
Nazi and imperial regimes both provided favorable conditions for
German business by disciplining labor and supporting industrial
development.

The West German Elites and Regime after 1945

Germany's defeat and unconditional surrender in 1945 constituted a
fundamental political crisis that involved the Nazi regime's total dis-

mantling. However, the western Allied Forces (the United States, Britain, France) had no inclination to replace basic social and economic structures in the western parts of Germany, which they controlled. Already in the summer of 1945, they permitted democratic parties to reorganize or form, and they thereafter gradually transferred governmental power to these parties. The first postwar state elections were held in 1946–47.

The United States High Command initiated two programs aimed at a far-reaching transformation of the political system and political culture within the American-occupied zone. Through a denazification program, all former Nazi collaborators were to be eliminated from public life. An accompanying reeducation program was supposed to promote democratic values, especially among young Germans. While the latter program was a success, the former was doomed to fail, because it falsely assumed the existence of a pool of anti-Nazi Germans who were capable of taking over all relevant elite positions. This seriously underestimated the extent to which the Nazis had penetrated German society. In reality, practically all holders of senior positions in the civil service had been actively involved with the Nazi regime, either as party members or as loyal supporters. Because there were no qualified candidates to replace them, they were allowed to remain in their positions, or they were only temporarily displaced. Thus, the extent of change in elite composition in 1945 and after was not as far-reaching as many had expected and hoped.

Only in the political and media elites was there thorough change, with persons unconnected to the Nazi regime taking all important positions. The western Allied Forces instituted a policy of licensing the political parties that could compete in electoral contests. This amounted to reconstructing the party system from top to bottom, and it fostered the emergence of a new political elite. Its core consisted of politicians such as the SPD's Kurt Schumacher, who had been prominent in centrist or left-wing parties (including communist) during the Weimar Republic. But the bulk of the new political elite were newcomers who started their political careers during the immediate postwar years and who could not have been involved in the Nazi regime because of their youth (Zapf, 1965, 148; Zelinsky, 1979).

The conditions in which reconstruction of the party system took place not only brought a substantially new group of politicians to power but also encouraged fundamental changes in the roles of political parties and the nature of party competition. The licensing policy resulted in the formation of a four-party system consisting of two new and two traditional parties. The founding of the Christian Democratic Party (CDU) and its Bavarian affiliate, the Christian Social Union (CSU), in 1945 was a deliberate attempt to overcome the religious cleavage between Catholics and Protestants. The formation of the Free Democratic Party (FDP) at about the same time ended the long-standing division of the liberal movement into left-wing libertarians and right-wing national liberals. Continuity in both organization and political outlook was, however, greater in the SPD, whose leaders conclusively abandoned their socialist, pacifist, and anticlerical orthodoxies only in the late 1950s. Like the SPD, the Communist Party was also able to rebuild its pre-Nazi organization. But the party failed to reestablish itself as an important political force, mainly because in the eyes of most voters it was associated with the simultaneous communist takeover in East Germany.

One of the major problems after any democratic transition is the fate of the former ruling party. The allied powers solved this by completely dismantling Nazi party organization and banning all organized Nazi-like political activities. This made it inevitable, however, that former Nazi party members would try to join other parties. Although a systematic study is still lacking, there is sufficient evidence that this never jeopardized the democratic character of the other parties, because they were able to make a firm commitment to democratic values and procedures a requirement for access to their leadership positions.[3]

The media elite and the outlets it operated were reorganized in similar fashion. Until 1949, a mandatory licensing system was in effect, and the editors who applied for a publishing license were scrutinized for possible collaboration with the Nazi regime. Initially, radio stations were controlled directly by the occupation authorities. After mid-1948, a broadcasting system run by Germans was gradually built under Allied supervision, which continued until 1955. As in the political realm, the result was a new media elite that was recruited from three different groups: journalists who had worked for newspapers that had been banned by the Nazis or that had at least retained some independent stance after 1933, public figures whose democratic credentials were beyond doubt but who had little or no previous media experience, and many young journalists who were still at early stages of their professional careers (Bausch, 1980; Meyn, 1968).

In other elite sectors, changes were less sweeping. Apart from individuals who had been prominent Nazi collaborators, no systematic purges took place, although the postwar careers of some persons were slowed temporarily. Because the overriding objective was rapid reconstruction from the war's ravages, criteria of professional expertise took precedence over considerations of political purity (Edinger, 1960; Zapf, 1965, 145 ff.). Elite continuity was greatest within the churches that had been able to retain a certain degree of autonomy throughout the years of Nazi dominance. Continuity was also pronounced in the civil service elite, where initial attempts at thorough denazification were soon abandoned in order to obtain effective administrators (Zelinsky, 1979, 226 ff.; Derlien and Lock, 1994, 62; Derlien, 1993, 328). The business organizations that had been part of the German Labor Front created by the Nazis but had otherwise carried on their activities with only minor Nazi interference were allowed to reinstate their old names and resume functioning. There was a high degree of continuity in the leadership of these business organizations between the Nazi and FRG regimes, with nearly half of all executive officers retaining their positions (Tornow, 1979, 250 ff.). Labor movement leaders, on the other hand, saw the necessity to reorganize trade unions fundamentally in order to overcome their marked weakness during the Weimar regime. A unified labor federation (*Deutscher Gewerkschaftsbund,* cf. Bernecker, 1979) was created, and its constituent unions were organized according to industries (*Industriegewerkschaften*) rather than occupations or ideological and party affiliations. Despite this organizational discontinuity, many trade union leaders from the pre-1933 period returned to elite positions.

Lewis Edinger (1960, 66–67), using data he collected on members of West German elites in 1956, summarizes the extent of elite continuity between the Nazi and FRG regimes. These data show that fewer than one-tenth of leading postwar politicians had been politically active between 1933 and 1940. By contrast, and with the exceptions of the labor union elite (0 percent) and the media elite (34 percent), at least two-fifths of the other West German elites in 1956 had worked in the same sector between 1933 and 1940.[4] These figures partly contradict critics who have charged that former Nazi officials continued to play an important role in the political life of postwar West Germany (e.g., Greiffenhagen and Greiffenhagen, 1979, 46). But this charge of an essential continuity in social structure and value orientations is certainly correct as regards the majority of West Germans. It is also true that most persons who had begun their professional careers during the Nazi period were able to continue their careers after the war. However, such career continuity is probably inevitable after the fall of any authoritarian or totalitarian regime with which the professionals who worked in public and private bureaucracies were forced to comply. The charge of Nazi continuity is, to this extent, misleading or innocuous.

Edinger's data also show that only about one-fifth of the elites in 1956 had participated in the political opposition against the Nazis. Some of those who did not participate had withdrawn to "inner exile" (*innere Emigration*) by giving up public office and working in the private sector or by forgoing careers that would have required political collaboration. But the dominant pattern had been acquiescence. To this extent, the majority of persons making up the elites of the early Federal Republic may justly be described as Nazi fellow travelers. Edinger concludes that, "[The] totalitarian elite was not succeeded by a counter-elite, but rather by a coalition of elites whose members were drawn largely from the ranks of those individuals who had been neither strong and consistent proponents nor opponents of the totalitarian regime" (Edinger, 1960, 76). According to Edinger, it is unrealistic to expect that a totalitarian elite can be replaced by a democratic counterelite (1960, 76 ff.). This is not because a totalitarian regime lacks opponents but because such opponents usually lack the experience and expertise necessary for effective elite position holding, a shortcoming many fellow travelers do not have.

The East German Elites and Regime after 1945

In Soviet-occupied eastern Germany during and after 1945, the Soviet military administration effected a systematic elite replacement, which was much more swift and extensive than that which took place after the Nazis came to power in 1933. In accordance with communist ideology, this replacement extended to the only major elite that had never been seriously bothered by the Nazis, the business elite. In all important eastern German sectors and organizations, old elites were replaced by members or loyal followers of the Socialist Unity Party (SED), which itself resulted from the forced merger of the preexisting Communist and Social Democratic parties. Criteria of expertise were of secondary importance in filling postwar elite positions, and this was a main reason why effective administrative and economic structures were rebuilt at a much slower pace than in western Germany.

Imposed from above, the new GDR elites and regime were not accepted as legitimate by most eastern Germans. The hierarchy of the SED quickly became the only channel for elite recruitment. A differentiation of elite groups by generation, societal sector, or party membership was, therefore, quite limited. In the late 1960s, Peter Christian Ludz (1968) argued that the underground, conspiratorial background of the post-1945 eastern German leadership had fostered the formation of a closed inner elite circle (*strategische Clique*) whose power rested entirely on the military power of the Soviet Union and whose members felt insecure in their positions. The elite's internal coherence derived from the uniform profession of a single ideology, which was the Marxist-Leninist variant of socialism. In the terms put forth by Dogan and Higley in chapter 1, the GDR elite was "ideocratically united."

After construction of the Berlin Wall in 1961, the GDR enjoyed a short period of economic and political consolidation. Cautious attempts at reforming the economic system led observers to expect that the generation of prewar communist leaders would be gradually replaced by a group of younger, more technocratically oriented elites. Ludz considered these new elites to be an "institutionalized counterelite." He predicted that the process of generational elite replacement would lead to a more pragmatic and successful set of economic policies such that the totalitarian state-socialist system would give way to a "consultative authoritarianism."[5] As it turned out, however, the old communist leaders held on to power, and the fledgling reform policies were soon abandoned. The GDR elite was, in fact, renewed only marginally during the regime's four-decade existence. Accordingly, the average age of its elite members increased considerably. For example, among members of the SED Central Committee, it went from forty-six during the 1960s to sixty-one during the late 1980s, and among Politburo members it went from fifty-two to sixty-five in the same period (Schneider, 1994, 78 ff.; Meyer, 1991, 151 ff.).

Scholars and other observers have debated whether the GDR regime's fall in 1989 was brought about by a revolution or by a process of collapse or implosion stemming from its sclerotic elites and organizational structures. The revolutionary interpretation is made plausible by the mass demonstrations that took place and that culminated in the communist leadership's swift exit. On the other hand, the gerontocratic and monopolistic nature of the GDR elite, whose most powerful members were completely out of touch with East German socioeconomic realities, is consistent with the thesis of a regime implosion. Because the implosion of a regime encourages widespread public protests (cf. Di Palma, 1993), the same crisis may look different from different theoretical perspectives, and this makes any firm classification of the 1989 crisis difficult.

Reunification and Elite Transfer After the 1989 Crisis

The elite changes that occurred in eastern Germany after 1989 were much more extensive than those which took place in western Germany after 1945. This was, to some extent, inevitable given the age structure of the SED elite and because state control of society had been much broader in the GDR than under the Nazi regime.[6] In particular, private business had been virtually wiped out. In GDR politics, the so-called bloc parties enjoyed only a formal independence and were in reality tied closely to the SED. Similarly, instead of independent voluntary associations, there were only the "mass organizations" created by the

SED for mobilizational purposes: the trade union federation (Allgemeiner Deutscher Gewerkschaftsbund, ADGB), cultural organizations (Kulturbund, Schriftstellerverband), the youth organization (FDJ), and a women's organization. The bloc parties and mass organizations all officially acknowledged the SED's "leading role." In elections, all candidates were included on joint candidate or "unity" lists (*Einheitslisten*) and the distribution of parliamentary seats among them was determined beforehand. Only the Protestant and Catholic churches were able to retain a limited amount of autonomy. But because the majority of East Germans were without religious affilliation, church influence was limited.

During the 1980s, a dissident movement began to form under the umbrella of the Protestant church and among artists and writers. But its opportunities for organized activity were quite restricted. Only after the numbers of legal and illegal emigrants began to swell in the late summer of 1989 did the dissidents became more assertive and start to form new parties. During the short period between autumn 1989 and spring 1990, the bloc parties and mass organizations of the GDR reorganized and claimed full autonomy from the SED. This reorganization involved the replacement of old leaders by younger ones. As new political parties and voluntary organizations proliferated, the media also claimed independence from political control. In rapid fashion, the elite structure was becoming more pluralistic.

This process of elite change accelerated throughout 1990. However, developments at both elite and mass levels were increasingly shaped by the dynamics of the reunification process. Once the border between East and West Germany was opened in November 1989, attempts to preserve an independent GDR were probably doomed, if for no other reason than that East Germany's economic condition relative to West Germany's simply did not permit the former's meaningful independence. As early as December 1989, West Germany's federal chancellor Helmut Kohl announced a ten-point plan for reunifying the two states. In East Germany, the former bloc parties and mass organizations immediately began to prepare for mergers with their West German counterparts.

It was obvious that the two states could not be reunified on equal terms; the much larger, richer, more powerful, and more stable West Germany would necessarily predominate. This quickly became apparent in the mergers of political parties and voluntary associations. In addition to their much smaller size, the East German parties and associations disposed of less well-developed organizational infrastructures, few or no funds, and they were greatly weakened by having to cope with turbulent internal conflicts triggered by the GDR regime's sudden collapse.

The sweeping elite change that took place in eastern Germany after 1945 had been accomplished by deliberately accepting a slower pace of postwar reconstruction. After 1989, in contrast, the shortage of candidates for leadership positions with the experience and expertise to work effectively within yet another new set of political and economic structures meant that vacant positions were frequently filled by western Germans with the necessary credentials. In other words, there was a widespread transfer of elites from western to eastern Germany. This was partly the consequence of the distinctive demographic configuration of Germany's division, in which western Germans outnumbered eastern Germans four to one. The result was a rapid and successful transformation of virtually all political and economic structures in eastern Germany. This widespread and probably historically unprecedented transfer of elites has often been perceived as a kind of "colonization" by western Germany. Consequently, eastern Germany today possesses only a few indigenous leaders who can serve as objects of political identification and loyalty, and this has fostered strong alienation and bitterness among many who live in that part of the country.

Data from a new study of German elites, carried out in 1995, reveal the extent of eastern German under-representation within the elites of united Germany (Büerklin and Rebenstorf, 1996). Only 11.9 percent of the more than three thousand elite persons studied lived in the GDR before 1989. The proportions of former GDR inhabitants are highest within the political elite (32 percent) and lowest in the military elite (0 percent), the business elite (0.4 percent) and the civil service elite (2.5 percent). When pre-1989 party memberships and political offices are examined, it becomes apparent that the old GDR political elite was swept away. Fewer than half of those elected to the parliaments of the five eastern German states in late 1990 had been members of the SED or one of the bloc parties before 1989, and only about one in ten had held a political office (Derlien and Lock, 1994, 75 ff.). Turnover in the political elite is equally apparent when the composition of the Party of Democratic Socialism (PDS), the successor to the SED, is examined. Only slightly more than a third (eleven out of thirty) of the PDS deputies in the present Bundestag were SED members before 1990. Another eleven deputies held political or administrative positions in the GDR, but their positions were at the local or regional level only. Most of the PDS leaders are fairly young persons who worked as teachers or academics before 1990. They come from professional backgrounds that are very different from those of the old SED leaders. On the other hand, continuity at subelite levels has been greater within the PDS than within the other parties now active in eastern Germany.

The East German dissident movement of the 1980s has not played much of a role as a recruitment reservoir for the new elites. As already noted, this movement in the GDR was especially weak, in part because, for discontented citizens of the GDR, "exit" was always a more promising alternative than "voice" (Hirschman, 1992). Veterans of the East German opposition groups that did manage to form have lacked the political experience and the organizational basis necessary for effective political parties in reunified Germany. As former dissidents, moreover, they mostly acted out of idealistic motives, without much clear idea of the kind of political system they sought and without really aspiring to elite positions. Only one of the several opposition groups in the GDR, Bündnis '90, enjoyed even modest electoral success in the reunified regime. However, its leadership soon recognized that the group could only survive by merging with the (formerly West) German Greens, and this was accomplished in 1993. A few former dissidents have found their way into the leadership of the established political parties. Others have held on to their ideals and become outspoken critics of parliamentary democracy, which in their eyes has little to do with their democratic ideals. The great majority of former dissidents, however, have given up politics in favor of professional careers (Pollack, 1995, 41).

The 1995 German elite study also reveals the composition of elites outside the political sphere (Bürklin and Rebenstorf, 1996). Given formal qualification requirements, it is not surprising that the elite transfer from western to eastern Germany was most pronounced in the civil service. In addition to the fact that most of the federal administration has remained in Bonn, where it is staffed overwhelmingly by western Germans, the proportion of western Germans among secretaries in the several eastern German state governments amounts to about one-third. In the academic and media elites located in eastern Germany, the proportion of western Germans is close to one-half. In other sectors, such as business, voluntary associations, the military, and the judiciary, no elite transfer occurred, since practically all major companies, interest associations, military bases, and federal courts have remained in the western part of the country. This may change, however, with the transfer of federal government institutions to Berlin planned for 1999.

In some sectors, one has to study a broader stratum of leadership positions in order to grasp the scope of the elite transfer that has occurred. Thus, only a fifth of the directors of East German enterprises privatized by the Treuhandanstalt[7] and only a quarter of the judges at the labor courts in the eastern German states are eastern Germans (Solga, 1996, 104). Within the bureaucracies of the eastern German states, the proportions of personnel from western Germany are espe-cially large where legal training is a job qualification, such as the minis-tries of justice, economics, and finance. They are smaller in ministries that deal mainly with technical matters, such as agriculture, environ-mental issues, and traffic management (Derlien, 1993, 328). Because the holders of these subelite and middle-level positions presumably constitute the pools from which elites will be recruited, it will be sev-eral decades until the western skewing in German elite composition is overcome.

The German Patterns and Their Implications

This review of political crises, regime change, and elite change in Ger-many leads to three major conclusions. The first concerns the extent and consequences of conflicts that derive from crises. Crises that result in regime changes usually stem from deep divisions within a society. Opposing groups of political elites normally blame one another for a crisis, and this mutual blaming is a serious liability for any new regime that follows. A crucial precondition for the success of the new political regime, especially if it is a newly created democracy, is, therefore, that the old regime has been so seriously discredited by the crisis that brought it down that it is no longer perceived as a viable political alter-native by the bulk of elite groups and the majority of citizens. This was the outcome in two of Germany's four major crises during the twenti-eth century. In 1945, there could not be the shadow of a doubt that Nazi Germany bore sole responsibility for the outbreak of World War II and for Germany's subsequent devastation. Similarly, the break-down of the GDR regime resulted from its obvious failure to govern East Germany effectively. A poor economic record, mass emigration, and widespread public protests testified to that failure. According to Guiseppi Di Palma (1993), dismal economic situations were especially delegitimizing for the state-socialist systems in Eastern Europe exactly because the promise of prosperity was so central a part of communist doctrine.

The outcomes of the 1918–19 and 1933 crises were very different be-cause of the elite disunity that existed both before and after them. Op-posing political camps offered conflicting explanations for the looming political crises and then, subsequently, for their occurrence. Samuel P. Huntington (1991) has observed that every regime change produces "losers" who indulge in nostalgia for the old system. In a similar vein, Guillermo O'Donnell (1992, 25 ff.) has argued that new democratic re-gimes encounter greater difficulties where a preceding authoritarian regime was relatively successful economically than where the preceding regime produced economic disaster. By the beginning of the twentieth century, Germany had become one of the major industrial nations of the world. The imperial regime was, therefore, widely seen as having fostered economic development and success. Because of the high costs of World War I, the country suffered a major economic setback. By 1918, industrial production had fallen to 57 percent of its prewar level. Moreover, economic recovery was achingly slow; it was only in 1927 that Germany regained its prewar level of industrial production (Bracher, Funke, and Jacobsen, 1988, 637). At the same time, governmental instability was pronounced. Elites on the right as well as the left blamed the democratic political system for the country's economic miseries. Right-wing elites denied that Germany had been one of the driving forces behind the outbreak of World War I, propagating instead the "stabbed-in-the-back" idea that it was revolution at home that caused Germany's defeat. On the left, communist and radical socialist elites blamed the capitalist economic system for the continuing miseries. They held the Social Democrats responsible for preventing necessary changes in the capitalist system and for collaborating with bourgeois forces. Thus, opposing elite explanations of the causes of the old regime's downfall and of subsequent difficulties were a central legacy of the 1918–19 political crisis, and it constituted one of the Weimar Republic's major liabilities. The legacy was erased only with the Nazis' ascendancy in 1933. Their legalistic strategy of claiming political leadership while at the same time preserving capitalist economic structures and permitting a high degree of elite continuity (except among left-wing parties and trade unions) contributed to the widespread expectation that the new Nazi regime would restore the stability and order for which German elites and their followers longed after the turbulent 1920s.

A second conclusion concerns the extent of elite change that is necessary to create a stable democratic regime. The German record suggests that a fundamental transformation of the political elite is the most crucial precondition for democratic stability. Only a new political elite can effect a clean and credible break with the old unstable and often undemocratic regime. Such an elite transformation involves creating a new and competitive party system. A previously dominant party must lose its preeminent position. The danger, of course, is that the new competitive system will be polarized, thereby ensuring governmental instability and undermining democratic legitimacy. Thus, it is necessary to avoid both extremes of continued single-party dominance and party-system polarization.

In western Germany after 1945, the presence of the Western occupying powers enforced the complete dismantling of the Nazi Party. Likewise, after 1989 in eastern Germany the SED, though it did not disappear altogether, lost its previously dominant position in several ways. It was largely discredited because of its responsibility for the GDR's poor economic performance. It was stripped of most of its substantial financial assets. And on the basis of large-scale infusions of money and personnel from western Germany, other parties soon became fully competitive. Thus, the elements of the SED that survived the 1989 crisis were forced to undertake a fundamental reorganization and find their place, in the guise of the PDS, as only one of several competing parties. We can say that in the crises of 1945 and 1989 outside help was crucial for the development of a competitive and nonpolarized party system (just as intervention from outside, in the form of Soviet occupation, was crucial to the sweeping regime and elite change in eastern Germany after 1945).

The third conclusion concerns the recruitment bases of new elites after democratization. The German experience of two transitions from totalitarian to democratic regimes (first from the Nazi regime to the FRG regime in western Germany and then from the state-socialist regime in eastern Germany to the reunified German state) confirms Edinger's (1960) observation that totalitarian regimes effectively prevent the development of a counterelite that is capable of running a country after the fall of such a regime. Opponents of a totalitarian regime are normally too weak and too politically inexperienced to constitute an important recruitment base for a posttotalitarian elite. Instead, the members of the new elite must come predominantly from the "grey zone" of individuals who were neither important leaders nor strong opponents of the totalitarian regime (Baylis, 1995, 10). As Edinger observes, in the wake of a totalitarian regime, extensive elite transformation is only possible in two ways: either by replacing existing local elites with "foreigners" or through extensive socioeconomic dislocation (Edinger, 1960, 80). Elite change in eastern Germany occurred in both ways. After 1945, the Nazi elite was completely replaced, amid total economic ruin and dislocation, by communist loyalists who mostly lacked the expertise needed to run complex organizations and who could therefore cling to power only by constructing and perpetuating another totalitarian regime. After 1989, elite transformation was accomplished through a massive transfer of "foreign" elites from western Germany. This latter process was, however, almost certainly a historical exception, and thus it cannot serve as a model for many countries.

Notes

1. The following are the major studies dealing with German elites that are based on systematically collected data: Zapf (1965) for the period 1919–69; Best (1988, 1989) for the period 1867–1933; Edinger (1960) for 1945; Hoffmann-Lange (1992) for the period 1968–81; and Bürklin and Rebenstorf (1997) for 1995. Additionally, the historical analysis by Bendix (1978) includes scattered evidence on German elites before World War I. Ralf Dahrendorf's (1967) well-known analysis of German elite structure is entirely based on the data collected by Wolfgang Zapf, who was his student, but it presents more sweeping generalizations about the changing character of German elites from national unification in 1871 until the early 1960s.

2. Among the constitutional factors, the excessive proportionality of the electoral law and the emergency powers of the president were of primary importance.

3. It is not known if this commitment was always sincere, and resulted from a true conversion, or if only lip service was paid to the altered situation. But this seems to be of only minor importance, because the postwar generation of party leaders were committed democrats. Moreover, as the parties became consolidated, a turn back towards nondemocratic politics became increasingly unlikely.

4. The numbers for the war years are smaller, since about one-tenth of the elites had served in the military between 1944 and 1945. Therefore, 1940 was taken as the year of reference.

5. As Higley, Kullberg, and Pakulski (1996, 135–37) have observed, an elite transformation of this kind did in fact occur in Hungary during the 1970s and 1980s, and it facilitated a relatively smooth transition to a democratic regime during 1989–90 (see also Jacek Wasilewski's discussion in chapter 7).

6. This is not to say that the GDR was more repressive than the Nazi regime, which in fact it was not. In the GDR, as in other Eastern European communist regimes, political repression was considerably relaxed during the 1980s, and a certain amount of political criticism was tolerated (cf. Di Palma, 1993; Higley, Kullberg, and Pakulski, 1996).

7. The Treuhandanstalt was a public agency created in 1990 to serve as a supervisory body for all state-owned enterprises of the former GDR. Its main purpose was to oversee the privatization of eastern German industry, finance corporations, and commercial enterprises by negotiating contracts with private buyers. It existed until the end of 1994, by which time its task had been largely accomplished.

References

Baum, Rainer, C. 1981. *The Holocaust and the German Elite*. Totowa N. J.: Rowman and Littlefield.

Bausch, Hans. 1980. *Rundfunkpolitik nach 1945. Erster Teil.* Munich: Deutscher Taschenbuch Verlag.

Baylis, Thomas A. 1995. "East German Leadership after Unification: The Search for Voice." Paper presented at the Fifth Conference of the East German Studies Group, Stanford University, November.

Bendix, Reinhard. 1978. *Kings or People. Power and the Mandate to Rule.* Berkeley: University of California Press.

Bernecker, Walther L. 1979. "Die Neugründung der Gewerkschaften in den Westzonen 1945–1949." In *Vorgeschichte der Bundesrepublik Deutschland*, ed. Josef Becker, Theo Stammen, and Peter Waldmann, 261–92. Munich: Wilhelm Fink Verlag.

Best, Heinrich. 1988. "Politische Modernisierung und parlamentarische Führungsgruppen in Deutschland, 1867–1918." *Historical Social Research* 13 (April): 5–74.

———. 1989. "Mandat ohne Macht: Strukturprobleme des deutschen Parlamentarismus, 1867–1933." In *Politik und Milieu. Wahl- und Elitenforschung im historischen und interkulturellenVergleich*, ed. Heinrich Best, 175–222. St. Katharinen, Ger.: Scripta Mercaturae Verlag.

Blackbourn, David and Geoff Eley. 1985. *The Peculiarities of German History.* Oxford: Oxford University Press.

Bracher, Karl Dietrich, Manfred Funke, and Hans-Adolf Jacobsen, eds. 1988. *Die Weimarer Republik, 1918–1933.* Düsseldorf: Droste Verlag.

Bürklin, Wilhelm. 1996. "Einstellungen und Wertorientierungen ost-und westdeutscher Eliten 1995: Gesellschaftliches Zusammenwachsen durch Integration der Elite?" In *Politische Einstellungen und politisches Verhalten im Transformationsprozeß.* ed. Oscar W. Gabriel. Opladen: Leske + Budrich.

Bürklin, Wilhelm, and Hilke Rebenstorf. 1996. "Die Eliten sind noch nicht zusammengewachsen." *Arbeitgeber* 13/14: 427–31.

———. 1997. *Eliten in Deutschland.* Opladen, Ger.: Leske + Budrich.

Dahrendorf, Ralf. 1967. *Society and Democracy in Germany.* New York: Doubleday.

Derlien, Hans-Ulrich. 1993. "German Unification and Bureaucratic Transformation." *International Political Science Review* 14: 319–34.

Derlien, Hans-Ulrich, and Stefan Lock. 1994. "Eine neue politische Elite? Rekrutierung und Karrieren der Abgeordneten in den fünf neuen Landtagen." *Zeitschrift für Parlamentsfragen* 1 (April): 61–94.

Diller, Ansgar. 1980. *Rundfunkpolitik im Dritten Reich.* Munich: Deutscher Taschenbuch Verlag.

Di Palma, Giuseppe. 1993. "Democratic Transitions: Puzzles and Surprises from West to East." In *Research on Democracy and Society I: Democratization in Eastern and Western Europe*, ed. Frederick D. Weil, 27–50. Greenwich, Conn.: JAI Press.

Edinger, Lewis J. 1960. "Post-Totalitarian Leadership: Elites in the German Federal Republic." *American Political Science Review* 54 (April): 58–82.

Greiffenhagen, Martin, and Sylvia Greiffenhagen. 1979. *Ein schwieriges Vaterland. Zur Politischen Kultur Deutschlands.* Munich: List.

Higley, John, Judith Kullberg, and Jan Pakulski. 1996. "The Persistence of Post-communist Elites." *Journal of Democracy* 7 (April): 133–47.

Hirschman, Albert O. 1992. "Abwanderung, Widerspruch und das Schicksal der Deutschen Demokratischen Republik." *Leviathan* 20: 330–58.

Hoffmann-Lange, Ursula. 1992. *Eliten, Macht und Konflikt in der Bundesrepublik.* Opladen, Ger.: Leske + Budrich.

Huntington, Samuel P. 1991. *The Third Wave: Democratization in the Late Twentieth Century.* Norman: University of Oklahoma Press.

Lepsius, M. Rainer. 1978. "From Fragmented Party Democracy to Government by Emergency Decree and National Socialist Takeover: Germany." In *The Breakdown of Democratic Regimes: Europe*, ed. Juan J. Linz and Alfred Stepan, 34–79. Baltimore: Johns Hopkins University Press.

Ludz, Peter Christian. 1968. *Parteielite im Wandel.* Opladen, Ger.: Westdeutscher Verlag.

Meyer, Gerd. 1991. *Die DDR-Machtelite in der Ära Honecker.* Tübingen: A. Francke Verlag.

Meyn, Hermann. 1968. *Massenmedien in der Bundesrepublik Deutschland.* Berlin: Colloquium Verlag.

O'Donnell, Guillermo. 1992. "Transitions, Continuities, and Paradoxes." In *Issues in Democratic Consolidation*, ed. Scott Mainwaring, Guillermo O'Donnell, and J. Samuel Valenzuela, 17–56. Notre Dame: University of Notre Dame Press.

Pollack, Detlev. 1995. "Was ist aus den Bürgerbewegungen und Oppositionsgruppen der DDR geworden?" *Aus Politik und Zeitgeschichte* B40/41: 34–45.

Sartori, Giovanni. 1976. *Parties and Party Systems. A Framework for Analysis.* Cambridge: Cambridge University Press.

Schneider, Eberhard. 1994. *Die politische Funktionselite der DDR.* Opladen, Ger.: Westdeutscher Verlag.

Solga, Heike. 1996. "Der Elitenimport nach Ostdeutschland: Transformationstypen und Veränderungen in der Elitenrekrutierung." In *Zwischenbilanz der Wiedervereinigung*, ed. Martin Diewald and Karl-Ulrich Mayer, 89–109. Opladen, Ger.: Leske + Budrich.

Tornow, Ingo. 1979. "Die deutschen Unternehmerverbände, 1945–1950: Kontinuität oder Diskontinuität?" In *Vorgeschichte der Bundesrepublik Deutschland*, ed. Josef Becker, Theo Stammen, and Peter Waldmann, 235–60. Munich: Wilhelm Fink Verlag.

Zapf, Wolfgang. 1965. *Wandlungen der deutschen Elite.* Munich: Piper.

Zelinsky, Ulrich. 1979. "Bedingungen und Probleme der Neubildung von Führungsgruppen in Deutschland 1945–1949." In *Vorgeschichte der Bundesrepublik Deutschland*, ed. Josef Becker, Theo Stammen, and Peter Waldmann, 217–33. Munich: Wilhelm Fink Verlag.

9

Japan: The Elite Legacies
of Meiji and World War II

Hiromitsu Kataoka

In its modern history, Japan has experienced two crises that led to re-gime changes, and both of them involved fundamental elite transfor-mations. The first crisis began with the surprising appearance of the black ships of the western powers off Japan's closed shores during the 1850s. The threat of foreign invasion triggered a deep power struggle between guardians of the status quo and reformers, a struggle that amounted to civil war. The crisis culminated in the overthrow of the feudalistic Tokugawa Shogunate regime by leaders of the lower samurai-warrior class allied with some feudal lords and court nobles who called for a return to a regime under the revered authority of an emperor. The Meiji Restoration of 1868 recreated such an imperial regime, albeit one that was bent on rapid economic and military modernization.

The second crisis occurred in 1945 with Japan's total defeat in World War II. The magnitude of this defeat was unequaled in the country's recorded history. The regime that resulted from it manifested Japan's forced acceptance of the Potsdam Declaration's promises of political freedom and democracy. Although this new regime was basically im-posed by external occupying forces, it entailed a fundamental reorga-nization of elites. This chapter examines the interconnected political crisis, regime change, and elite transformation at the end of World War II and considers how this upheaval shaped Japan's subsequent politics. In order to do this, however, we must first take a brief look at the regime and elite configurations that preceded and contributed to the 1945 crisis.

Elites and the Imperial Regime, 1868–1945

The Meiji Restoration of 1868 was a revolutionary event because it sought to build a modern unified national state strong enough to stave off western domination by overcoming feudalistic parochialism and stagnation. But the Restoration was simultaneously reactionary, in that it sought to legitimize this modernizing effort by invoking the ancient authority of an emperor. The trauma of the foreigners' black ships and the threat of foreign invasion were yoked to a mythology about the emperor's ancient and divine origins to create an intense national identity and mobilization.

In seeking to inspire nationalist sentiments among a population that was being freed from feudal class distinctions, the Meiji regime proclaimed the twin goals of "National Wealth and Power" and "Industrialization and Development," and it made state bureaucrats the principal agents of modernization. Yet the victorious Meiji leaders could not readily agree about how to organize the new regime. Discussions about its constitutional form continued until 1881, when a leading court noble, Tomomi Iwakura, successfully persuaded many of the Meiji leaders and their lieutenants to adopt the Prussian form of a constitutional monarchy. The most vehement advocate of a parliamentary system of government along British lines, Okuma Shigenobu, was effectively excluded from the final constitutional deliberations. As a consequence, the principle that a constitutional monarch must be responsible to a freely elected parliament was altered to accommodate the idea of an emperor who ruled by divine right.

In the Imperial Constitution of 1889, all government powers were viewed as flowing in principle from the divine and virtuous person who was emperor (Shima, 1992). Ministers of state, including the prime minister, were to be appointed by and responsible to the emperor, who was above any earthly authority and who, therefore, merely received advice about questions of rulership. An elected House of Representatives was established in the Imperial Diet as a response to popular demands for political representation, but it played no role in constituting cabinets and governments, and it could not overthrow them through no-confidence votes. Governments were, therefore, free to be as autocratic as they wished, needing to justify their actions only to the emperor.

Reflecting the Meiji Restoration's ambiguously revolutionary and reactionary character, a two-tier structure of elites emerged. One tier consisted of the active political elites who were engaged in governing and decision making, the other consisted of more or less honorific, privileged court nobles and feudal lords who exercised little practical political power but who constituted an aristocracy charged with defending the imperial household. Although they did not often participate directly in political decision making that affected the course of Japan's development, these aristocratic elites could influence decisions through the House of Lords and the Privy Council, their two citadels. The tier of active political elites was connected to the aristocratic tier by a system for ennobling the distinguished Meiji revolutionary leaders and their immediate successors, as well as leaders who contributed meritoriously to the state. A body of distinguished elders (*genro*) formed the core of the aristocratic elites and advised the emperor in his choice of prime ministers.

The tier of political elites who were able to exert regular influence on government decisions included persons and groups both inside and outside the government. The chief insider groups were the prime ministers and other ministers of state, as well as bureaucratic and military leaders. In their efforts to build national power, these governmental or state elites became more and more autocratic and unresponsive to popular demands for democratization. The political elites outside immediate governing circles consisted of business leaders and intellectuals. Some intellectuals assisted governmental leaders as advisers and experts, but the bulk of them formed counterelites demanding restraints upon autocratic power wielding. A significant number of parliamentarians began their careers in the counterelite camp. Some counterelite persons and groups eventually accepted the imperial regime and swore fidelity to the emperor, explaining that, after all, his political role was essentially nominal. But in general, the counterelites remained hostile to the regime, though their calls for greater democracy served only to push the governmental-state elites in ever more autocratic and reactionary directions.

Because modernization and industrialization were the overriding priorities, and because governmental and bureaucratic elites were the principal agents of these processes, they clearly had the upper hand. As early as 1880, the government began to privatize state-owned factories, shipyards, and mines while retaining responsibility for developing the infrastructure necessary to an industrializing society. This enabled giant industrial and financial conglomerates (*Zaibatsu*) to thrive by buying government-owned assets cheaply. The enormous wealth and economic power the Zaibatsu rapidly accumulated meant that government leaders could not easily ignore them. But as commoners, Zaibatsu owners and managers received little official deference. Heads of Zaibatsu families were ennobled only to the level of barons, the lowest aristocratic rank. Only one Zaibatsu leader, Eiichi Shibusawa, was granted the higher rank of viscount in recognition of his wide business leadership.

Within the political elite, prime ministers were at the apex of governmental power. There were twenty-nine prime ministers between the introduction of cabinet government in 1885 and the end of World War II. The first five were close associates of the Meiji revolutionary leaders, and they had already established themselves as important political figures before 1885. These five men rotated in the prime ministership until 1901 and even later. Of the remaining twenty-four prime ministers, two were court nobles, five were former bureaucrats, four were parliamentarians, and fully thirteen were military leaders (seven army generals and six navy admirals). A few of these military leaders were chosen because they hailed from the local fiefs (*han*) of the illustrious Meiji revolutionaries. A few others were chosen because of their proven statesmanship. But in general, the selection of military leaders as prime ministers reflected the military's takeover of the cabinet.

Professional political leaders were adept at persuasion and intrigue, while the heads of Zaibatsu families possessed great wealth and economic power. Bureaucratic and military leaders, by contrast, were institutional elites in the sense that their eminence and influence depended upon the incumbency of strategic posts in large organizations of national importance. This enabled them to mobilize and deploy organizational resources and information. The bureaucratic and military elites came mainly from the former samurai-warrior class. With the construction of a universal system of education, however, meritocratic processes gradually displaced ascriptive practices in elite recruitment, so that the bureaucratic and military elites increasingly attracted young and ambitious persons from every nook and corner of Japanese society, irrespective of social origins. This more open system of social and occupational mobility enhanced national unity (Passin, 1965, 55 ff.), and it tended to institutionalize a significant degree of elite circulation.

At first, the military elite was content merely to influence, or if necessary circumvent, cabinet decisions and government policies by advising the emperor directly about military promotions and the choice of top commanders. This back-door channel to the emperor enabled military leaders to veto and otherwise influence the selection of cabinet ministers responsible for the army and navy and to have considerable influence on the making and remaking of cabinets more broadly. After 1937 and the outbreak of war with China, however, military leaders took overt control of the cabinet. In 1941, General Hideki Tojo became prime minister and merged the army and interior portfolios into his prime ministerial position. This enabled him to order the attack on

Pearl Harbor on December 8, 1941, and to align Japan with Germany and Italy in World War II.

The war was presented to the Japanese people as a sacred struggle that was vital for the nation's survival in the face of dire threats by the Allied powers and in cooperation with all the peoples of Asia. This portrayal played on traumatic memories of imminent foreign conquest during the years before the Meiji Restoration. Obsessed with avoiding such a conquest, Japan had long bent its energies to acquiring the wealth and military power that would allow it to compete with foreign powers on an equal footing. Through a successful war with China in 1894–95 and an even more spectacular victory over Russia in 1904, the Japanese had gained much confidence and a sense of national identity amounting to xenophobic nationalism.

Yet, the demands for democratization awakened by the Meiji Restoration never disappeared entirely. Indeed, they were to some extent realized during the so-called Taisho democracy of the 1920s, when male suffrage was made universal and electoral competitions between parties became central to politics. In that same period, however, disputes with foreign powers over control of Manchuria and foreign demands for arms reduction fueled the Japanese obsession with avoiding foreign subjugation. With the rise of ultranationalism during the turbulent 1930s, the Japanese people were gradually persuaded that invading and colonizing other East Asian countries was essential to avoid foreign conquest. Swayed by constant military preachments that the war that began in 1941 was inevitable, the Japanese people were easily mobilized for the cataclysmic struggle.

Foreign Conquest, Political Crisis, and Regime Change in 1945

For Japan, World War II was a disaster virtually from the start, though it lasted four years. Scarce resources were quickly exhausted, and social life was thoroughly undermined. Suffering serious food and many other shortages, the Japanese people nevertheless prepared in early 1945 for a final defense of the homeland, even by honing bamboo spears. Thus, the emperor's unprecedented radio broadcast on August 15, 1945, following the atomic bombing of Hiroshima and Nagasaki, announcing that Japan would surrender came as a complete shock. The military government unconditionally accepted the Potsdam Declaration, which stipulated that the country would be occupied by Allied Forces until a civilian government could be established and freely endorsed by the Japanese people.

Except for Okinawa, which had already been conquered by the

United States and brought under its direct military rule, Japan escaped the fate of being further divided territorially. Because the United States decided to rule Japan indirectly, the country also retained the ability to form its own government, though national sovereignty was vested in the Supreme Commander, Allied Powers (SCAP). The United States appointed General Douglas MacArthur as supreme commander, and he was empowered to issue interim directives without consulting the Far Eastern Advisory Commission specified by the Potsdam Declaration. In this manner, Japan was controlled militarily until the San Francisco Peace Treaty took effect in April 1952.

General MacArthur was determined to demilitarize and democratize Japan as thoroughly as possible in order to make the country pacific and unthreatening to the United States and the rest of the world. Demobilization of the armed forces was completed by mid-October 1945, although arrests of alleged war criminals continued for several more months. Incrementally over the next several years, the secret police were abolished, restraints on political, civil, and religious freedoms were lifted, political prisoners were released, electoral reforms were instituted, the suffrage was extended to women, an autonomous labor movement was encouraged, and reforms in land ownership and the education system were instituted.

The need to revise the Imperial Constitution of 1889, which was technically still in effect, loomed large if Japan was to be entirely reconstructed along democratic lines. Political leaders who had survived the war and who were not prosecuted under Allied occupation became preoccupied with the question of how to reconstruct the political system while keeping the emperor at its head. Circumstances were not favorable for this project, however. On January 1, 1946, the emperor made a declaration in which he denied his own divinity, and in so doing he gained MacArthur's sympathy. Nevertheless, MacArthur rejected the guidelines political leaders presented for reforming the constitution in ways that would retain the emperor as ruler while making cabinet ministers responsible to a Diet with strengthened powers. MacArthur ordered his own staff to draft a new constitution, and this was done in the space of a week. The Japanese government had no alternative but to accept the American draft, altering it only in small details. The final draft, in which the emperor was deprived of all power and relegated to a strictly symbolic role, was to be adopted in accordance with the procedures for constitutional revision contained in the Imperial Constitution. In the course of debates in the House of Lords of the still extant old Diet, this discontinuity with the imperial regime was hotly disputed. But political leaders hurried to adopt the new constitution, lest MacArthur and his staff judge them as hostile and intransigent (Miyamura, 1995).

Article 9 of the constitution adopted on May 3, 1947, renounced war as a means for solving international disputes, as well as the maintenance of armed forces and other war-making capacities. In his memoirs, MacArthur writes that it was not he but Prime Minister Shidehara Kijuro who proposed the insertion of this article (MacArthur, 1964). Nevertheless, it was widely believed that in a meeting with Shidehara, MacArthur suggested the article and Shidehara agreed with it as a tradeoff for retaining the emperor. Shidehara was chosen as the second postwar prime minister, after Prince Higashikuni, because as foreign minister before the outbreak of war he had urged peaceful relations with the United States. Nevertheless, he was an ardent supporter of the old imperial regime, despite its autocratic and militaristic bent. In his memoirs, Shidehara (1951) discloses that after the war he was so convinced of the necessity for peace that he did not feel that he was forced to accept Article 9. This somewhat contorted reasoning was characteristic not only of governmental and other elites but of ordinary citizens. Devastated by the war, without self-confidence or a sense of direction, most Japanese welcomed the new constitution in spite of various qualms and reservations about its details.

In step with the constitutional reforms, SCAP proceeded to purge from public office all those who had been closely associated with prosecuting the war. It disbanded the Zaibatsu groups, and it undertook a mass reeducation program aimed at inculcating democratic values. The purge of elites and cadres who prosecuted the war began in early January 1946, and it was subsequently carried out in cooperation with investigative committees staffed by Japanese personnel whom SCAP judged trustworthy. In the end, a total of 210,288 persons were purged. The elite and cadre groups to which these persons belonged are shown in table 9.1. Not included in table 9.1, however, are 6,001 members of the disbanded secret police, 121,878 persons removed from teaching and university positions, and 21,195 leaders and activists in labor unions and organizations associated with the imperial regime. An additional 272,590 persons were prohibited from standing for election to mayoral and other local positions and from taking any other prominent roles in local communities. The purge ended in May 1948, and those imprisoned were gradually released. In 1950, however, SCAP again used its power to purge 12,253 persons from positions connected with the Communist Party. Altogether, some 640,000 persons were purged from Japanese public life after 1945 (Momose, 1995, 121).

As a result of this sweeping purge, which necessarily involved mistakes and injustices, Japanese elites were greatly altered. The old mili-

TABLE 9.1
Japanese Political Elite Groups and Cadres Purged after 1945
(N = 210,288)

Sector	Number	Percentage
Military officers	167,035	79.4
Bureaucrats	1,809	0.9
Politicians	34,892	16.6
Ultranationalists	3,438	1.6
Businessmen	1,898	0.9
Journalists	1,216	0.6

Source: Masuda (1995, 109).

tary elite disappeared entirely, with two dozen of its top leaders being tried for war crimes and sentenced to death or life imprisonment by the Tokyo war crimes tribunal. The political elite's makeup changed substantially, and the business elite was quite severely affected not only by the purge but also by the disbanding of Zaibatsu groups. It is estimated that about two thousand business leaders failed to retain their top-level positions after the war. The bureaucratic elite was, however, comparatively unscathed. Most of the small number of purged bureaucrats had worked in the Ministry of the Interior, where they were closely connected to the secret police. The purge of bureaucrats in other ministries was confined mainly to those who had directed war mobilization programs, a relatively small number. Of the major elites, in other words, only the bureaucrats survived as a group. Overall, the postwar purge of elites and cadres dispelled the militaristic atmosphere of prewar and wartime Japan, and it contributed to a fresh democratic start. The purge opened many elite positions to new persons unconnected with the imperial regime or the war, and in this way it rejuvenated the elites. To be sure, some purged politicians later returned to public life as parliamentarians or other political officeholders, but the prewar business leaders and journalists were substantially replaced and the military elite was eradicated.

Some foreign observers of the political changes feared that Japan would revoke the new constitution as soon as it regained independence (Miyamura, 1995). Some Japanese governmental leaders apparently did view acceptance of the new constitution as little more than a maneuver aimed at achieving international approval and thus early independence (Nakamura, 1995). By 1952, when the San Francisco Peace Treaty took effect, however, the new democratic regime was so well established that no significant group was willing to seek its overthrow. Ideologically, Japanese politics were then clearly divided between right and left. With support by moderate and independent groups in the Diet, conservative parties dominated the government initially. But when conservative leaders started to talk about revising the 1947 constitution, the moderates and independents threw their support to the Socialists. In 1956, some proponents of constitutional revision within the newly formed Liberal Democratic Party (LDP) were successful in passing a law that established a Research Council on the Constitution. After seven years of investigation and discussion, this council published a report that assessed in an even-handed way the pros and cons of constitutional revision. But shortly after the report appeared, the LDP lost any prospect of gaining the two-thirds parliamentary majority that was required for proposing a constitutional referendum. With this political turn of events, the divisive issue of revising the Allied-imposed constitution receded.

As a consequence of the 1945 crisis and the purges that followed it, the old two-tier structure of elites was replaced by what was in effect a single tier of competing and cooperating elite groups. At the same time, there was large elite circulation. The longer-term result has been a configuration of plural, institutionalized, and professionalized elites.

The Political Elite and Regime Change

Cabinets in the imperial regime were not responsible to the popularly elected House of Representatives, and this was a principal reason why the military elite was able to exert so much influence before and during World War II. By contrast, postwar cabinets have been directly responsible to the House, and they are strengthened by the concentration of administrative powers in the hands of ministers. In the old regime, a prime minister had been no more than *primus inter pares,* but in the new regime he is clearly the principal government leader. Despite these changes, however, the new cabinet system appears to have inherited the instability and weakness of the old system. Exactly because the Japanese prime minister has been such a preeminent figure in postwar governments, competition for the post has been intense. During the fifty-one years between 1945 and 1996, there have been twenty-four prime ministers whose average tenure in office has been about the same as that in the imperial regime. During the same half century, Great Britain has had only ten prime ministers, and West Germany had only half a dozen chancellors. Still more striking, the average tenure of other cabinet ministers has been half that of prime ministers. This is because ministerial portfolios are scarce resources that are frequently rotated in order to garner support from party factions and from coalition partners. In Italy and France, by contrast, there is greater continuity among the holders of ministerial portfolios, despite frequent changes of cabinets.

The first eight postwar prime ministers had achieved elite positions under the old regime. One had been crown prince, four were top-level bureaucrats, one was a Socialist leader, one was a prominent parliamentarian, and one a prominent journalist. Three of these men returned to national politics after being purged and then released from prison. Only two or three of them had been openly critical of the war effort; the others had for various reasons been uninvolved in prosecuting the war and thus were considered acceptable by SCAP. Of the sixteen remaining postwar prime ministers, six were previously high-level bureaucrats, and ten were leaders of parliamentary factions and parties. As Japanese politics have become more professionalized, high-level bureaucrats have found it increasingly necessary to enter parliament and join the queue of parliamentarians waiting for a shot at the prime ministership. Interestingly, the average tenure of former bureaucrats in the prime ministership has been longer than the average tenure of parliamentarians in that post.

The 1947 constitution required that a majority of cabinet members be persons elected to the Diet. The cabinets organized by Tetsu Katayama and Hitoshi Ashida during 1947–48 contained many more parliamentarians than bureaucrats. This pattern continued during the second Shigeru Yoshida cabinet, which began in 1948, although Yoshida appointed the nonelected Eisaku Sato as secretary general of his cabinet. But in his third cabinet during the early 1950s, Yoshida gave Hayato Ikeda, a novice parliamentarian with a bureaucratic background, the important Finance portfolio, and he further increased the number of former bureaucrats in the cabinet. The increased bureaucratic coloration of the cabinet made for significant political elite continuity between the old and new regimes. The principal difference was that bureaucrats first needed to obtain election to the Diet before they could gain ministerial posts.

There were several reasons for this elite continuity. First, most established and influential prewar parliamentarians were purged by SCAP, while emerging postwar parliamentarians were too young to hold ministerial positions. Second, the difficult tasks of postwar recovery and economic management placed a premium on the knowledge possessed by bureaucrats. Third, bureaucrats had shown much political dexterity in negotiating with SCAP. Fourth, because he himself had been a bureaucrat in the Foreign Service, Yoshida had a greater affinity with bureaucrats than with parliamentarians. In his *Memoir of Ten Years*

(1957), Yoshida states that he tried to mix parliamentarians and bureaucrats in order to supplement each other's skills while also training administrators politically and parliamentarians administratively. He reshuffled his cabinets regularly toward these ends. Even in Yoshida's heavily bureaucratic cabinets, however, ministers who had been bureaucrats still fell short of a majority. The pattern of heavy reliance on former bureaucrats was followed by Yoshida's successor, Ichiro Hatoyama, who fought bitterly with Yoshida and who took power from Yoshida's hands. The prevalence of former bureaucrats reached its climax during the cabinets of Prime Ministers Eisaku Sato and Hayato Ikeda, both of whom were honor student graduates of the so-called Yoshida School for training bureaucrats in politics.

When Kakuei Tanaka displaced his mentor Sato as prime minister in 1972, the tide shifted in favor of parliamentarians without bureaucratic backgrounds. Among the thirteen prime ministers who followed Tanaka, for example, there have been only four former bureaucrats, and all four spent more years in politics than in the bureaucracy. The increased prevalence of parliamentarians reflected the growing professionalization of politics and the primacy of electoral competitions. Professionalization occurred in two ways: by observing the criterion of seniority when selecting cabinet ministers and as a consequence of the increased centrality of parliamentarians in policy-making networks.

As mentioned, parliamentarians were second only to the military elite in being most affected by the postwar purge. Of the 466 parliamentarians who made up the last House of Representatives of the Imperial Diet, 381, or 82 percent, were disqualified from standing for election to the new House of Representatives in 1946 (Momose, 1995, 115). As a result of that election, novice parliamentarians accounted for 80 percent of the House, and they for the first time included thirty-nine women. However, the prewar pattern of local politicians dominating the House continued after the war, though their aggregate power was to some extent decreased. After the land reforms dictated by SCAP, however, the background of local politicians changed from that of large landowners to that of independent farmers who were organized in agricultural cooperatives. With a few exceptions, these independent farmers became strong supporters of the conservative parties, especially the LDP. There was also an abundance of bureaucrats, lawyers, journalists, and businessmen, as well as leaders of various social, labor, and agrarian movements, in the early postwar parliaments. With the increasing professionalization of politics, however, the numbers of lawyers, journalists and businessmen waned, although former bureaucrats managed to remain prominent numerically. But former bureaucrats have had to compete on an equal footing with local politicians, members of parliamentarians' staffs, and second-generation parliamentarians. The sons and sons-in-law of parliamentarians have significant advantages in this competition, because elections are fought with personal rather than party organizations of supporters, and these are frequently transferred from one generation to the next. If anything, this pattern will be reinforced by the system of smaller constituencies that Japan is now implementing.

The Bureaucratic Elite and Regime Change

To use a term employed by Max Weber (1958, 100), the prewar Japanese bureaucracy was "autokephalic" in character. An *autokephalic* bureaucracy is one that is headed by persons who are promoted through the bureaucratic hierarchy and who are, therefore, homogeneous with the bureaucrats they lead. Because the emperor appointed prime ministers and other ministers of state, irrespective of party strength in the House of Representatives of the Imperial Diet, it was not unusual to select ministers of state from among the highest-ranking bureaucrats, and in this respect there was no clear distinction between the cabinet and the top echelon of the bureaucracy. This pattern became entrenched after Tokyo University was reshaped into the Imperial University of Tokyo in 1886 with a mandate to train the most talented persons to meet the state's needs. A higher civil service examination was created the following year. In 1899 it was ordained that the vice minister (or undersecretary) and bureau chief of each ministry had to be chosen from among those who had passed the higher civil service examination. Before 1899, it had been possible to appoint vice ministers and bureau chiefs politically, using a government's discretionary powers. From 1899, however, such political appointments were banned.

Just after the turn of the century, graduates of the Imperial University of Tokyo began to appear among bureau chiefs, and after about 1910 they could be found among vice ministers, as well. After a few more years, Tokyo graduates were appointed as ministers. During the heyday of party politics in the 1920s, a sizable number of parliamentarians were also appointed as ministers, but they rarely constituted a cabinet majority. In 1926, Reijiro Wakatsuki became the first graduate of the Imperial University of Tokyo to become prime minister after pursuing a bureaucratic career, and he was followed by Osachi Hamaguchi in 1929, Koki Hirota in 1936, and Kichiro Hiranuma in 1939. Thus, the autokephalic bureaucracy became a major force in the old regime, and the ability to sustain its autokephalic character was one measure of its power. It needs to be added that bureaucrats, of course, had to display strong personal leadership as well as much political dexterity before they could be appointed prime minister.

The Public Service Decree of 1877 mandated that bureaucrats were the emperor's servants. While in Europe servants of the Crown were in reality servants of the state. Because the corporate nature of the state was distinct from the Crown, Japanese bureaucrats continued to think of themselves and be thought of as servants of the divinely ordained and virtuous emperor until the end of World War II. The idea that the emperor was merely an organ of the state was officially rejected as incompatible with his divinity. Although they were recruited from every part of Japan according to meritocratic procedures, bureaucrats were endowed with titles and honors that made them into a privileged stratum distinct from ordinary citizens. The latter were encouraged to respect and defer even to lower-ranking bureaucrats. Acting as modernizing agents and tutelary stewards in accordance with Confucian principles, the bureaucrats believed that they ruled Japan on behalf of the emperor.

Immediately following the Meiji Restoration, bureaucrats played the roles of transitional planners and developers of the modernizing nation-state. But as the Meiji regime took firm root, bureaucrats became not only more arrogant but also more conservative politically. Because their educations were primarily legalistic, they were assiduous in avoiding misapplications of the law. After the war in Manchuria during 1931 and the assassination of Prime Minister Tsuyoshi Inukai by disgruntled naval officers on May 15, 1932, a group of so-called New Bureaucrats who were sympathetic to the military leadership emerged. But they were destined to be replaced by another group, called the Renovating Bureaucrats, after the military revolt and further assassinations of government leaders in Tokyo in February 1936 and the outbreak of war with China in 1937.

The Renovating Bureaucrats were technocrats committed to total mobilization and control of what amounted to a war economy. They characterized themselves as more creative and innovative than the bureaucrats they displaced. They were critical of the profit motives of Zaibatsu groups, and they demanded a separation between business ownership and management along with a subordination of profit motives to the public goal of military preparedness. Overriding opponents, the Renovating Bureaucrats got the cabinet to adopt Guidelines for the Establishment of a New Economic System, and they steered mobilization laws through the Diet. They and their sympathizers proposed a New Bureaucratic System to replace the old and somewhat stagnated one. Nevertheless, many of the young Renovating Bureaucrats were arrested and imprisoned on suspicion of communist sympathies because of their opposition to profit motives. Their Planning Office citadel, which was directly responsible to the cabinet, was eventually absorbed into a new Ministry of Military Supply (Kataoka, 1996).

One element of the regime change that began in 1945 was replacing this autokephalic bureaucracy with a heterokephalic one to be headed by ministers chosen from among parliamentarians. Elected by the sovereign people, these new ministers were to be distinct from the bureaucrats, though, as noted, the constitution of 1947 required that only a majority of cabinet ministers come from the Diet. At first many academics and business leaders were appointed ministers. But with the professionalization of politics it became increasingly difficult to have nonparliamentarian ministers of state because, as also noted, the post of minister became an important resource in securing political support. Following Max Weber, changing the bureaucracy's character from autokephalic to heterokephalic meant that it could be turned into an instrument for serving a democratic regime. But the post-1945 change turned out to be less sweeping than was intended. For one thing, newly elected parliamentarians lacked the know-how necessary for directing and managing the bureaucracy, not to mention actually initiating policies. For another, the vice administrative ministers who stood next to the presiding ministers were placed in the general category of civil servants instead of the "political" category consisting of ministers of state and vice parliamentary ministers.

Power to appoint vice administrative ministers and bureau chiefs was given to ministers in the new regime. But they rarely had a chance to use this power, because the order of promotion among top-level civil servants was already firmly established by an esoteric process of selection operated by incumbent and former vice administrative ministers and chiefs of the cabinet secretariat. In this process, a given year's cohort of recruits to the bureaucracy is promoted more or less equally until, after about twenty years, its members reach the level of division chief, at which time a more severe selection process begins. Although some ministers have ignored this formal system and promoted their favorite bureaucrats, as soon as such defiant ministers leave their posts the formal system returns, almost as though it had remained undisturbed and unchallenged. In this respect, there have been important vestiges of the old autokephalic bureaucracy in the new postwar regime. Although bureaucrats are politicized by working with ministers hailing from parliament and by mobilizing support for ministers' policies, they essentially cohabit with their political superiors while keeping their own civil service domain largely free from political intervention (Kataoka, 1996).

The bureaucratic elite thus not only survived the regime change, but it has retained its self-consciously tutelary and stewardlike role. Its members still believe that only they can judge the public interest correctly. Whereas they formerly ruled Japan on behalf of and as the agent of the emperor, during the postwar period they have ruled the country on behalf of and as the agent of the people. But because "the people" lack an effective voice, the power of the bureaucratic elite has not been much diminished.

In the process of managing postwar recovery, the bureaucratic elite made heavy use of regulations and rationing that had been used to manage the wartime economy. In his book *The Regime of the 1940s,* Yukio Noguchi (1995) observes that the postwar regime was a continuation of the wartime one because administrative techniques remained largely unchanged. But we must be careful not to overlook the fact that the totally controlled wartime economy was replaced by a free market economy at an early point after 1945. Under this free market economy, regulations and rationing could not be employed as systematically and intensively, and their impacts were accordingly more moderate and indirect. Indicative economic planning after the war was quite different from imperatively coordinated wartime planning. Moreover, regulations and rationing measures were discarded incrementally as economic recovery progressed.

Noguchi also argues that the postwar bureaucratic elite has been the direct descendant of the Renovating Bureaucrats. Many postwar bureaucrats have confessed that they also believe this to be the case. But the Renovating Bureaucrats flowered in the fertile soil of a war economy, and they were destined to disappear with the war's end. As mentioned above, moreover, younger Renovating Bureaucrats were suspected of communist leanings and had been ousted from government before and during the war, while top-level Renovating Bureaucrats were purged starting in 1945. It is thus quite difficult to find any remnant of them among the postwar bureaucratic elite. After the purge was abandoned, some went into politics and others became economic analysts or commentators, but none returned to bureaucratic posts. After the war's end, to be sure, one member of the Renovating group, Hayato Ikeda, was made vice administrative minister of Finance. But when the Renovating Bureaucrats had held sway before and during the war, Ikeda was in a rather lowly position from which he could have observed the top Renovating Bureaucrats in the Finance Ministry only from a considerable distance. Another former bureaucrat in the Finance Ministry, Takeo Fukuda, was part of the entourage of Nobusuke Kishi, one of the top Renovating Bureaucrats. But it was, in fact, only after Kishi was freed from imprisonment as a war criminal that the two men met each other personally for the first time. Postwar industrial and financial policies aimed at economic recovery were innovated by bureaucrats but also by economics professors such as Hiromi Arisawa and Hyoe Ohuchi. In his book *The Memoir of Ninety Years*, Takeo Fukuda (1995) confesses that bureaucrats translated the ideas of Ohuchi into concrete monetary policy during the early stage of postwar recovery.

In the immediate wake of wartime defeat, the bureaucratic elite lost its self-confidence and felt itself to be disgraced. Its members were embarrassed by SCAP's demand for radical bureaucratic reform, and they were uncertain about their future roles. Because all of them had been educated under the old regime, they were not familiar with the concept of popular sovereignty or with the idea of serving the whole people, as ordained by the new constitution. A U.S. Civil Service Mission, led by Brian Hoover, proposed to transform the prewar bureaucratic system as one of the keys to pacifying and democratizing Japan (Hoover, 1949). This proposal increased the elite's anxieties. But as postwar recovery gained speed, top bureaucrats regained their self-confidence and sense of power. They succeeded in sabotaging the Hoover mission's reform efforts, whether intentionally or unintentionally. Although a new system for classifying civil servants was adopted, the old practice of using different levels of civil service examinations was maintained. Increasingly, bureaucratic leaders began to claim that only they could judge the public interest correctly amid a citizenry that did not know how to be sovereign. In this respect, too, there was greater continuity than discontinuity between the prewar and postwar bureaucratic elite.

According to the Hoover mission, politicians were to make laws and civil servants were to implement them faithfully. This meant eliminating the former involvement of bureaucrats in making and proposing the drafts of laws, not to mention the preparation of imperial decrees. In a parliamentary regime, however, it is quite customary that a government proposes drafts of laws that are in fact prepared by civil servants. In Japan, bureaucrats have, therefore, continued to draft laws unabashed. For them, laws are indispensable instruments for intervening in society and for leading societal sectors through administrative guidelines framed under the laws. In this sense, the bureaucratic elite has altered constitutional notions about the rule of law by making laws into instruments of administration. Of course, bureaucratic leaders need more than the help of governmental leaders and parliamentarians to get laws passed. Having daily contact with parliamentarians to secure their support is one of the reasons that the bureaucratic elite has become politicized in the postwar regime.

The Business Elite and Regime Change

Although industrialization began after the Meiji Restoration under state hegemony with bureaucrats as the modernizing agents, the economic role of government remained somewhat limited until the 1930s, when military leaders and their sympathizers ushered in a command economy fit for waging war. Zaibatsu groups controlled the main economic sectors in an oligopolistic manner, but they also competed intensively with each other. In the less central economic sectors, small and medium-sized businesses flourished. Some Zaibatsu groups had originated in the Tokugawa era, and they survived the Meiji Restoration by supporting the new regime with money and the supply of armaments. Other Zaibatsu groups emerged under the imperial regime, and they established close ties with it. Each group kept good relations with one or two key government leaders and received favorable treatment in return for its support. In the successive wars with China and Russia, the Zaibatsu accumulated huge fortunes.

A Zaibatsu group was a huge conglomerate formed around a Zaibatsu family, the head of which had the entrepreneurial ingenuity to organize his own firm and find lucrative business opportunities for it. The Zaibatsu system was thus strongly personalistic, and its distinctive, idiosyncratic leaders initially constituted an informal and fluid business elite. Starting in 1890, the elite status of the most prominent Zaibatsu leaders was officially acknowledged by co-opting them into the House of Lords of the Imperial Diet. Following Japan's defeat of Russia in 1904, the organization of Zaibatsu groups became more modern, with each group consisting of a headquarters company with unlimited financial liability and several satellite or subsidiary and sub-subsidiary companies with limited liabilities. All stocks in the satellite or subsidiary companies were owned by the headquarters company, whose stocks were, in turn, totally owned by the Zaibatsu family. In this way, the capital of a Zaibatsu group was entirely closed to the market. The headquarters company controlled satellite and subsidiary companies both financially and personally by putting members of the Zaibatsu family on their boards. The Mitsui, Mitsubishi, Sumitomo, and Yasuda groups each owned a bank and had satellite companies in virtually all main economic sectors. A group such as Kawasaki controlled many companies indirectly through its bank. Still other groups were concentrated in specific economic sectors without having a bank (Suzuki, 1934).

During the 1930s, the strong profit orientation of the Zaibatsu groups came under severe attack by young and radical military officers, right-wing forces, and the Renovating Bureaucrats. After the chairman of Mitsui Unlimited was assassinated, members of Zaibatsu families started to retire from the boards of satellite and subsidiary companies, and in order to meet the need for capital with which to finance heavy industry, they began to sell their stock in those companies. The attacks on them nevertheless persisted. Shintaro Ryu, of the Asahi Newspaper group, proposed separating Zaibatsu ownership and management in order to better utilize the companies both for wartime needs and in the interest of public justice. The Renovating Bureaucrats sought to make the separation of ownership and management part of their new economic system, although they did so without success. After 1941, however, companies were grouped into "control associations," which cut across Zaibatsu group lines on an industry-by-industry basis. These control associations were formally autonomous, but they were expected to work under governmental direction according to purposes that the government ordained (Hoashi, 1941).

Despite the criticisms leveled at them, the Zaibatsu groups were heavily involved in the war effort from its outset. It was therefore not surprising that SCAP decided as early as September 1945 to disband the Zaibatsu in order to eliminate a perceived cause of the war. Two months later, SCAP dictated the disbanding of the Mitsui, Mitsubishi, Sumitomo, and Yasuda groups, and it gradually extended this treatment to a total of eighty-three groups. The headquarters companies of the groups were annihilated by having all their stock confiscated. Some satellite and subsidiary companies were also summarily divided. Other companies were left intact but were made independent of their former Zaibatsu owners. Designated members of Zaibatsu families were prohibited from serving on these companies' boards of directors. At the same time, older managers of Zaibatsu groups were purged. As a result, very young managers who had been either branch or factory chiefs in 1940 were quickly promoted to the presidencies of these companies.

Quite fortuitously, in other words, Japan underwent the kind of sweeping "managerial revolution" that James Burnham described a few years earlier (Burnham, 1941). The members of Zaibatsu families were forced into retirement. With few exceptions, the purged older managers had no chance to return to their former posts. Thus, the Japanese economy was invigorated with young and energetic leaders (Higuchi, 1953; Miyamura, 1995). Although Zaibatsu families and their headquarters companies disappeared, the former satellite and subsidiary companies kept close relations with each other through banks that escaped dismemberment.

As a result of this managerial revolution, the business elite became institutionalized in the guise of presidents and other top officials of large and crucially important companies employing major segments of the workforce and deploying vast economic resources. The power and prestige of these individuals has been enhanced by their leadership positions in industry-specific business associations, especially the four largest associations, which are harnessed into the Federation of Economic Organizations (FEO). The president of the FEO has generally been seen as the prime minister of the business world. Still, his power is institutional rather than personalistic in the fashion of the old Zaibatsu family heads. Because the business associations resemble the control associations of the war years, some historians argue that the postwar business system and its elite actually originate in the imperial regime (Okazaki and Okuno, 1995). However, whereas the old control associations tried to direct their member companies toward state-ordained goals, the postwar business associations seek to promote the more or less strictly private interests of their members and industries. Although there are certainly some similarities between the prewar and postwar business associations, they should not be exaggerated. In particular, the changed economic system within which the postwar associations function is a critical difference; there is no government plan aimed at controlling them in a totalistic way.

During the early years of the postwar regime, the business elite was involved in politics in various ways. Some business leaders were appointed as ministers of state or were advisers to the prime minister. Others stood successfully for election to the House of Representatives. As long as Japanese politics were deeply divided between proponents of socialism and capitalism, as they were during the 1950s and 1960s, business leaders were drawn ineluctably into politics. But as the free market economy strengthened, the business elite became more apolitical and peripheral to the political arena. This change preceded by several years the professionalization of politics discussed above. The prestige and power of business leaders actually increased as they become more and more apolitical and as they directed more of their attention to advisory committees located in the economic realm and also in the fields of education and welfare. Suffering from cabinet instabilities, government leaders have often relied on business leaders to legitimate particular government programs. The halo effects of endorsements by top business leaders have been invaluable for governments. Especially in implementing administrative reforms, the business elite's approval and support has been crucial. For their part, business leaders stick with their rallying cries for more privatization and deregulation, though they do not hesitate to ask governments for special favors.

Japanese Elites and Regimes in Historical Perspective

In 1943, Robert A. Brady wrote that in Japan, feudalistic carryovers, mercantilist practices, and monopoly-oriented capitalism had long gone hand in hand. He claimed that this symbiosis of an old social order and new economic and political forms made business and military expansion easier than in the Nazi streamlining of Germany (Brady, 1943, 84). He might be right. After the Meiji Restoration there emerged the two-tier elite structure consisting of active elites of political power and action and honorific elites of aristocratic privilege and influence. The active tier of elites could promote modernization and industrialization vigorously by relying on governmental power legitimized by the ancient authority of the emperor and backed up by the honorific and aristocratic tier of elites, including newly ennobled governmental and military leaders. This dual elite structure probably contributed importantly to Japan's exaggerated nationalism and military adventurism.

Governmental elites composed of prime ministers, ministers of state, top bureaucrats, and military leaders took precedence over parliamentary and business elites, not to mention other nongovernmental elites and counterelites. In a word, modernization and industrialization were imposed from above. Patron-client relations developed between some governmental leaders and some heads of Zaibatsu families, but these relations were to some extent reversed once Zaibatsu groups accumulated wealth and controlled heavy industries. On the eve of the 1904 war with Russia, bureaucrats had to ask for the help of Zaibatsu groups in selling government bonds. Kamekichi Takahashi (1966) encapsulated this relationship by saying that bureaucrats wagged the business elite's tail. Yet, the status and privileges of business elites were not so great in the eyes of government officials. After the war with Russia, military leaders, not businessmen, quickly gained the dominant position among governmental leaders.

Before and during World War II, the distance between elites and ordinary people was very great. Despite the abolition of a class system and the spread of an achievement orientation, the government followed the practice of distinguishing the elites by endowing their members with titles and privileges. In the early stage of the Meiji era, young people could have a realistic hope of attaining bureaucratic elite status by studying hard. But this hope gradually became less realistic. Military officer schools became the surest route to elite status, but only a few could expect to emerge eventually as generals or admirals. Under the imperial regime, ordinary citizens were subservient and obedient, and they formed what Gabriel Almond and Sidney Verba (1963) have termed a "subject" political culture.

With the regime change that began in the 1945 crisis, the dual elite structure was replaced by a single structure consisting of active, plural, and increasingly institutionalized elite groups. This elite transformation not only reflected the regime change and the war-induced crisis that generated it, but the transformation was also the product of more glacial social changes that accompanied the slow demise of feudal organization and the spread of democratic sentiments. As a consequence of the disappearance of the aristocratic elite tier, which had often undercut the active elites' leadership, the latter now had to lead and manage a democratized country without recourse to any authority other than the sovereign people. Whereas governments under the old regime suffered from the lack of a firm base of popular support, governments under the new postwar regime could be stable to the extent that the parties making them up enjoyed such support. But intense competitions among prospective prime ministers kept governments as unstable as before. Thus, the tenures of prime ministers were as short as before. However, there was a crucial difference, and it lay in the ability to change prime ministers peacefully and thereby to stem and survive several economic and foreign policy crises. Since the end of LDP hegemony in 1993, political instability has, if anything, increased, despite, or perhaps because of, the fact that ideological differences among the parties competing for government power have all but disappeared.

Chalmers Johnson points out that postwar Japan has been one of the "capitalist regulatory states" that have displayed a "soft authoritarianism" because it has fused in ad hoc manner the effectiveness of an absolutist state with the effectiveness of a bourgeois market (Johnson, 1995, 29 ff). In this way, he highlights continuities between the prewar and postwar regimes, albeit mediated by occupational reforms. If a capitalist regulatory state involves a regime in which the goals of society are set by bureaucrats, however, Johnson is wrong about Japan. It is true that in the current regime's early years the overriding goal was to regain prewar levels of productivity and then to catch up with Western countries' productivity levels. But unlike the prewar goals of "National Wealth and Power" and "Industrialization and Development," these postwar goals lacked any concrete measures for guiding markets and inspiring the Japanese people. Although the postwar goals may have been dictated by bureaucrats and other elites, there has been little that resembles the rational plan that Johnson imputes. The bureaucratic elite has had only a gaggle of loose strategies with which to tackle social problems as they arose. To use a term that has sometimes been applied to the British system of governance, there has at most been a "directionless consensus" among Japanese elites under the new regime. Although some westerners fear Japanese economic power, that power in fact exists only in statistics or in an abstract aggregate of wealthy business firms. There is neither the will nor a consensus among elites about how to use Japan's economic power to accomplish some new set of goals.

In the minds of most Japanese people since the 1945 crisis, business leaders have formed the most respected and prestigious elite. Politicians, by contrast, are regularly caricatured as impotent and ignorant, while bureaucrats are viewed as power usurpers. In reality, however, the business, political, and bureaucratic elites have formed a kind of iron triangle or power elite. Although business leaders profess to be apolitical, they do not hesitate to ask politicians and bureaucrats for favors, at the same time denying responsibility for economic difficulties and turning economic problems over to the politicians and bureaucrats. Thus far, bureaucrats have been willing to tackle the difficult problems caused by economic development with the support of politicians when necessary. The iron triangle connecting political, bureaucratic, and business elites is likely to break down when really large costs of policy failures come to be apportioned among the three elites, as has recently been the case in the wake of bankrupted housing finance companies. But failing this elite triangle's complete rupture, it is likely to go on drifting, directionlessly.

Democratization has shortened the distance between elites and ordinary citizens, or between leaders and followers, quite remarkably. There is no longer an unbridgeable chasm between them. Although Japan's subject culture has not as yet been replaced by a robust civic culture, democratization has had the effect of reducing the reverence and respect of ordinary people for the elites, who consequently find it more and more difficult to get their way and to lead the citizenry, especially because they must share information with the public. On the other hand, because the bureaucratic and business elites are institutionalized, politicians are professionalized, and there is substantial intraelite circulation, there has emerged an invisible or psychological gulf between elites and the mass public. The many who are unable to join one of the indispensable organizations and the many who fail to reach the top in such organizations are excluded or marginalized politically, and they tend to display much apathy and frustration. Under future but as yet unspecifiable circumstances, they may become antagonistic toward the regime. To this extent, both elite credibility and Japan's governability may confront another crisis to which some solution other than a new regime change will have to be found.

References

Almond, Gabriel A. and Sidney Verba. 1993. *The Civic Culture.* Princeton: Princeton University Press.

Brady, Robert A. 1943. *Business as a System of Power.* New York: Columbia University Press.

Burnham, James. 1941. *The Managerial Revolution.* New York: John Day.

Fukuda, Takeo. 1995. *Memoir of Ninety Years.* Tokyo: Iwanami Books, Inc.

Higuchi, Hiroshi. 1953. *The Resurgence of Zaibatsu.* Tokyo: Naigai Keizai.

Hoashi, Kei. 1941. *Theory and Practices of Control Associations.* Tokyo: Economy Press.

Hoover, Brian. 1949. *A Modern Civil Service System.* Washington D.C.: U.S. Civil Service Commission.

Johnson, Chalmers. 1995. *Japan: Who Governs? The Rise of the Developmental State.* New York: W. W. Norton.

Kataoka, Hiromitsu. 1996. *Elitology of Bureaucrats.* Tokyo: Waseda University Press.

MacArthur, Douglas. 1964. *Reminiscences.* New York: Time.

Masuda, Hiroshi. 1995. "The Impact of the Purge." In *Occupation and Reforms,* ed. Masanori Nakamura. Tokyo: Iwanami Books.

Miyamura, Haruo. 1995. "Aspects of the Post-War Discussions Concering the Emperor." In *Postwar Thoughts and Consciousness,* ed. Masanori Nakamura. Tokyo: Iwanami Books.

Momose, Takashi. 1995. *Dictionary of Japan's Showa Era After the End of the War: Occupation and Reforms.* Tokyo: Yoshikawa Kobunkan.

Noguchi, Yukio. 1995. *The Regime of the 1940's.* Tokyo: Toyokkeizai.

Okazaki, Tetsuji, and Hasahiro Okuno. 1995. *The Origins of the Present Japanese Economic System.* Tokyo: Soshisha.

Passin, Herbert. 1965. *Society and Education in Japan.* New York: Teachers College of Columbia University.

Shidehara, Kijuro. 1951. *Fifty Years of Diplomacy.* Tokyo: Yomiurishinbuhshya.

Shima, Yositaka. 1992. "An Interpretation of the Shirasu Theory of Kowashi Inoueh." In *The Formation of the Meiji Government,* ed. Goin Library. Tokyo: Mokutakusha.

Suzuki, Mosaburo. 1934. *The Zaibatsu of Japan.* Tokyo: Kaizosha.

Takahashi, Kamekichi. 1966. *Industrial Development of the Meiji and Taishyo Eras.* Tokyo: Kashiwa Books.

Weber, Max. 1958. *Staatssoziologie.* Berlin: Duncker und Humblot.

Yoshida, Shigeru. 1957. *Memoir of Ten Years.* Vol. 1. Tokyo: Shinchoshiya.

10

South Africa:
From Apartheid to Democracy

Hennie J. Kotzé

South African politics underwent more dramatic changes between 1985 and 1995 than in any period since the union was established in 1910. Throughout that decade, and especially during the four years that led to acceptance of a new, interim constitution in late 1993, the most important actors were political elites. Their behavior and interactions bore out Arend Lijphart's "self-negating prediction" that in some ethnically plural societies, "elites cooperate in spite of the segmental differences dividing them because to do otherwise would mean to call forth the prophesied consequences of the plural character of the society" (Lijphart, 1977, 100). In South Africa, Steven Friedman observes, the critical element in the regime transition was "acceptance by its elites . . . that they had no option but to live with each other . . . somehow; the abyss always seemed to hold less appeal than the option of shifting ground" (Friedman, 1994, 331).

The reorganization of elite relations in South Africa occurred in the midst of a deep crisis involving rapid economic decline, intense ethnic mobilization and violence, and severe international pressure. A longitudinal study of elite attitudes that I conducted throughout the transition period sheds much light on how this crisis brought about fundamental elite and regime change. My study rested on three propositions. The first was that for a successful democratic transition to occur, the most important elite groups had to build a significant degree of consensus about democratic game rules, and their attitudes on key economic and political issues had to converge. Second, opposing elite groups in the principal political and social arenas had to establish formal and informal interaction networks for the sharing of power. Finally, I thought that if these elite changes occurred, then clear signs of a regime change toward stable democracy would follow. What was necessary in South Africa, in short, was something approximating an "elite settlement" through which "warring elite factions suddenly and deliberately reorganize their relations by negotiating compromises on their most basic disagreements" (Burton and Higley, 1987, 295; see also chapter 3, this volume).

When one looks at the extent of consensus and attitudinal convergence among South African elites in the late 1990s, it is clear that a great shift has occurred.[1] One notable change is the emergence of elite consensus. The interim constitution that was agreed to in 1993 embodied basic elite compromises, and the successful foundational elections of April 1994 showed greatly increased elite "game-rule" consensus. These developments cleared the way for South Africa's Constitutional Assembly to adopt a permanent constitution in May 1996, and this consitution was duly implemented in February 1997. Integrated elite networks, the second important element in a settlement, have also clearly emerged, though the full extent of this integrative process will be apparent only when the African National Congress (ANC) government led by President Nelson Mandela has had more time to fill important state positions with its supporters—an aspect of the so-called redistribution of gains. My assumption about a consequent change to stable democracy should be born out once Mandela steps down from the presidency and a second round of free and democratic elections takes place, in 1999.

White Domination and Regime Crisis

South Africa is one of the most deeply divided societies in the world.[2] The fact that several distinct and large racial and cultural groups live, work, and act politically in close proximity to one another virtually guarantees a continuous struggle between forces binding society together and those threatening to tear it apart. A major complicating factor is a highly unequal distribution of wealth. Racial and class divisions coincide to a large extent. As in other countries where great differences in material welfare coincide with ethnic cleavages, the cumulative effect in South Africa has been ever more intense conflicts. The white minority long deprived other groups of voting rights in order to maintain a state in which white privileges were institutionalized. At the time of union in 1910, a very small and relatively prosperous segment of the nonwhite population in the Cape Province and Natal had the suffrage, but in the northern provinces the vote was restricted to whites. The deliberate and sustained exclusion of the majority of the population from political influence and power is the most conspicuous feature of South Africa's modern political history.

From its beginning, therefore, the new state lacked much political legitimacy. However, because the vast majority of nonwhites were also to a large extent excluded from the capitalist economy, and because only a relatively small proportion of the nonwhite population lived in "white" areas, the resistance of nonwhites to their exclusion was for a while subdued. The state's chronic legitimacy deficit flared up periodically when its racist nature was challenged by various contenders. These flare-ups were usually linked to what have been termed "crises of accumulation"—situations in which the capitalist base of the state was threatened. The large mobilization of resistance during the late 1950s and early 1960s, in which the African National Congress and, to a lesser extent, the Pan-Africanist Congress (PAC) emerged as direct challengers to the state, was one such crisis.

A relatively favorable economic climate allowed the state to allay the accumulation crisis that fueled the political struggles of the late 1950s and early 1960s. That crisis was followed by the "silent sixties," during which the National Party (NP) government severely repressed resisters, forcing those ANC and PAC elites and cadres who were not imprisoned to go underground or into exile. During the 1970s, however, recurring illegal strikes and violent manifestations of unrest in the black townships impinged in unprecedented ways on the NP government led by B. J. Vorster. P. W. Botha, who succeeded Vorster as prime minister in 1978, was compelled to initiate major restructuring measures to stem spiraling political and economic difficulties. Although Botha's restructuring measures were complex and somewhat confused, their basic aims were clear enough: to increase both the legitimacy of the state and to garner additional capital with which to resume strong economic growth.

The main political thrusts of the Botha government's policies from the mid-1970s to the mid-1980s can be summarized as follows:

—unilateral development of the subordinate structures of homeland governments *(bantustans)* in order to accommodate the political aspirations of the different nonwhite population segments
—limited "power sharing" with the Coloured segment and, as an afterthought, also with the Asian segment
—development of separate local authorities to embody a distinction made in the 1983 Tricameral Constitution between what were termed "own affairs" and "general affairs" in order to entrench the principle of group differentiation

—gradual extension of the "power sharing" with Coloureds and Asians to the black population

These rather cumbersome "reform" efforts between 1978 and 1984 did not alter the fact that effective power remained in the hands of the white population and its elites. It was, therefore, not surprising that the Botha government's attempts at restructuring precipitated the most widespread resistance to racial exclusivism in the country's history. The government's unveiling of the racially discriminatory tricameral constitutional framework in 1983–84 led to mass mobilizations and large-scale violence. During those upheavals, which culminated in the 1985 declaration of what proved to be a continuing state of emergency, political power became concentrated in the office and person of the state president to an unprecedented degree. None of the Botha government's restructuring measures could stave off international condemnations of the political violence, increased international economic sanctions, and an ensuing loss of confidence in government.

Facing the financial costs of apartheid, increased pressures from the resistance movements, and enormous problems stemming from rapid urbanization, massive unemployment, severe housing shortages, and gross deficiencies in public education, a new government headed by F. W. de Klerk took office in 1989. It inaugurated a period of regime transition with the unbanning of black resistance movements and the Communist Party (SACP) on February 2, 1990, and nine days later with the release of Nelson Mandela, the ANC leader, from his quarter-century imprisonment on Robbin Island.

Elites and Pacts

President de Klerk's speech at the opening of Parliament on February 2, 1990, began a fundamental change in South Africa's political game rules. In terms of the literature on democratization, the initiatives signaled by de Klerk's speech can be described as constituting the "liberalization" of South African politics.[3] Alternatively, his speech can be seen as declaring the start of a negotiated regime transition following the limited liberalization accomplished by Botha's reforms during the 1980s. Either way, de Klerk's initiatives put South Africa irreversibly on the road leading away from white domination and the system of apartheid. Without a more probing study it is impossible to determine which factors or forces played the most important role in bringing de Klerk and his government to the conviction that a regime transition was necessary. V. Z. Slabbert (1990) writes that, in addition to various internal pressures, there were various anticipated and unanticipated external pressures. Taken together, the pressures constituted a crisis of major proportions to which de Klerk's government had to react.

After de Klerk's speech in early 1990, South African politics were punctuated by a series of pacts between the most important contenders for power.[4] Initially, the pacts were directed at agreeing on a set of rules to which all key elite groups would adhere in subsequent negotiations; it was only much later that talks about alternative "regime models" got under way. The most important initial pacts were the Groote Schuur Minute (May 1990), the Pretoria Minute (August 1990), the D. F. Malan Accord (February 1991), and The National Peace Accord (September 1991), all of which had to do with guaranteeing organizational security for the main opposing groups. It should be noted that one of the greatest threats to both the transition and the creation of a climate of national reconciliation was—and even today continues to be—the high level of interethnic violence. For more than ten years, there has been a low-intensity war in some areas of the country, and a number of political parties have used violence as a weapon in pursuing their specific political goals.

The initial pacts were followed by the Convention for a Democratic South Africa (CODESA I), which was convened in December 1991. CODESA I is best viewed as officially commencing a process of multilateral elite negotiations.[5] Between November 1991 and late 1993, the efforts to achieve a negotiated elite settlement were led by South Africa's main and more or less moderate political groupings, anchored by the ANC on one side and de Klerk's National Party on the other.

The first part of 1992 was dominated by the March referendum de Klerk called to counter white right-wing resistance to negotiations. This referendum had several impacts on the political process. First of all, it constituted a massive popular endorsement of negotiations. Second, white voters gave their representatives in CODESA I a mandate to negotiate for minority protections in fairly specific terms. Third, although 68.7 percent of white voters endorsed de Klerk's position and strategy in the referendum, its result reminded all negotiating groups that close to a million white voters felt so threatened by the prospects of change that they could not support even the very qualified negotiating mandate the referendum provided.

The March 1992 referendum gave de Klerk a personal psychological boost, and it bolstered his leadership of the NP, which was being threatened by several by-election losses, increasing unemployment, rising crime rates, and escalating political violence. However, the mandate de Klerk obtained could not be interpreted as expressing the unified support of National Party voters for the government's constitutional proposals, because many of the "yes" voters belonged to the moderate Democratic Party (DP) or were white supporters of the ANC and other extraparliamentary groups. On the other hand, the competing Conservative Party's (CP) claim to represent the "white nation's" desire for self-determination was disproved by the referendum result. Internal Conservative Party policy divisions were soon exposed when a CP wing split off to join the intransigent Afrikaner-Volksunie under the leadership of Andries Beyers. Ultimately, the Conservatives aligned themselves with the militant Afrikaner Weerstands Beweging. The right-wing Afrikaner camp became irrevocably divided when the Freedom Front (FF) was establish in March 1994 under the leadership of General Constand Viljoen, a former head of the Defence Force under the P. W. Botha government.

One of the most important implications of the March 1992 referendum for the ANC was that it would henceforth be negotiating with opponents who had a strong mandate for a settlement that might produce restricted majority rule. The need to match demands for minority protections with provisions for majority rule had become the crucial issue confronting CODESA I. Negotiations did not go smoothly, however, and CODESA II, which was a continuation of Codesa I, deadlocked in May 1992, when the ANC suspended bilateral negotiations and brought about CODESA II's collapse. At that point in the process, nevertheless, all main parties were convinced of the need for negotiations. Even the CP and the PAC, who had not participated in the two CODESA rounds, had moved closer to a pronegotiation stance. Given this embryonic elite consensus on the need for a negotiated settlement, why did the CODESA II breakdown occur? The most important reasons were as follows:

—Fundamental differences existed among the main participants about the meaning and content of democracy. Although these principled differences could not be reconciled, the parties nevertheless sought consensus about the "nuts and bolts" of a new constitution.

—The ANC-led alliance held a populist conception of democracy and was wedded to the principle that the "will of the people" (in practice, majorities consisting of 50 percent plus one) must be decisive in elections and government decisions. This meant that government policy would have to give content to the overriding principle of equality, to be achieved through a redistribution of wealth and occupational opportunities.

—The NP-led alliance, as well as the Inkatha Freedom Party (IFP) and the moderate, English-speaking Democratic Party, had more classically liberal conceptions of democracy, in which the primary principle is that majority government must be reconciled with the protection of minorities. All three groups thus rejected the ANC alliance's 50 percent-plus-one conception of democracy.

—Rhetorical consensus at CODESA on the need for negotiation concealed a difference in principle about what could be achieved in such a process. Among certain factions of the ANC and the NP, the prevailing view was that a negotiating forum is just another site of "struggle" (in ANC terms) or "strife" (a *strydperk* in NP terms) where the aim is to talk your opponents into submission. Compromising, making mutual concessions, and achieving agreements were seen as tactical moves on the road to absolute victory for one's own side.

—The longevity of an interim, power-sharing government was also in dispute. For the NP, an interim government should be in office over a relatively long transition period; for the ANC, it should be limited to drawing up a constitution for the final transfer of power during a relatively short period in office.

—Once the NP alliance began to fear that it had overestimated its domestic and foreign support, its leaders insisted on a mechanism to give special protection to regional governments in an eventual constitution-writing body. But this was vehemently opposed by the ANC and its allies.

—Owing to poor communication between the leaders of the ANC alliance and their supporters, many of the latter suspected that their leaders were on the verge of "selling out" at CODESA, and some cadre personnel in the ANC alliance, therefore, started to demand a more radical and uncompromising stance.

Adding to the elite standoff were the ways in which both the government and the ANC alliance handled the black mass-action campaign up to and including a confrontation at Bisho in September 1992, where members of the Ciskei Defence Force opened fire on ANC marchers, killing twenty-nine persons and wounding several hundred. Each side wanted to make political capital at the other's expense, with both camps playing "election politics" even before there was any agreement about the rules and scheduling of elections. It appeared that each side was attempting to clear the political playing field of opponents rather than leveling it for fair competition. Quite possibly, the bloody confrontation at Bisho brought the main sides to a moment of truth. The domestic and international pressures that had built up after a massacre at Boipatong in June 1992, when thirty-nine people were killed, developed still greater momentum after Bisho early in September, and they prompted bilateral negotiations between the top leaders of the two sides. Later that month the ANC and the government signed the Record of Understanding, an agreement (or pact) that had a strong positive influence on subsequent negotiations. The Boipatong and Bisho massacres thus stand out, bracketing the period of greatest crisis, and the NP government's important concessions in the negotiations that followed the Bisho blood-letting suggest that this period of crisis drastically weakened its resolve.

At this critical juncture, the distribution of support for and against the state had important implications for a settlement. Leaders of the ANC-SACP alliance, the main challengers, realized after protracted attempts—which included well-organized mass actions—that it was impossible to displace the forces that controlled the state. The principal leaders of the state, in turn, realized that the challengers could harm the state through prolonged mass actions to such an extent that compromise was the only way out. Hindsight suggests that lasting compromises would probably not have been possible without the "test of strength" that took place during the middle of 1992.

Important mutual concessions thus put the transition process back on track. The NP agreed to an elected constituent assembly, and the ANC agreed to its multiparty character (a reconstituted CODESA), even supplying a brief detailing the guidelines for the assembly's actions. Although the government tried to draw the Inkatha Freedom Party into the talks, the IFP was not interested, and it instead formed a Concerned South Africans Group (COSAG) with right-wing organizations and with the black leaders of Ciskei, Kwa-Zulu, and Bophu-thatswana. This group later became known as the Freedom Alliance. Not even the ANC alliance's dramatic acceptance of power sharing, embodied in SACP leader Joe Slovo's so-called sunset clauses, which called for a Government of National Unity that would last for five years following the first free elections, could persuade the COSAG forces to participate in negotiations.

After a planning conference in March 1993, which was attended by twenty-six parties, including the COSAG groups as onlookers, a new negotiating forum was established in the following month. This Multi-Party Negotiating Process (MPNP) was a more streamlined structure than CODESA. Whereas CODESA II had involved four delegates and two advisers per party, a new Negotiating Council (which became known as the "engine room"), containing two delegates and two advisers per party, was created to speed deliberations. This produced the desired goods in late July 1993. Not only were twenty-six constitutional principles agreed and published (later increased to thirty-four principles) to serve as the "building blocks" for a new constitution, but a provisional map of nine proposed regions or provinces was also agreed in early August.

By mid-September 1993, the Negotiating Council was able, after difficult and often acerbic deliberations and without the support of the Freedom Alliance, to send to Parliament for its approval four draft bills that specified the mechanisms for transiting to a new regime. The four bills were made into a single law, the primary purpose of which was to level the political playing field by ensuring that the electoral process would proceed fairly.

Once a Transitional Executive Council was instituted in December 1993 and an agreement on an interim constitution was reached, three years of elite negotiations were, for the most part, ended. The date for South Africa's first nonracial democratic elections was set for April 27, 1994. At the last minute, the IFP agreed to contest the elections. This meant that, with the exception of far-right parties such as the CP and the Reconstituted National Party and the hard-left Azanian People's Organization, all significant political parties and groupings finally contested the elections. The IFP's last-minute decision to participate enhanced the legitimacy of the election and the Government of National Unity (GNU) that was subsequently formed.

An interim constitution had been adopted by Parliament in December 1993. It took effect with the election in April 1994, and it established a parliamentary system with cabinet government. As Doreen Atkinson has observed, "Constitutionalism was born out of the ANC's willingness to constrain majority rule, as long as the NP abandoned its demand for veiled racial privilege" (Atkinson, 1994, 93). The Parliament elected in April 1994 was empowered to function also as a constitutional assembly, charged with writing a final constitution by May 8, 1996. However, this new constitution had to accord with the thirty-four constitutional principles laid down in the interim constitution (see Schedule 4, Constitution Act of South Africa, 1993).

The new Parliament was one of the most important products of the negotiated regime transition between 1990 and 1994. As the process of political change shifted from the phase of democratic transition to that of democratic consolidation after the April 1994 elections, Parliament became the main locus of political developments.[6] It has continued to face the difficult task of finding and institutionalizing some compromise between the different conceptions of democracy that remain apparent in South Africa.

In many democratic transitions, conflicts arise over competing procedural and substantive conceptions of democracy, with the former stressing procedural fairness and the latter social justice. In South Africa it is quite clear that these contrasting conceptions divide the main political camps even today. The now-dominant camp, led by the ANC, embraces the substantive conception and calls for genuine equality between groups and cultures. This informs policies that seek income distributions that bear no relation to skin color or culture. The other camp, consisting of the NP and minority parties such as the IFP and the FF, holds to the view that South Africa comprises a variety of cultures and must therefore be managed as a state with a plurality of cultures in which radical egalitarian redistributive policies, undertaken in service to democracy, will succeed only in marginalizing the predominantly white middle class and various nonwhite minorities. These competing conceptions of democracy and lines of policy are reflected in a debate about the further restructuring of South African political institutions and society in general. They underlie the fears of some elites that a "transplacement by erosion"[7]—a gradual erosion of the elites who started the transition and their replacement by new elites—is taking place.

Elite Settlement and Regime Change

In 1990, two mutually exclusive elite camps, which could be described as competing hegemonies or types of political domination, faced each other. One camp contained the holders of state power, the other consisted of those seeking to overthrow that power. This dichotomous elite lineup and the intransigence of the two camps account in large measure for the spiraling violence of the late 1980s. An important reason for the rigidity of the main elites was the way in which the state and the political regime were fused in South Africa. In the words of Robert Fishman, "A regime may be thought of as the formal and informal organization of the center of political power, and of its relations with the broader society. A regime determines who has access to political power, and how those who are in power deal with those who are not."[8] A state, by contrast, is best thought of as "a (normally) more permanent structure of domination and coordination including a coercive apparatus and the means to administer a society and extract resources from it" (Fishman, 1990, 428).

In South Africa, the state in Fishman's sense was an organic part of the wider political regime. Consequently, there was no possibility that the holders of state power could be displaced from their positions by competing political groups. It is virtually an axiom of revolutionary theory that if a ruling group can retain its cohesion it can withstand the revolutionary onslaught of almost any challenger.[9] But at the start of the 1990s in South Africa, both state power holders and state challengers believed that they could win a complete victory over the other. Lijphart's "self-negating prediction" was therefore set in motion only when the opposing elites jointly experienced the constraining effects of a mutually costly stalemate and when they began to comprehend the degree to which they were in fact mutually dependent on each other. Gradually, in other words, elites perceived that the conflict between them and their respective camps must not be zero-sum in its character. But to capitalize on this growing perception and to effect an outcome that would be beneficial to both sides, a situation of "mutual security" (to use Robert A. Dahl's term) first had to be created.[10] This could only be achieved if the state shifted to a more neutral position as guardian of the peace for everyone—if, in other words, the fusion of state and regime was broken.

My longitudinal study of elite attitudes between 1990 and 1995 showed clearly that both power holders and challengers initially saw the NP government as fully controlling the state and as constituting the entire political regime. This is hardly surprising; no one would doubt that elites opposing the white-dominated regime had such perceptions at the outset of the process I have summarized. The interesting aspect of my study is the extent of change in these perceptions during the period. To get at this, let me focus on the surveys of elite attitudes that I conducted in the latter half of 1992 and in 1995.[11]

The 1992 survey was conducted well before a final elite settlement was in sight, while the 1995 survey was conducted nearly eighteen months after the new ANC-led Government of National Unity took power. In both surveys, elites were defined as those persons who hold authoritative positions in powerful public and private organizations and influential movements, and who are therefore able to affect strategic decisions regularly.[12] A positional method was used to operationalize this definition, so that persons who occupied the highest positions in the most important sectors of society were asked to participate in the surveys.[13] A total of 1,007 position holders responded to the 1992 survey, and 635 responded to the 1995 survey. The institutional sectors in which these elite respondents were located are shown in table 10.1.

The apartheid and postapartheid political systems that existed in 1992 and 1995, respectively, are reflected in the two sample compositions. In 1992, recruitment to top positions in most sectors was still confined largely to whites; it was only after the April 1994 elections that blacks began to acquire meaningful access to high-level positions in most political, economic, and social institutions. The racial makeup of the 1995 sample, though still skewed heavily toward whites, reflected this change: 82.2 percent whites; 12.2 percent Africans; 2.2 percent Coloureds; and 2.4 percent Asians. Because of the racially skewed

TABLE 10.1
Sector Locations of Elite Respondents in 1992 and 1995

Institutional Sector	1992 Sample	1995 Sample
N	1,007	635
Agriculture	50	54
Labor	23	30
State bureaucracy	105	102
Business	74	86
Academic	74	51
Right-wing political organizations	56	50
Members of Parliament	164	132
Local politicians	61	—
Extraparliamentary organizations	108	—
Media	70	34
Parastatal organizations	54	—
CODESA delegates	49	—
Church	76	60
Military	43	36

patterns of recruitment to top institutional positions, the racial makeup of the 1995 sample did not parallel the racial makeup of the Parliament elected in April 1994. Nor did the party affiliations of persons in the 1995 sample parallel the party composition of Parliament—there being much greater proportions of whites and NP supporters still in elite positions in the various institutional sectors than in Parliament. Finally, there were virtually no adherents of the small PAC and African Christian Democratic Party (ACDP, which was founded just prior to the 1994 elections) in top positions in the various institutional sectors in 1995, and I have therefore excluded PAC and ACDP members from my analysis.

To probe the attachments of respondents to the different institutions of state and society, I attempted to gauge their sympathy or antipathy toward those institutions by analyzing a number of multi-item indexes and measurements constructed through a factor analysis (orthogonal rotation method) and interitem correlation. Specifically, each respondent was asked: "Please indicate how sympathetic or unsympathetic you feel towards the following institutions," and each was presented with a Likert-type scale: very sympathetic/sympathetic/neutral/unsympathetic/very unsympathetic.

The 1992 Survey

To analyze responses to the foregoing question in my 1992 survey, forty-six variables were subjected to factor analysis. Six factors emerged, and the first three of them explained 53.2 percent of the variation in respondents' answers, with the first factor alone explaining 28.9 percent of the variation.[14] Only the first factor, with a cut-off point of 0.4, is used in the present analysis. This factor combined the core institutions in the system of state hegemony that existed in 1992, and it suggested the existence of a set of values, rendered in terms of sympathies and antipathies, with regard to this hegemony (i.e., values can be favorable or unfavorable).[15]

From this factor, an index called "core state" was constructed. It encompassed the largest part of the state's administrative, bureaucratic, and coercive system and included the following entities: the South African Broadcasting Corporation, the House of Assembly, the South African Defence Force, the Civil Service, the state president, the courts, and the South African Police. Table 10.2 shows how sympathies and antipathies of respondents toward the "core state" institutions were arrayed in 1992 according to the political parties and movements respondents supported.

The pattern shown in table 10.2 is predictable in view of the racial composition of the parties. It was primarily those parties that could participate in the system whose elite supporters would presumably have much sympathy for the core state. Accordingly, 89 percent of the respondents who identified with the National Party were sympathetic

TABLE 10.2
Elite Sympathy for "Core State" in 1992, by Political Party Supported (percentage) (*N* = 1,007)

Party Supported	N	Sympathetic	Neutral	Unsympathetic
National Party	470	89	7	4
Democratic Party	148	39	30	31
Right-wing parties	70	69	17	14
Indian parties	22	77	9	14
ANC/SACP	80	6	13	81
Inkatha Freedom Party	51	71	16	14
Pan-African Congress	35	6	11	83
Other	103	50	18	32
No party specified	28	29	25	46

toward the core state.[16] Only 7 percent were neutral, and a mere handful (4 percent) were unsympathetic. This pattern corresponds with the
view that it was the NP that created state hegemony over the years
and that, as a party, was inseparable from the state. As regards elite
respondents who identified with the English-speaking Democratic
Party, the pattern was much more mixed: almost 40 percent felt sympathy toward core state institutions, but 30 percent were neutral, and 30
percent were unsympathetic (of whom, however, only 3 percent described themselves as "very unsympathetic"). Considering the DP's
generally liberal stance, this relatively high degree of sympathy among
its elite adherents toward institutions they had criticized over the years
as authoritarian instruments of NP rule was somewhat surprising. It
can, perhaps, be explained by postulating the existence of a somewhat
diffuse, but nonetheless real, sense of cohesion among white elites in
the face of the crisis that unfolded during 1992.

Supporters of right-wing political parties and organizations such as
the Conservative Party, the Reconstituted National Party (HNP), and
the Afrikaner Volkswag (AV) showed, of course, a high degree of sympathy toward the core state: almost 69 percent were sympathetic and
17 percent were neutral, while only 14 percent were unsympathetic
(only 4 percent of them "very unsympathetic"). This pattern shows
that, in spite of the militant, often subversive rhetoric emanating from
right-wing circles, the core state still had a high degree of legitimacy
in those circles. In the case of the Conservatives, it could in fact be
argued that the strong Afrikaans ethnic link between them and NP
holders of top positions in the core state underlay this sympathetic
attitude, whereas in the case of Democratic Party supporters, the majority of whom were English speaking and members of the English
community, no such ethnic link existed, so that one has to look for
other reasons for their sympathy, such as the sense of cohesion among
whites who all felt embattled. This underlying sense of cohesion
shown by—mainly white—respondents who supported the NP, the DP
and the CP has been described by Jannie Gagiano as follows:

> The White group is a political community by virtue of the operation of
> the rules of a political regime that gives them differential and superior
> access to the levels of power in the state. This is the structural cement that
> binds them together. The social cement that binds whites together—the
> principle of cohesion—is at most a vague notion that because of a com-
> mon European ancestry it is incumbent upon them to act in concert to
> preserve Western values and a commensurate Western way of life in
> South Africa. Misguided as it might be, they might also share an anxiety
> that if black people are given unencumbered access to the levers of power

in the state, the conditions for preserving these values could be seriously damaged. Conditions like retaining the capitalist parameters of the economy and the "first world" standards of public administration are at stake. (Gagiano, 1989, 10)

Respondents who identified with the smaller Indian parties that associated themselves with the state system also showed a high degree of sympathy for the core state: 77 percent were sympathetic, 9 percent neutral and 14 percent unsympathetic. Respondents supporting the Labour Party are not included in table 10.2 because of their small number, but they also reported a high degree of sympathy (45.5 percent) in spite of the fact that the Labour Party formed part of the "patriotic front" with the ANC-SACP. Wholly unsurprising, of course, was the exceptionally few ANC-SACP supporters (6 percent) with sympathy for the core state.[17] Conversely, elite supporters of the Inkatha Freedom Party, the majority of whom were black, showed a large measure of sympathy for the core state: just over 70 percent were sympathetic, 16 percent were neutral, and only 14 percent were unsympathetic.

Table 10.3 aggregates all 1992 elite respondents by race and shows the extent to which each racial category was sympathetic or antipathetic toward the core state. The distribution in table 10.3 shows that the majority of white (72 percent), Coloured (50 percent) and Indian (62 percent) elites had sympathy for the core state, whereas African elites (53 percent) were primarily unsympathetic. Most of the African elites who were sympathetic were IFP supporters. But table 10.3 also suggests that, given the 14 percent of unsympathetic white elites and the 36 percent of African elites with some sympathy toward the core state, there was no simple elite division along racial lines. To complicate matters further, there was a major ideological division between, on the one side, African elites in the ANC-SACP alliance and more radical "Africanists" in the PAC and, on the other side, Zulu nationalist elites in the IFP.

TABLE 10.3
Elite Sympathy for the "Core State" in 1992, by Racial Categories
(percentage) (N = 1,007)

Racial Category	N	Sympathetic	Neutral	Unsympathetic
White	729	72	15	14
African	171	36	12	53
Coloured	56	50	16	34
Indian	52	62	10	29

In sum, it is clear from tables 10.2 and 10.3 that during the second half of 1992 white elites retained a significant amount of cohesion, even though the process of regime transition was already under way. It is also clear that there was still significant sympathy among Coloured and Indian elites for the state and its institutions and, by implication, for the NP government's policies. To the extent that these nonwhite elites chose to cooperate with the government, they were part of the "established" elite camp. Although a number of reasons could be suggested for their cooperation, the most important was probably overlapping social values.[18] Another important reason was that the state, in its attempts to counter the ANC/SACP-led revolutionary mobilization, had obtained a measure of support among African, Coloured, and Indian groups by co-opting some of their leaders into state managerial positions in the process of trying to make apartheid work.[19] The data also show that white elites who supported parties represented in Parliament generally had a relatively high degree of sympathy for the state and, by implication, for the wider political regime in which their parties and the institutions they controlled still had the upper hand.

The 1995 Survey

In my 1995 survey there were twenty-nine variables or items included in the "sympathy scale." A factor analysis using the same techniques that were applied to the 1992 survey identified five factors. The first factor explained 31.2 percent of the variance and the first three factors together explained 53 percent of the variance (a cut-off point of 0.4 was again used). Eighteen months after the 1994 elections, the institutionally based elites clustered quite differently.[20]

The first factor included elites in the institutions that could in 1995 be described as the "new regime" because of their strong link with the ANC, which was by then the dominant party in the Government of National Unity. An interesting contrast with the 1992 survey is that elites in the most important institutions of the state, namely the police service, civil service, national defense force, and courts loaded on a separate factor. In the perceptions of elite respondents, these institutions were not as yet parts of the new regime. What was also significant, however, was that most of the statutory bodies, such as the Land Claims Court, the Truth and Reconciliation Commission, the National Economic, Development, and Labour Council and the South African Broadcasting Corporation, were viewed as part of the new regime. Still more remarkable was the perception that the guardian of the interim constitution, the Constitutional Court, was also part of the new regime.

Table 10.4 correlates party support with an index compiled from the

TABLE 10.4

Elite Perceptions of the "New Regime" in 1995, by Party supported
(percentage) (*N* = 635)

Party Supported	N	Sympathetic	Neutral	Unsympathetic
NP	251	16	13	71
DP	97	37	19	44
Extraparliamentary right-wing	21	0	0	100
ANC	135	95	2	3
Freedom Front	51	2	2	96
IFP	12	8	25	67
Other	68	38	21	41

institutions perceived as making up the new regime. It shows noticeable antipathy among supporters of parties other than the ANC toward the institutions in the new regime. Antipathy was total (100 percent) among supporters of extraparliamentary right-wing groups, and it was marked among elite supporters of the Freedom Front (96 percent), the NP (71 percent), the IFP (68 percent), and the DP (44 percent).[21] Among ANC supporters, by contrast, there was a very high level of sympathy for the "new regime" (no less than 95 percent, with only 3 percent unsympathetic).

In table 10.5, the specific state institutions associated with the new regime—the police, the defense force, the civil Service, and the courts—which emerged as Factor 4 and which I call "the new state," are examined in terms of the sympathies and antipathies of elite per-

TABLE 10.5

Elite Perceptions of the "New State" Institutions in 1995, by Party Supported
(percentage) (*N* = 635)

Party Supported	N	Sympathetic	Neutral	Unsympathetic
NP	251	78	17	5
DP	97	65	28	7
Extraparliamentary right-wing	21	52	24	24
ANC	135	71	24	5
Freedom Front	51	57	31	12
IFP	12	67	17	17
Other	68	65	19	16

sons toward them, again arrayed according to the parties supported by respondents. It can be seen that in 1995 sympathy for the new state's key institutions was quite widespread among elites, ranging from a high of 78 percent among NP supporters to 52 percent among supporters of extraparliamentary, right-wing parties and organizations. Significantly, most ANC supporters (71 percent) were sympathetic to the "new state" institutions that had, only a few years earlier, been most centrally involved in suppressing the ANC and its allies.

There are two possible explanations for the patterns in table 10.5. First, elite supporters of the old apartheid regime may have believed in 1995 that most of the top positions in these key state institutions were still held by persons associated with the old regime. Second, ANC supporters may have believed that because the ANC controlled the presidency and Parliament it was now in full control of the key state institutions and no longer needed to fear them. In the eyes of ANC supporters, moreover, the affirmative action program adopted by the Government of National Unity, which aimed at replacing position holders associated with the old regime with newly recruited persons from the opposition, was already having the desired effect of ensuring that the key state institutions would be loyal to the new government.

Overall, it appears that most elites perceived that a new postapartheid regime peopled mainly by ANC-aligned elites had replaced the old NP-dominated apartheid regime. Unlike the old authoritarian configuration, however, the most important state insitutions were now seen to be more autonomous from the wider political regime. Whether this will prove to be a fleeting or a lasting perception of the postapartheid power structure depends to a great extent on the process of institutionalization and on the success of specific policies that the postapartheid, ANC-led government is pursuing.

Elites and Regime Institutionalization

A notable feature of recent studies of democratization is the stress on institutions.[22] This is part of the revival of institutional analysis, which emphasizes the formal and informal rules that structure political life. Institutions constitute the frameworks within which elites and the public are expected to act, providing incentives and rewards for cooperative behavior as well as sanctions for noncooperative behavior. Cooperative behavior involves attitudes that are "supportive of the political system and that, in turn, result in stability" (Mezey, 1995).[23]

If the maintenance of stability and order is a problem that is common to all modern states, it has to be remembered that newly democratized states, especially those which, like South Africa, lack robust economies and the widely shared identity that Juan Linz and Alfred Stepan (1996) call "stateness," are especially vulnerable if their institutions do not generate cooperative elite attitudes and behavior. In South Africa at present, we are dealing with emerging institutions whose future performance is still in the domain of what Giuseppe Di Palma terms "the probable and expected." He writes, "Whether the risk of a breakdown stays out of the agenda of a new democracy depends . . . on how institutions turn out. Thus, on the one hand, as institutions emerge, they should become valued per se and should make the chances of players backing out ever more remote. They should at least render inoperative any residual reservations that players may hold. On the other hand, such players' 'socialization' (following, as it were, their recruitment to the game) remains contingent, and consent relies on institutional performance" (Di Palma, 1990, 39).

More concretely, the perception elites have of the performance and worth of new institutions is crucial for the stability of a newly democratized regime. If it is assumed that a majority of the South African population are prepared to grant legitimacy to new political institutions that operate according to electoral and other procedural rules of democracy, one still has to answer the vexing question of how the new institutions can become accepted by all significant groups in the society. In reality, the process of institutionalization has much in common with the process of building a nation. According to Samuel P. Huntington (1968, 397), the success of nation building depends first on a "horizontal" integration of the diverse groupings that must be molded into a national unit. It depends second on a "vertical" assimilation of economic and social classes. In South Africa a tension between the two forms of integration—horizontal and vertical—may well lie at the root of the differing levels of sympathy for postapartheid institutions that are evidenced by supporters of the ANC-aligned parties and supporters of parties opposing the ANC alignment.

The process of institutionalization has progressed some distance in South Africa. In this chapter, the orientations of elites toward both old and new political institutions have been analyzed. Although the 1995 data were collected quite soon after new institutions were established, the data show that they were already receiving considerable elite sympathy (and legitimacy?). The data, therefore, suggest that a process of institutionalization propitious for stable democracy had begun. The patterns I have summarized are consistent with the assumption that there is a causal connection between the ability of the groups my elite respondents headed to achieve their main interests in the new regime and the extent of elite sympathy for the regime. The time dimension is, of course, crucial for any process of institutionalization, and only an extension of my longitudinal study will show whether the South African process is continuing and gaining strength. Eighteen months after the origin of a fundamentally new regime in 1994, the signs were encouraging.

Notes

1. For a summary of the shift in attitudes of elites and the most important consequences for the "logic of ongoing elite convergence," see Kotzé (1993, 171–74).

2. This section draws on Kotzé and Lourens (1988).

3. O'Donnell and Schmitter (1986, 7) define liberalization as "the process of making effective certain rights that protect both individuals and social groups from arbitrary or illegal acts committed by the state or third parties."

4. For most students of democratization, political pacts—negotiated elite agreements that remove from the political agenda sources of potentially destabilizing conflict—are one of the most acceptable forms of democratization. For a discussion of types of pacts, see Hagopian (1990, 149–50).

5. See Friedman (1994) and Sisk (1995, 202–45) for excellent overviews of CODESA's creation and functioning.

6. See the discussion by Liebert and Cotta (1990, 14) of the different roles played by parliaments in democratic consolidation: (1) as the "central site" of consolidation; (2) as but one of several consolidation paths, with party interactions and charismatic leadership being other important paths; or (3) as being "nearly superfluous in the setting up of the original consensus on the rules of the new game."

7. This concept is used by Nel (1995, 85) to describe the process in South Africa.

8. This conception of regimes is slightly more elaborate, but not inconsistent with, Dogan and Higley's conception of a regime, in chapter 1, as "the basic pattern by which government decision-making power is organized, exercised, and transferred in a society."

9. See Skocpol (1979, 32–33) for elaboration of this statement.

10. See Dahl (1971, 123–34).

11. These two surveys are selected from those conducted annually between 1990 and 1995 in my "Longitudinal Study of the South African Elite and Their Attitudes Regarding Political Change."

12. This definition of elites is a slightly modified version of the one used by Dogan and Higley, in chapter 1 of this volume, and by Field, Higley, and Burton (1990, 152).

13. For a full description of the methodology, see Kotzé (1991, 7–13). See also Kotzé and Du Toit (1995, 35–41). It is virtually impossible to determine the boundaries of some elite sectors. A fairly wide operationalization of the

definition was implemented; this was necessary not only to cover the wide range of interest groups but also to include the leadership of both parliamentary and extraparliamentary groupings.

14. The contending theoretical interpretations of South African society do not rest on compatible assumptions about the interrelatedness of the underlying dimensions of society. The orthogonal method of rotation, which makes no assumption about the interrelatedness of factors, was therefore used to generate these factors.

15. For discussion of this conception of state hegemony, see Kotze and Du Toit (1995). The factor loaded as follows (asterisks indicate civic bodies):

*Broederbond	.79115	S.A. Defense Force	.59076
*Fed. of African Culture	.78040	*Large corporations	.58399
*Dutch Reform Church	.75515	Civil Service	.56656
*African Trade Institute	.71416	State president	.52991
*Afrikaanse Press	.70027	*S.A. Agriculture Union	.52527
S.A. Broadcasting Corp.	.68375	Courts	.50961
National Party	.63156	S.A. Police Service	.48105
House of Assembly	.59076		

16. "Very sympathetic" and "sympathetic" and then "unsympathetic" and "very unsympathetic" are combined respectively as "sympathetic" and "unsympathetic."

17. At the time of the 1992 survey the ANC and SACP still saw themselves as liberation movements, and they had not officially registered as political parties.

18. For an analysis of the elites' social values, see Kotzé (1991, 77–81).

19. For further discussion of the reasons for co-optation, see Gagiano (1990, 12–14).

20. The factor loadings were as follows (asterisks indicate civic bodies):

Factor 1: The New Regime

*S.A. Council of Churches	.83510	Govt. of Nat'l Unity	.71280
ANC	.83890	Parliament	.68669
Congress of Trade Unions	.83151	President	.68877
Truth & Reconciliation Comm.	.79737	Constitutional Court	.68650
Land Claims Court	.80931	Develop./Labour Council	.69854
*Civic Associations	.80400	PAC	.64801
SACP	.74391	S.A. Broadcasting Corp.	.66823

(Standardized item alpha is 0.9452)

Factor 2: The Afrikaaner Establishment

*Fed. of Afrikaanse Culture	.82742	Afrikaanse Trade Inst.	.78136
*Dutch Reform Church	.88231	NP	.76434
*Broederbond	.80127	S.A. Agriculture Union	.51229

(standardized item alpha is 0.8874)

Factor 3: The Ethnic Nationalists

Volkstaatraad	.86406	Inkatha Freedom Party	.56769
Freedom Front	.78024	Cong. of Traditional Ldrs.	.55586

(standardized item alpha is 0.7688)

Factor 4: The State Elites

S.A. Police Service	.71859	S.A. Defence Force	.67881
Civil Service	.68615	Courts	.49692

(standardized item alpha is 0.6631)

Factor 5: The Liberals

Democratic Party	.80208

21. The N''s for supporters of the extraparliamentary right-wing groups and for the IFP are relatively small, but they are included in table 10.4 as indications of the general trends among supporters of these forces.

22. See Apter (1991). Note, however, that according to Steinmo, Thelen, and Longstreth (1992, 12–13), "an institutional approach does not replace attention to other variables—the players, their interests and strategies, and the distribution of power among them"; rather, "it puts these factors in context, showing how they relate to one another by drawing attention to the way political situations are structured."

23. According to Pontusson (1995, 118–19), some of the claims advanced by "institutionalists" about the role of institutions are that they determine "the capacity of political or economic actors; the distribution of power among political or economic actors; and, who the actors are and/or how the actors conceive their interests." See also Weaver and Rockman (1991), and Steinmo, Thelen, and Longstreth (1992).

References

Apter, David E. 1991. "Institutionalism Reconsidered." *International Social Science Journal* 43.

Atkinson, Doreen. 1994. "Principle born of Pragmatism?: Central Government in the Constitution."In *South African Review 7: The Small Miracle of South Africa's Negotiated Settlement,* ed. Steven Friedman and Doreen Atkinson. Johannesburg: Ravan Press, 1994.

Burton, Michael G., and John Higley. 1987. "Elite Settlements." *American Sociological Review* 52 (June): 295–307.

Dahl, Robert A. 1971. *Polyarchy: Participation and Opposition.* New Haven: Yale University Press.

De Villiers, B. 1994. *The New Constitution: Framework and Protection of Human Rights.* Occasional paper series, July. Johannesburg: Konrad Adenauer Foundation.

Di Palma, Giuseppe. 1990. "Parliaments, Consolidation, Institutionalization: A Minimalist View." In *Parliament and Democratic Consolidation in Southern Europe,* ed. Ulrike Liebert and Maurizio Cotta. London: Pinter.

Field, G. Lowell, and John Higley. 1985. "National Elites and Political Stability." In *Research in Politics and Society: Studies of the Structure of National Elite Groups,* ed. Gwen Moore, 1–44. Greenwich, Conn.: JAI Press.

Field, G. Lowell, John Higley, and Michael G. Burton. 1990. "A New Elite Framework for Political Sociology." *Revue Européene de Sciences Sociales* 28: 149–82.

Fishman, Robert. 1990. "Rethinking State and Regime: Southern Europe's Transition to Democracy." *World Politics* 42 (August).

Friedman, Steven. 1994. "Afterword: The Brief Miracle?" in *South African Review, 7,* ed. S. Friedman and D. Atkinson. Johannesburg: Ravan Press.

Gagiano, Jannie. 1989. "The Scope of Regime Support: A Case Study." In *Negotiating South Africa's Future,* ed. H. Giliomee and L. Schlemmer. Johannesburg: Southern Books.

Hagopian, Frances. 1990. " 'Democracy by Undemocratic Means'?: Elites, Political Pacts, and Regime Transition in Brazil." *Comparative Political Studies* 23 (July).

Hungtington, Samuel P. 1968. *Political Order in Changing Societies.* New Haven, Conn.: Yale Univ Press.

Kotzé, Hennie J., and E. Lourens. 1988. "Towards a Non-Racial Alternative: Extra-Parliamentary Resistance to the 'Reformist' Apartheid State." In *South Africa: The Challenge of Reform,* ed. D. J. Van Vuuren, Hillcrest: Owen Burgess.

Kotzé. Hennie J. 1991. *Elites and Democratization: An Exploratory Survey of South African Elites.* Stellenbosch. S.A.: Centre for South African Politics.

―――. 1993. *A Negotiated Democracy?: A Survey of Elite Attitudes Towards Political, Economic and Social Transformation.* Stellenbosch, S.A.: Centre for International and Comparative Politics.

Kotzé, Hennie J., and Pierre Du Toit. 1995. "The State, Civil Society, and Democratic Transition in South Africa." *Journal of Conflict Resolution* 39 (April): 27–48.

Liebert, Ulrike, and Maurizio Cotta, eds. 1990. *Parliament and Democratic Consolidation in Southern Europe.* London: Pinter.

Lijphart, Arend. 1977. *Democracy in Plural Societies: A Comparative Exploration.* New Haven: Yale University Press.

―――. 1985. *Power-Sharing in South Africa.* Policy Papers in International Affairs, 24. Berkeley: Institute of International Studies, University of California.

Linz, Juan J., and Alfred Stepan. 1996. *Problems of Democratic Transition and Consolidation.* Baltimore: Johns Hopkins University Press.

Mezey, M. 1995. "Legislatures and the Creation of Consensus in Divided Societies." Unpublished paper prepared for the International Political Science Association Research Committee on Politics and Ethnicity, University of the Witwatersrand, Johannesburg.

Nel, P. 1995. "Transition through erosion: Comparing South Africa's Democratisation. *Aussenpolitik* 1.

O'Donnell, Guillermo, and Philippe Schmitter. 1986. *Tentative Conclusions about Uncertain Democracies.* Baltimore: Johns Hopkins University Press.

Pontusson, Jonas. 1995. "From Comparative Public Policy to Political Economy: Putting Political Institutions in Their Place and Taking Interests Seriously." *Comparative Political Studies* 28 (April).

Sisk, T. 1995. *Democratization in South Africa: The Elusive Social Contract.* Princeton, New Jersey: Princeton University Press.

Skocpol, Theda. 1979. *States and Social Revolutions.* New York: Oxford University Press.

Slabbert, V. Z. 1990. "The Causes of Transition in South Africa." In *Transition: South Africa and Transition from Authoritarian Rule,* ed. P. du Toit and V.Z. Slabbert. Cape Town: Idasa.

Steinmo, Stein, Kathleen Thelen, and Frank Longstreth, eds. 1992. *Structuring Politics: Historical Institutionalism in Comparative Analysis.* Cambridge: Cambridge University Press.

Weaver, Robert K. and Bert A. Rockman. 1991. *Do Institutions Matter? Government Capabilities in the United States and Abroad.* Washington, D.C.: Brookings Institution, 1991.

11

Conclusion

Mattei Dogan and John Higley

The chapters in this volume highlight a need to refocus the study of political regime change. Instead of viewing regimes as the products of gradual processes of socioeconomic modernization, cultural evolution, political institutionalization, and the emergence of civil society, an approach analogous to that of "complexity theory" in the natural sciences should be explored. Like the abrupt changes in structures of natural phenomena with which complexity theory deals, political regimes should be regarded as subject to profound ruptures and discontinuities. Political crises are episodes, or bifurcation points, at which regimes embodying established elites and modes of politics are pushed into relatively unpredictable states where basic changes become possible (cf. Prigogine and Stengers, 1984; Eve, Horsfall, and Lee, 1997). Studying crises and what happens to elites during them can reveal much about why and how different types of regimes are born.

This is substantially new theoretical territory, and in venturing into it the preceding chapters have raised difficult questions and problems. In this concluding chapter, we try to pull together various theses in order to evaluate the framework of elites, crises, and regime origins with which we began in chapter 1. What are the framework's strengths and weaknesses? How might it be revised in light of the questions and problems encountered? In short, what have we learned, and where do we go from here?

We have divided the chapters into two groups, and this is how we propose to discuss them. Chapters 1 through 4 deal with conceptual issues and with wide historical and comparative contexts. In our introductory chapter, we called attention to "crisis" as a critical factor in the relation between elite change and regime change, and we alluded to

dozens of crises that constituted major turning points in countries' politics. In chapter 2, Alan Knight questions our initial treatment by pointing out that crisis needs a better definition, with more unequivocal
indicators, if it is to be linked persuasively to elite and regime change.
In addition, by arguing that elites do not act in political, economic,
and social vacuums, Knight attacks the view that elites are sufficiently
autonomous from mass and external pressures during crises to control
what happens and to shape new regimes. In chapter 3, Michael Burton
and John Higley partially rebut Knight and a number of other scholars
who adopt mass-centered frameworks that minimize the scope for independent elite action. They contend that in twelve disparate cases of
elite settlements during the past three centuries, it was precisely elite
autonomy and choice in the midst of crises that made settlements and
fundamentally changed regimes possible. In chapter 4, Knight returns
to his attack by arguing that during eight crises in Mexico over the past
fifty years, neither the elite configuration nor the regime was substantially altered; instead, Mexican elites and the PRI regime mainly reacted, often in fumbling ways, to crises that sprang from mass
discontents or external pressures. He tries to show, moreover, that this
pattern has not been peculiar to Mexico; in most other Latin American
countries during the past half-century, elites and regimes also primarily reacted to mass-induced or externally induced political crises.
Clearly, the collision between Knight's position and ours requires further comment.

Because they deal with the effects of one or more crises on elites and
regimes in individual countries, chapters 5 through 10, together with
the consideration of Mexico in chapter 4, constitute the second group
we want to discuss. The authors of these chapters look closely at crisis-
induced elite and regime changes (but also important continuities) in
seven countries: Mexico, the Soviet Union/Russia plus Hungary and
Poland, Germany since World War I, Japan since the Meiji Restoration
in 1868, and South Africa during the first half of the 1990s. Rich in
details, these case studies focus on how crises affected the composition
and functioning of political elites. But their findings are quite diverse,
and it is important to ask how they collectively advance our understanding of the interaction between crises, elites, and regimes.

The Conceptual Issues Reconsidered

Let us return to the problem of how to capture "crises." In chapter 2,
Knight makes a plausible distinction between their objective (etic) and
subjective (emic) dimensions, between what we as scholars and observ-

ers think are crises and what political actors perceive to be crises. Knight's distinction sensitizes us to the twin dangers of ignoring some major crises in which no political earthquakes are outwardly apparent and of concentrating on others that look like earthquakes but are regarded by the actors as manageable tremors. We doubt, however, that these dangers are as great as Knight claims. We are not deterred by his example of Prime Minister James Callaghan's breezy dismissal of the troubles besetting Britain in the winter of 1978–79. We would have said, "etically," that Callaghan was right: the public-sector strikes of those winter months hardly constituted an "abrupt and brutal challenge to the survival" of the regime, which was our definition of "crisis" in chapter 1. Knight overlooks the possibility that political actors have mental hierarchies of crises. Although, as we warned, politicians tend to call more or less any and all political upsets "crises," surely most of them know the difference between embarrassing revelations, policy fiascoes, factional deadlocks, ministerial instabilities, and so forth, and regime-threatening ruptures. We submit that actors' perceptions of the latter coincide with the perceptions of outside observers much more than the etic/emic distinction implies.

We also think that Knight goes too far in equating the emic or subjective dimension of crises with "moods of crisis" and "panics" that sweep through mass publics. Without denying that such moods and panics occur, we suspect that they seldom, if ever, constitute the principal challenge to a regime's survival. The protests of students and the strikes of workers during May 1968 in Paris and other French cities spawned a dramatic "mood of crisis" or "panic"; yet it is a matter of record that, having assured himself of the French army's readiness to defend the Fifth Republic, President Charles de Gaulle and the top-level political elite prevailed simply by dissolving the National Assembly and holding elections, in which, be it recalled, the left-wing parties allied with the protesters and strikers were decimated politically. Manifestations of mass discontents punctuate the politics of all countries, but by themselves they seldom challenge the survival of regimes. They are normally contained or repressed by sheer force, they wither for want of strong elite leadership, or, as in France during 1968, they trigger parliamentary dissolutions and elections that divert or reduce much of the discontent.

Knight is, of course, right to highlight the causal bafflements that our focus on crises confronts. He asks: Do elites bring crises on themselves through their mistakes and ineptitudes, or are they the "hapless victims of *fortuna*?" Do regime-challenging crises result from "bad politics" or "bad luck"? Is there a direct and causal relation between the relative severity of crises and the probability of regime change? What about exogenous causes of crises? Are they not at least as important as endogenous ones, and can the two kinds of causes be disentangled?

Our general answer is that a theory of crisis that solves these bafflements is not yet possible; certainly, this volume does not offer such a theory. Although we believe that the main components of such a theory can be seen in the preceding chapters, it must be recognized that these components never recombine in identical ways across the many crises with which a theory must deal. This is why we suggest an analogy between our focus on crises and how complexity theorists try to explain abrupt and greatly varying discontinuities in the physical world. Just as the static physical world assumed by Isaac Newton has been found to be much more complexly discontinuous, so the political world of deterministic properties assumed by Marxian, modernization, and cultural theories is in reality much more disjunctive. What needs greater attention in comparative politics and comparative political sociology is the occurrence of crises and what happens during them, rather than elaboration of the view that crises are integral parts of linear socioeconomic and sociopolitical processes.

Sometimes elites are the perpetrators, and sometimes they are the victims, of crises. Research is needed on the relation between the relative severity of crises (beyond our basic stipulation that they challenge the survival or equilibrium and effectiveness of a regime) and the probability of regime change. As for the importance of exogenous causes of crises, we certainly did not ignore their importance in our introductory chapter. Clearly, any configuration of elites and type of regime can be destroyed by "asteroidal" events and forces. However, as Knight himself observes in his comparative survey of Latin America in chapter 4, the emphasis on exogenous causes of regime change has been fashionable but probably overdone. Most politics, an American politician has famously said, are local, and this is true of many countries.

Contributors to this volume disagree about the extent of elite autonomy and thus about the importance of elite choice and action during crises. Knight advances two claims. The first is that "precisely in times of crises, elites become more fluid, open, and unpredictable . . . New elites suddenly surface, old elites find they can no longer command allegiance; ergo, they lose elite status." He cites the sudden entrance of Subcommandante Marcos and a small band of Chiapas Indian followers onto the Mexican political stage in the first days of 1994. His second claim is that "it is particularly at times of crisis—classically of revolution—that mass publics achieve leverage, putting elite power and status at a discount," and he instances the Bogotazo uprising in Colombia during 1948. Knight argues, in short, that elites' power and autonomy are so weakened in crises that it is implausible to view them as the critical actors.

In chapter 3, as we have noted, Burton and Higley counter that these claims are clearly wrong as regards crises that trigger elite settlements. In situations propitious for settlements, elites, instead of becoming "more fluid, open, and unpredictable," are arrayed in two or three well-articulated and opposing camps. Spurred by a crisis, the leaders of the camps negotiate secretly and extensively with one another, hammer out compromises of basic disputes, and see to the writing, adoption, and implementation of new constitutions or other formal arrangements. Throughout, these leaders maintain the support of their respective camps, and they contain elite groups and mass movements that would destroy the nascent settlement if left to act freely.

Crises that generate settlements are rare, however, and Knight is right to claim that in many crises, especially revolutionary ones, elite autonomy and control are weakened. Yet, we think that he again goes too far. The emergence of Subcommandante Marcos and his rebel band of Indians during 1994 did not effect a discernible change in the autonomy and control of Mexican elites; rather, Marcos and his followers were contained and marginalized politically. One cannot today speak of a new Marcos-led elite group in Mexico, not even, so far as we are aware, in the state of Chiapas. Although we do not dispute Knight's point that in mass national revolutionary crises (as distinct from local uprisings like that in Chiapas) elites lose autonomy and control, it is wrong to generalize from such revolutionary crises, because they are at least as rare as the settlement-generating crises in which elite autonomy and control are conspicuous. As Burton and Higley suggest, revolutionary crises are at one end of a continuum and settlement crises are near its other end. Nor is it clear that elite autonomy and control are shattered by major uprisings like the 1948 Bogotazo in Colombia; as often as not, such uprisings simply spark takeovers by military elites. Thus, a military dictatorship under General Rojas Pinilla was the eventual outcome in Colombia, just as a military dictatorship under General Suharto resulted from the mass blood-letting in Indonesia during 1965.

In the wide middle of the continuum between revolutionary and settlement crises, there is clearly a mixed picture. Elite autonomy and control are significant, but so are mass pressures and exogenous forces. However, no one has said otherwise. Even the most dogmatic elite theorists acknowledge the political importance of mass publics, the need of elites for mass support, and the difficulties elites have in gaining and maintaining that support. The autonomy of elites and their ability to shape political outcomes are never more than "relative," as Knight also concludes. Elite theorists are distinctive not in denying the political importance of mass publics but in contending that the choices and actions of elites constitute the single critical determinant of regimes. Our focus on crises and their effects on elites and regimes underscores this contention by spotlighting the circumstances and situations in which the elite determinant of regimes is usually most apparent.

The Case Studies Compared

In addition to the treatment of Mexico in chapter 4, the studies in chapters 5 through 10 concentrate on how regimes originated in elite circulations and changed elite functioning during and after different kinds of crises. Three crises arising from defeats in warfare are examined: Germany in 1918–19 and 1945, and Japan in 1945. A regime-destroying crisis arising primarily from economic disaster—Germany in 1932–33—is reviewed. A seminal implosion crisis, also fueled by economic disaster, is analyzed: the Soviet Union between 1989–91 and the first years of the succeeding Russian regime. Two crises primarily involving the sudden withdrawal of foreign (Soviet) support are considered: Poland and Hungary in 1989–89. A hybrid crisis involving the withdrawal of foreign (Soviet) support and a sudden regime implosion is reviewed: East Germany in late 1989, followed by that territory's unique incorporation into the German Federal Republic. Finally, a crisis that combined elements of a revolutionary uprising, withdrawal of foreign support, and spiraling economic problems—South Africa between 1992–94—is studied.

Different types of regimes resulted from these crises: quite unstable democracies in Weimar Germany, early postwar Japan, and postcommunist Russia; an authoritarian-cum-totalitarian regime in Nazi Germany after 1933–34, and a totalitarian regime in communist East Germany after 1945; stable democracies in West Germany after 1945–49, in Poland and Hungary after 1990, and in eastern Germany as a part of the Federal Republic after 1991; and a much more inclusive democratic regime in South Africa, which may or may not prove to be stable, after 1994.[1] Do the kinds of crises and elite changes in which these regimes were born help to account for their varying characteristics?

Let us consider the elite circulations that occurred. Surveying the preceding chapters, at least four patterns can be discerned:

—the near total replacement of existing elites as a consequence of the Soviet Union's conquest of eastern Germany in 1945

—replacement of the explicitly political elite and gradual strangulation of other elites in Nazi Germany after 1933–34

—replacement of political and military, but not administrative and business, elites in Weimar Germany after World War I and in western Germany and Japan after 1945

—the survival of most elite persons and groups in Mexico since the PRI regime's inception in 1929 despite recurring crises, in Hungary, Poland, and Russia, during and after 1989–91 and in South Africa during and after 1992–94

Looking at these patterns, one observation is that the extent of elite circulation and the extent of regime change are at least loosely correlated. Where elite circulation was wholesale in scope (eastern Germany under Soviet occupation after 1945), there was radical regime change, from the Nazi totalitarian regime to an entirely different state-socialist regime. Where circulation was comprehensive among political and military elites but much less extensive among administrative, business, and cultural elites (Germany and Japan after 1945), there was also quite profound regime change, from harshly authoritarian or totalitarian regimes to democracies that soon became quite stable. Where, on the other hand, circulation was mainly limited, at least initially, to the topmost political office holders (Germany after World War I and again in the first years of the Nazi ascendancy), regime change was less immediate and clear-cut: though significantly more democratic in form than the old imperial regime, Weimar Germany quickly became polarized politically, and its democratic regime was highly unstable; several years passed before the Nazi regime clearly displayed a totalitarian character.

The Soviet/Russian, Polish, Hungarian, and South African cases indicate, however, that the correlation between extent of elite circulation and extent of regime change is by no means tight. In those countries, circulation mainly took the form of horizontal movements of elites rather than their vertical replacement. Yet, regime change was extensive: from what was clearly an embattled authoritarian regime dominated by the military in 1980s Poland, and from what had become a posttotalitarian state-socialist regime in 1980s Hungary, to stable democracies in both countries during the 1990s; from a less clearly posttotalitarian state-socialist regime in the Soviet Union to a quite unstable democracy in Russia; and from the repressive apartheid regime to a fully democratic one in South Africa.

The relation between elite circulation and regime change is thus anything but straightforward. There is always much else going on, and we have assembled only a handful of cases on which to base generalizations. The safest generalization seems to be that crises in which elites are thoroughly replaced lead most readily to basic regime changes. But this is neither surprising nor mysterious. Emerging from a revolutionary crisis or imposed from outside through conquest in warfare, an entirely new set of elites will have no ties to the previous regime, they will almost certainly be the bearers of a radically different ideology and political program, and during their first years in power they will suffer much insecurity. Although there are no doubt many other reasons, these three are sufficient to explain why a regime erected by entirely new elites is virtually certain to differ greatly from its predecessor.

More puzzling is the converse pattern of limited elite circulation but sharp regime change (the Soviet/Russian, Hungarian, Polish, and South African cases). In chapter 3, Burton and Higley propose that it is precisely this pattern that is conducive to fundamental elite settlements, and they go on to argue that this is what took place in Hungary and Poland during 1989 and what occurred in South Africa between 1992 and 1994. The more detailed analyses of those three countries in chapters 7 and 10 are consistent with their proposal. In all three cases, opposing elite camps did not displace each other, nor were they replaced through revolutionary or other mass uprisings; rather, and in their mutual survival interests, the leaders of opposing elite camps negotiated power-sharing arrangements that opened the way to the restrained elite competitions necessary for well-functioning democratic regimes.

No settlement occurred among elites in the dying Soviet Union or during the first years of the Russian Republic. Instead, with the Soviet regime imploding around them, elites mostly survived, but they have fought each other for ascendancy in postcommunist Russia. It is perhaps significant that, with the exception of the armed but extremely brief confrontation over control of the Moscow White House during the first days of October 1993, this elite fighting has been nonviolent, and that on more than one occasion a contending camp has extended an olive branch to its opponents. Still, the Soviet/Russian case strongly suggests that an indigenous implosion crisis has dynamics and consequences that stand in the way of an elite settlement or other direct route to a stable democratic regime.

It is also necessary to ask if the different patterns of elite circulation uncovered in this volume are related to the different kinds of crises distinguished in chapter 1. Here again, there appears to be a correlation, but one that requires several qualifications. First, defeat in warfare produced wholesale circulation in eastern Germany after World War II but more limited circulations in Germany as a whole after World War

I and in western Germany and Japan after World War II. Obviously, the type of elite and regime that exist in the country or countries that inflict a defeat in warfare have a strong impact on the extent of elite circulation in the defeated country. Second, an indigenous implosion crisis left Soviet *nomenklatura* elites substantially in place, though this kind of crisis eradicated their East German counterparts in one fell swoop. It would seem that whether implosion crises have internal or external causes makes a big difference in what happens to elites during them. Third, economic disaster contributed mightily to the Nazi takeover in Weimar Germany, but it also loomed large in the Soviet Union's demise where, as we have just said, elites largely survived (albeit often by changing positions and sectors). In economic disasters, the kind of opposition elite that is available to capitalize on them politically—Hitler and the NSDAP in Germany, but no comparable challenging elite in the Soviet Union—is clearly a factor that shapes the extent of circulation. Fourth, withdrawal of foreign support confronted communist regimes in Hungary and Poland with crises during the late 1980s, but sizable proportions of the old nomenklatura elites nevertheless survived; meanwhile, the same withdrawal of Soviet support led to the comprehensive demise of East German elites. A crucial variable was apparently the character of the "late communist" regimes: substantially reformist in Hungary, demoralized and confronted by a well-organized opposition in Poland, but frozen in dogmatism and fear in East Germany. Finally, in South Africa a compound crisis involving rapid economic deterioration, withdrawal of foreign support, and a revolutionary uprising left elite camps substantially intact but contributed to a major power shift between them. We can identify among our cases no compound crisis similar to that which unfolded in South Africa, and we must, therefore, regard it as sui generis.

We said in chapter 1 that circulation is only half the story of elite change. Equally important are fundamental alterations in elite behavior and functioning. To capture them, we distinguished between disunited and two types of united elites: consensually united and ideocratically united. We argued that changes from one to another type are most likely to occur during crises, which is another reason for paying greater attention to crises in comparative political analysis. In addition to Burton and Higley's analysis of how consensually united elites emerged in a dozen crisis-induced elite settlements, each of the case studies in this volume has addressed this problematic.

Alan Knight in chapter 4 portrays Mexican elites as at present moving, uncertainly, away from the always rough and incomplete ideocratically united configuration that was the principal residue of Mexico's seminal political crisis in 1928–29. During the past two decades in particular, major economic crises have not so much threatened the Mexican regime's survival as they have undermined the PRI establishment's long political dominance. Knight is thus prepared to entertain the possibility that this gradual, crisis-driven change in elite type will reach its conclusion should the PRI be defeated at the next presidential election in the year 2000. In place of the disintegrating ideocratic configuration there would then be something approximating the consensually united configuration. In our own view, the PRI's defeat in the mid-1997 congressional and mayoral elections and the subsequent necessity for the government headed by President Ernesto Zedillo to cooperate on a more or less equal footing with the opposing party elites, who now control the Chamber of Deputies, has made even more likely the change that Knight contemplates.

With one exception, the other case studies in this volume all conclude that deep crises were the occasions for consensual unifications of previously disunited or ideocratically united elites. In her nuanced account of German elites and regimes during the twentieth century, Ursula Hoffmann-Lange, in chapter 8, highlights the disunited condition of elites during the imperial and Weimar regimes and how this led to the Nazi takeover. She then shows how the complete destruction of the Nazi regime at the end of World War II cleared the way for implanting a consensually united elite in West Germany but also for imposing an ideocratically united elite in East Germany. Finally, she shows how the East German regime's implosion in 1989 facilitated a unique "elite transfer" from western to eastern Germany, as the result of which a consensually united elite now presides over the whole country.

In chapter 9, Hiromitsu Kataoka traces a similar pattern among Japanese elites. Emphasizing the two-tier elite structure that emanated from the Meiji Restoration in 1868, he shows that elites were deeply disunited down to Japan's devastating defeat in 1945. In terms of elite structure, he further shows, the main effect of that defeat was the elimination of the top elite tier and all the authoritarian principles and practices it embodied. Since the 1945 crisis and initially under American tutelage, a single-tier elite has functioned in accord with democratic institutions and procedures. However, the consensus among Japanese elites has been "directionless" in Kataoka's view, and political, business, and bureaucratic elites have constituted a cozy and exclusionary "iron triangle" or "power elite" formation. Kataoka is thus not sanguine about the ability of Japanese elites to withstand the costs of deep policy mistakes and failures, when and if they materialize. We may add that as this volume goes to press in early 1998, Japanese elites appear to be facing, as a consequence of persistent economic stagnation and reverberations from an Asian financial "meltdown," precisely the kinds of costs Kataoka worries about, with probably disruptive consequences for the elite formation he describes.

In chapter 10, Hennie Kotzé provides a detailed account of the deep and increasingly violent struggles between South African elites from early in the twentieth century, but especially after the apartheid regime was put in place between 1948 and 1958. He shows how these struggles led, in fits and starts, but still inexorably, to the profound crisis of the early 1990s, in which a host of pressures and inconclusive "tests of strength" led opposing elites to open negotiations aimed at transforming the apartheid regime. Employing uniquely comprehensive and comparable sets of data on all major elite groups' perceptions of the regime and state institutions in late 1992 and mid-1995, Kotzé shows how the orientations of elites were substantially reversed in the course of collectively extricating themselves and the country from that crisis. The result has been, Kotzé concludes, a consensually united configuration of elites who, however, confront massive and possibly insurmountable problems and cleavages in South African society.

Jacek Wasilewski shows in chapter 7 that the crises Hungarian and Polish elites confronted in 1988–89—deep-seated and highly volatile in Poland, more gradual and somewhat less threatening in Hungary—were weathered through negotiations. He finds that this negotiated way out of the crises had by 1993 enabled roughly half of the previously dominant nomenklatura elites to retain their elite status. They accomplished this by sharing power with reformist and oppositional elite groups, an arrangement that has created much public cynicism and scholarly controversy about the fates of the nomenklatura elites. Wasilewski's data show the extent to which those elites converted their political capital into economic and cultural capital, and in this way his analysis undergirds the thesis of Burton and Higley, in chapter 3, that elite settlements and consensually united elites were the principal political outcomes of the 1988–89 Hungarian and Polish crises.

The Soviet/Russian case is the glaring exception to the pattern of crisis-induced consensual unifications of previously disunited or ideocratically united elites. Reflecting the complexity and importance of the Soviet/Russian case, three chapters examine it. In chapter 5, Jack A. Goldstone portrays the Soviet Union's demise as a genuine revolution, albeit a revolution mainly "from above." He shows how the increasingly sclerotic Soviet economy undermined the Soviet state's credibility and impelled politically counterproductive reform efforts, the main consequence of which was the fragmentation of Soviet elites. Elite infighting culminated in the failed state coup of August 1991 and the banning of the Communist Party and dismantling of the state in the

months that followed. The debris from this dramatic revolutionary crisis, Goldstone contends, is a disunited set of Russian elites that as yet
show no signs of moving toward the consensually united configuration.

Using several bodies of data, Olga Kryshtanovskaya and Stephen
White, in chapter 6, and Jacek Wasilewski in chapter 7, show the success with which large proportions of the Soviet nomenklatura elites
reproduced their elite status in Russia after 1991. Their investigations
reveal that, depending on which Soviet elite baseline is employed, between one-half and three-quarters of Russian elites in 1993–94 had held
important nomenklatura positions under the old regime. All three
scholars, therefore, hesitate to view the crisis of 1989–91 in the Soviet
Union as revolutionary in scope and depth. Kryshtanovskaya and
White are prepared to say only that the monolithic Soviet elite has
reconstituted itself as a plural elite; Wasilewski concludes that elite
continuity has been the dominant feature of the Soviet/Russian case.
Neither analysis denies that important changes in both the elite and
the regime occurred, but both assess those changes as much more limited than casual observers have assumed. To the extent that elites had
fragmented badly during the Soviet Union's final years, as Goldstone
shows in chapter 5, it follows that in reproducing their elite status so
extensively, the elites now dominating Russia have also reproduced
their divisions.

Closing Observations

This book has explored the role of elites in political crises, most of
which result in regime changes. We have tried to relate phenomena—
elites, crises, and regimes—that are too often treated in isolation by
comparativists. We have at the same time tried to widen the distance
between the elite-crisis-regime relation and the various societal processes on which many comparativists focus. Like us, the reader will feel
that more questions have been raised than answered. Still, we think it
so evident that regime changes are closely associated with crises, that
elites are the critical actors in crises and thus in regime changes, and
that this is a seriously underinvestigated area in comparative studies
that even a question-raising effort is a step forward.

Much more work is needed. "Crisis" obviously needs better operational indicators. There is fairly broad scholarly agreement about the
definition of *elites*, but as with any macro concept in social science (cf.
"social classes," "state actors," or "institutions"), the boundaries between elites and other population segments are too vague, and this is

also the case as regards the boundary between "political" elites and "nonpolitical" elite groups. There is, of course, no real scholarly agreement about types of political regimes, though we urge that, if only for reasons of heuristic expediency, roughly the typology we have used, which derives mainly from the careful distinctions that Juan Linz has drawn over many years, be adopted.

The largest barriers to progress in the area we have explored are not hard to find, and they are entwined. One is the equivocal status of elite theory in social science. This is a subject that each of us has treated at length elsewhere, and we shall avoid further ruminations here. But it will be apparent that this volume is an effort to shift thinking toward elite theory. If we have prompted readers to ponder the problems that elite theory confronts, then a basic aim has been achieved. The greatest strength, but also the greatest puzzle of elite theory, is the large place it assigns to historical contingency. Elite theorists hold that the circumstances in which elites act are often contingent, and the choices they make are also contingent. Just as the natural sciences are discovering that the physical world is more complexly contingent than was previously believed, so elite theory grapples with this characteristic of the political and social world. Political crises exhibit contingency in extreme form. The study of how these contingent episodes affect elites, and through elites, regimes, will help us deal more effectively with this basic problem in political explanation.

Note

1. If we employ four basic types of political regimes (democratic, authoritarian, totalitarian, and traditional-monarchical), sixteen kinds of regime changes are theoretically possible. But as Leonardo Morlino (1980) rightly remarks, there cannot be changes from the first three types to the traditional-monarchical type, because the democratic, authoritarian, and totalitarian types manifest a modernization process away from, or beyond, the traditional-monarchical type.

References

Eve, Raymond A., Sara Horsfall, and Mary E. Lee, eds. 1997. *Chaos, Complexity, and Sociology*. Thousand Oaks, Calif.: Sage Publications.

Morlino, Leonardo. 1980. *Come Cambiano i Regimi Politici*. Milan, Italy: Angeli.

Prigogine, Ilya and I. Stengers. 1984. *Order Out of Chaos*. New York: Bantam Books.

Index

accidents, historical, 54–55, 56, 68
accommodation, 67, 172. *See also* compromise; elite settlements; negotiation
actions, mass. *See* mass actions
actions, political, 7
actors, 66, 85; collective, 38, 55 (*see also* mass publics); decisive, 26; elites as, 15, 240–41 (*see also* elite action); number of, 57, 62. *See also* elites
administrations, 20
administrative elites, 16, 243; in Japan (*see* Japan)
affairs, 7
Africa, implosion of regimes in, 11. *See also* South Africa
African National Congress (ANC), 214, 215, 217. *See also* South Africa
age, 135–36, 137, 154, 157, 179. *See also* continuity of elites
Allende, Salvador, 6, 66, 86
Almond, Gabriel, 209
ANC. *See* African National Congress
Anderson, Richard, 132
Andropov, Yuri, 103, 110
apartheid. *See* South Africa
Argentina, 9
Arisawa, Hiromi, 204
aristocratic (honorific) elites, 190, 191, 208, 209
Ash, Timothy Garton, 95, 150
Ashida, Hitoshi, 198

Ataturk, Kamal, 13
Athens, 8
Atkinson, Doreen, 221
Austria, 4; elite settlements in, 49
authoritarian regimes, 20; economic success and, 183–84; elite composition and functioning in, 21; ideocratically united elites and, 18; Latin American, 37–38, 83, 85 (*see also* Latin America); modernization and, 79, 81; modes of transition, 13–14, 17; Soviet Union (*see* Soviet Union); treatment of opposition, 85
authoritarianism, 87–88, 179
autocratic regimes, 52, 56; coups, 56; opposing elites, 52
autokephalic bureaucracy, 200
autonomy of elites, 39–42, 87, 238; during crises, 3, 15, 25, 26, 63, 240; democratization and, 86; domestic, 87; of elite leadership, 56; mass publics and, 85–86; PRI (Mexico), 78; relative, 41
autonomy of state institutions, 230

Baerwald, Hans, 16
Baum, Rainer, 174
Beyers, Andries, 218
Botha, P. W., 55, 215
Brady, Robert A., 208
Braun, Herbert, 40

251

About the Editors and Contributors

Michael Burton is professor of sociology at Loyola College in Maryland and the author and coauthor of numerous articles on elite theory and the sociology of elites, mass movements, and political change.

Mattei Dogan is director of research at the National Center of Scientific Research in Paris, and he has also been professor of political science at the University of California at Los Angeles. He is chairperson of the Research Committee on Political Elites of the International Political Science Association.

Jack A. Goldstone is professor of sociology at the University of California at Davis and is editor in chief of the forthcoming *Encyclopedia of Political Revolutions.*

John Higley is professor of government and sociology and holds the Jack S. Blanton Chair in Australian Studies at the University of Texas at Austin. He has written extensively on elite theory and conducted survey studies of Norwegian and Australian elites.

Ursula Hoffmann-Lange is professor of political science at the University of Bamberg, and she has conducted major survey studies of West German elites from the 1960s through the 1980s.

Hiromitsu Kataoka is professor of public administration and dean of the Graduate School of Political Science at Waseda University in Tokyo. He has published numerous works on Japanese bureaucratic elites and public policy.

Alan Knight is professor of Latin American history at Oxford University, where he also directs the Centre for Latin American Studies at St.

Antony's College. His two-volume study, *The Mexican Revolution*, is a standard work.

Hennie J. Kotzé is professor of political science at the University of Stellenbosch in South Africa. He has led a five-year survey study of South African elites during the recently completed regime transition in that country.

Olga Kryshtanovskaya is head of the Department of Elite Studies in the Russian Academy of Science, Moscow. She is also a press and television commentator on Russian politics.

Jacek Wasilewski is professor of sociology at Jagjellonian University in Krakow, Poland. He is the author and coauthor of numerous books and articles on Polish and other East European elites in the postcommunist period.

Stephen White is professor of politics and head of the Department of Politics at the University of Glasgow. He is one of the best-known students of Russian politics.